John J. Riemer, MLS
Editor

Cataloging and Classification Standards and Rules

Pre-publication
REVIEWS,
COMMENTARIES,
EVALUATIONS . . .

"**S**tandards are the backbone of the cost-effective, shared cataloging enviroment of today's technical services world. This book takes a look at the development and continuing role of such basic and widely accepted standards as AACR2, LCRIs, MARC, and LC's subject heading and classification schemes, placing them in the context of a cataloging community whose scope has changed from local to national and, now, international.

Written from the viewpoint of an impressive group of experts, each closely involved with standards in a specialized area, this book presents a unique opportunity to survey the history, continuing implementation and future initiatives of bibliographic standards."

Ruth S. Haas, MLS
Senior Cataloger
and Serials Team Leader
Harvard College Library

"To paraphrase an old adage, we are well into a time when the unexamined standard is not worth keeping. In the new volume, *Cataloging and Classification Standards and Rules*, editor John J. Riemer gathers papers from library experts that examine the standards now used to support bibliographic access and control. As a whole, these provide an excellent resource for library administrators and practitioners who continue to work on evolving these standards to make them more international in scope and more applicable to networked resources. The collection well documents how *de facto* standards have developed, internationally and within the United States, as shared cataloging has become more convenient, commonplace, and economical. For the most part, the authors have firsthand knowledge of the standard setting process in general and the particular developments they describe. *Cataloging and Classification Standards and Rules* is fairly comprehensive in its treatment of all facets of cataloging. It touches on international issues, as well as the LC Rule Interpretations, the MARC format, the Core bibliographic record, name and series authority records, subject access, implementing the USMARC format for classification data. All the papers, and particularly those on sequential bibliographic relationships and meta-information structures for networked resources, identify issues and possible actions, critical to adapting cataloging standards to an internationally networked environment. I recommend the book to those who want to help keep cataloging relevant to all kinds of information resources."

Martha Hruska
University of Florida

More pre-publication
REVIEWS, COMMENTARIES, EVALUATIONS . . .

"**C**ataloging and Classification Standards and Rules (edited by John Riemer) provides a comprehensive overview of the state of cataloging standards and rules. This collection of separately authored articles covers just about every aspect of rules and standards, from a basic overview of how standards are made to detailed accounts on the development of the LCRI's, authority records, and AACR2 itself. A good introduction to the basic history of our cataloging tools, the work provides valuable perspectives on the definitive rules and standards and how they evolved to their present forms.

"**T**he first chapter on "What Makes a Standard" sets the tone very well with the basic information it provides. Readers without much knowledge of the international cataloging scene will find the entry on the adoption and translation of AACR2 for use in non-English-speaking countries fascinating. Subsequent chapters provide valuable insight and information on the development of the MARC format, the role of LCRI's in library standards, standards for subject access, and standards for authority records. Riemer has not only assembled an extensive collection of topics but also a distinguised list of contributors from the library field."

Elizabeth Brown, MLS

The Haworth Press, Inc.

Cataloging and Classification Standards and Rules

Cataloging and Classification Standards and Rules

John J. Riemer, MLS
Editor

The Haworth Press, Inc.
New York · London

Cataloging and Classification Standards and Rules has also been published as *Cataloging & Classification Quarterly*, Volume 21, Numbers 3/4 1996.

The development, preparation, and publication of this work has been undertaken with great care. However, the publisher, employees, editors, and agents of The Haworth Press and all imprints of The Haworth Press, Inc., including The Haworth Medical Press and Pharmaceutical Products Press, are not responsible for any errors contained herein or for consequences that may ensue from use of materials or information contained in this work. Opinions expressed by the author(s) are not necessarily those of The Haworth Press, Inc.

The Haworth Press, Inc., 10 Alice Street, Binghamton, NY 13904-1580 USA

Library of Congress Cataloging-in-Publication Data

Cataloging and classification standards and rules / John J. Riemer, editor.
      p. cm.
      "Has also been published as Cataloging & classification quarterly, volume 21, numbers 3/4 1996" T.p. verso
      Includes bibliographical references and index.
      ISBN 1-56024-806-8
      1. Cataloging–Rules. 2. Cataloging–United States–Rules. 3. Classification–Books. 1. Riemer, John J.
Z693.C377 1996
025.3'0973–dc20

96-12747
CIP

INDEXING & ABSTRACTING

Contributions to this publication are selectively indexed or abstracted in print, electronic, online, or CD-ROM version(s) of the reference tools and information services listed below. This list is current as of the copyright date of this publication. See the end of this section for additional notes.

- *CNPIEC Reference Guide: Chinese National Directory of Foreign Periodicals*, P.O. Box 88, Beijing, Peoples Republic of China
- *Computing Reviews*, Association for Computing Machinery, 1515 Broadway, 17th Floor, New York, NY 10036
- *Current Awareness Bulletin*, Association for Information Management, Information House, 20-24 Old Street, London EC1V 9AP, England
- *IBZ International Bibliography of Periodical Literature*, Zeller Verlag GmbH & Co., P.O.B. 1949, D-49009 Osnabruck, Germany
- *Index to Periodical Articles Related to Law*, University of Texas, 727 East 26th Street, Austin, TX 78705
- *Information Science Abstracts*, Plenum Publishing Company, 233 Spring Street, New York, NY 10013-1578
- *Informed Librarian, The,* Infosources Publishing, 140 Norma Road, Teaneck, NJ 07666
- *INSPEC Information Services,* Institution of Electrical Engineers, Michael Faraday House, Six Hills Way, Stevenage, Herts SG1 2AY, England
- *INTERNET ACCESS (& additional networks) Bulletin Board for Libraries ("BUBL"), coverage of information resources on INTERNET, JANET, and other networks.*
  - JANET X.29:UK.AC.BATH.BUBL or 00006012101300
  - TELNET: BUBL.BATH.AC.UK or 138.38.32.45 login 'bubl'
  - Gopher: BUBL.BATH.AC.UK (138.32.32.45). Port 7070
  - World Wide Web: http: //www. bubl.bath.ac.uk./BUBL/home.html
  - NISSWAIS: telnetniss.ac.uk (for the NISS gateway) The Andersonian Library, Curran Building, 101 St. James Road, Glasgow G4 0NS, Scotland
- *Konyvtari Figyelo-Library Review,* National Szechenyi Library, Centre for Library and Information Science, H-1827 Budapest, Hungary
- *Library & Information Science Abstracts (LISA),* Bowker-Saur Limited, Maypole House, Maypole Road, East Grinstead, West Sussex RH19 1HH, England
- *Library Hi Tech News*, Pierian Press, P. O. Box 1808, Ann Arbor, MI 48106
- *Library Literature,* The H.W. Wilson Company, 950 University Avenue, Bronx, NY 10452

(continued)

- *National Clearinghouse for Primary Care information (NCPCI),* 8201 Greensboro Drive, Suite 600, McLean, VA 22102

- *Newsletter of Library and Information Services,* China Sci-Tech Book Review, Library of Academia Sinica, 8 Kexueyuan Nanlu, Zhongguancun, Beijing 100080, People's Republic of China

- *Periodica Islamica,* Berita Publishing, 22 Jalan Liku, 59100 Kuala Lumpur, Malaysia

- *Referativnyi Zhurnal (Abstracts Journal of the Institute of Scientific Information of the Republic of Russia),* The Institute of Scientific Information, Baltijskaja ul., 14, Moscow A-219, Republic of Russia

SPECIAL BIBLIOGRAPHIC NOTES

*related to special journal issues (separates)
and indexing/abstracting*

❑ indexing/abstracting services in this list will also cover material in any "separate" that is co-published simultaneously with Haworth's special thematic journal issue or DocuSerial. Indexing/abstracting usually covers material at the article/chapter level.

❑ monographic co-editions are intended for either non-subscribers or libraries which intend to purchase a second copy for their circulating collections.

❑ monographic co-editions are reported to all jobbers/wholesalers/approval plans. The source journal is listed as the "series" to assist the prevention of duplicate purchasing in the same manner utilized for books-in-series.

❑ to facilitate user/access services all indexing/abstracting services are encouraged to utilize the co-indexing entry note indicated at the bottom of the first page of each article/chapter/contribution.

❑ this is intended to assist a library user of any reference tool (whether print, electronic, online, or CD-ROM) to locate the monographic version if the library has purchased this version but not a subscription to the source journal.

❑ individual articles/chapters in any Haworth publication are also available through the Haworth Document Delivery Services (HDDS).

Cataloging and Classification Standards and Rules

CONTENTS

Introduction   1
John J. Riemer

What Makes a Standard?   5
Sally McCallum

IFLA and International Standards in the Area
of Bibliographic Control   17
Robert P. Holley

Internationalizing the Rules in AACR2: Adopting
and Translating AACR2 for Use in Non-Anglo-American
and Non-English-Speaking Cataloging Environments   37
Barbara Stern

The Evolution of LCRIs–From *De Facto* Standard to ?   61
Kay Guiles
Robert Ewald
Barbara Tillett

The Development of the MARC Format   75
Karen M. Spicher

The Core Bibliographic Record and the Program
for Cooperative Cataloging   91
Sarah E. Thomas

Meta-Information Structures for Networked Information
Resources   109
Casey Palowitch
Lisa Horowitz

Standards for Name and Series Authority Records   131
    Judith A. Kuhagen

Standards and Rules for Subject Access   155
    Nancy J. Williamson

Automating the Library of Congress Classification Scheme:
    Implementation of the USMARC Format
    for Classification Data   177
    Rebecca S. Guenther

Recent Research on the Sequential Bibliographic
    Relationship and Its Implications for Standards
    and the Library Catalog: An Examination of Serials   205
    Gregory H. Leazer

Index   221

ABOUT THE EDITOR

John J. Riemer, MLS, is Assistant Head of Cataloging, Coordinator of LC National Programs, and Head of Serials Cataloging at the University of Georgia Libraries. Previously, he held cataloging positions at the University of California, Los Angeles. Since 1987, Mr. Riemer has served as Libraries' CONSER Operations Committee Representative and NACO Coordinator. He is the author of a module on subject headings for serials in the CONSER Cataloging Manual and is currently a member-at-large on the Association for Library Collections & Technical Services' Cataloging and Classification Section Executive Committee, within the American Library Association.

To the Memory of My Mother

In Her Words:

In your twenties you plan to set the world on fire.
In your thirties you think you are setting the world on fire.
In your forties you think you have set the world on fire.
In your fifties you wonder if you have set the world on fire.
In your sixties you realize you didn't set the world on fire.
In your seventies you can relax and enjoy the world as it is.

–Mary Marcella Riemer (1920-1989)

Introduction

John J. Riemer

Standards enable us to see where we are in our growth. They signify the extent to which consensus has developed in our cataloging and classification practices. They represent criteria by which we may measure current and future progress, such as comparing an online catalog's adequacy in terms of fulfilling Cutter's objects[1] or evaluating drafts of a new cataloging code against Lubetzky's two objectives for the catalog.[2]

Standards help build a sense of community in much the same way as does speaking a common language. By representing jointly-held values about the service we are rendering to users, standards thus give meaning to our work. By fostering a sense of continuity with the past, standards can keep our attention focused on overall purpose when what we do undergoes a transition from one medium or technology to another.

Standards make it much more possible to collaborate with others when we find we share common interests. Combine adequate education and training for catalogers with a learned willingness "to practice tolerance bibliographically,"[3] and we will be able to use with confidence the products of cooperative cataloging programs. Combine leadership that advocates needed changes, democratic deliberation processes, and imaginative application of lessons learned from all relevant areas of our profession, and we will have the standards we need for tomorrow.

As Walt Crawford has observed, "To use standards effectively,

---

[Haworth co-indexing entry note]: "Introduction." Riemer, John J. Co-published simultaneously in *Cataloging & Classification Quarterly* (The Haworth Press, Inc.) Vol. 21, No. 3/4, 1996, pp. 1-4; and: *Cataloging and Classification Standards and Rules* (ed: John J. Riemer) The Haworth Press, Inc., 1996, pp. 1-4. Single or multiple copies of this article are available from The Haworth Document Delivery Service [1-800-342-9678, 9:00 a.m. - 5:00 p.m. (EST)].

1

you must first understand what they are, how they are created, and how they relate to one another."[4] This collection of papers on standards and rules is offered in that spirit. The articles take stock of where we stand in a variety of areas. They take a broad view and trace many interconnections to other standards. They offer commentary and attempt insight into the future.

Sally McCallum introduces this volume by reviewing the standards landscape. She discusses the various kinds of standards used in the library and information science community, and she notes differences in their nature, structure, purpose, formality, and methods of development. As examples she calls on three key standards: governing structure of bibliographic data, facilitating markup of documents, and defining specifications of orders for library materials.

Robert Holley reviews the role the International Federation of Library Associations and Institutions (IFLA) has played to date in developing bibliographic control standards. Drawing from his years of experience in that organization, he comments on its standards setting process. The paper also examines the role of standards within the international library community.

The extent of international acceptance of *AACR2* is the focus of Barbara Stern's paper. In it, she looks at various nations which have translated or adopted the code, in whole or in part, and what problems they have encountered in doing so. Those charged with future revision of the code can learn from these experiences.

Kay Guiles, Robert Ewald, and Barbara Tillett anticipate the future role to be played by the *Library of Congress Rule Interpretations*. To set the stage for this, they trace the history of this *de facto* standard. What once was in-house documentation is now a key component of cooperative cataloging programs.

As McCallum notes in her introductory paper, the bibliographic community's farsightedness in developing the MARC bibliographic format continues to pay enormous benefits in the form of exchangeable data and interchangeable vendor systems. Karen Spicher analyzes the historical development behind this success story. Her examination of primary sources sheds light on the early automation experiences and other factors influencing MARC's design.

Sarah Thomas provides the background and rationale for a brand-new standard. The Core Record is crafted to deliver a maximum of bibliographic content for a viable, reasonable, and potentially universal expenditure of effort to create the record. This standard is to serve as the foundation of future cooperative cataloging activity.

Casey Palowitch and Lisa Horowitz take on another frontier, electronic documents. Considering "meta-information" generally to be documentation supplied in, about, but not as an intrinsic part of an item (e.g., a book's title page or microfiche's header), they look at various possibilities for structuring this kind of data in electronic documents. The authors suggest that the headers used in the Text Encoding Initiative (TEI) standards could greatly expedite the cataloging process for this new material.

Judith Kuhagen reviews what is standardly included in the name and series authority records created and maintained by the Library of Congress and its cooperating partners. Carefully, she has culled the significant from the detailed; she has noted how and why practices have changed over the years. In so doing, she affords us the chance to become more informed consumers of authority work.

Nancy Williamson offers a comprehensive overview of the subject half of bibliographic control. For each of the significant "standards," "guidelines," and "rules" she has selected, she writes of its origins, characteristics, maintenance, and importance to bibliographic retrieval systems. She highlights interrelationships among the various tools, especially the one between alphabetic and systematic access.

The Library of Congress is currently taking the new classification standard for "test flights" as it converts the LC classification schedules to USMARC. Rebecca Guenther demonstrates how actual implementation inevitably entails refinement and further development. Her article also reviews features of the format and anticipates some of its benefits to catalogs and catalogers.

In the final paper, using serials as a case study, Gregory Leazer reviews recent research on sequential bibliographic relationships. He questions whether the MARC bibliographic format can adequately relate records, and he challenges custodians of the standard to find out if it can do so. The result could be anything from its abandonment to radical reform to development of a new, complementary format.

In conclusion, I would like to acknowledge receiving invaluable ideas, support, and advice from Ruth Carter, Marty Joachim, Nolan Pope, Dorothy McGarry, Barry Baker, Karen Morgenroth, Katha Massey, and others throughout the course of this project. I also appreciate the encouragement my wife Diana Kirkpatrick has given me. Responsibility for the shortcomings of this volume lies solely with me.

NOTES

1. Charles A. Cutter, *Rules for a Printed Dictionary Catalog.* U.S. Bureau of Education, Special Report on Public Libraries, Part II. (Washington: Government Printing Office, 1876), 10.

2. Seymour Lubetzky, *Principles of Cataloging. Final Report. Phase I: Descriptive Cataloging* (Los Angeles: Institute of Library Research, University of California, Los Angeles, 1969), 14.

3. Sarah E. Thomas, speaking at the CONSER Policy Committee meeting, May 5, 1995, Library of Congress, Washington.

4. Walt Crawford, *Technical Standards: An Introduction for Librarians.* 2d ed. (Boston: G. K. Hall, 1991), 13.

What Makes a Standard?

Sally McCallum

SUMMARY. The author describes the characteristics of *de jure* standards developed by the formal standards organizations, ISO, ANSI, and NISO, and formal industry groups, and *de facto* standards developed by informal, self-selected groups and companies. A comparison with the process used to develop Internet standards is made. Three key standards for the Library community are examined against this background: those that form the basis for encoding bibliographic data (MARC), electronic documents (SGML-based), and for ordering and purchasing bibliographic items (EDIFACT-based). *[Article copies available from The Haworth Document Delivery Service: 1-800-342-9678.]*

INTRODUCTION

Standards are the backbone of bibliographic control. The bibliographic community's function is to organize information, making it retrievable by users of every type. Yet the information itself is massive in amount and takes all forms, and the users have very different needs and skills. Information specialists are challenged to build retrieval aids that are universally (and easily) understandable and reasonably precise, and standards are the primary tools. But concern for retrieval is not the only motive for standardization in library work. Librarians discovered long ago that their collections

---

Sally McCallum is currently chief of the Network Development and MARC Standards Office at the Library of Congress.

[Haworth co-indexing entry note]: "What Makes a Standard?" McCallum, Sally. Co-published simultaneously in *Cataloging & Classification Quarterly* (The Haworth Press, Inc.) Vol. 21, No. 3/4, 1996, pp. 5-15; and: *Cataloging and Classification Standards and Rules* (ed: John J. Riemer) The Haworth Press, Inc., 1996, pp. 5-15. Single or multiple copies of this article are available from The Haworth Document Delivery Service [1-800-342-9678, 9:00 a.m. - 5:00 p.m. (EST)].

overlap; therefore if one library prepared cataloging to the satisfaction of all, then the rest could adopt the result. This also requires common practices and standards. Thus the information community is rife with standards of all kinds: USMARC, AACR2, LCSH, DDC, LCC, LCRI, etc.

Standards generally take the form of an assortment of shared practices, established by authority, custom, or general use, and endorsed formally or informally. One way to review the standards landscape is to consider the processes by which the common practices were agreed upon. These processes vary due to differences in formality of procedures, breadth of consensus required for approval, speed of development, and methodology for documenting the standard.

This paper outlines the sources and rules for development of both formal and informal standards, followed by a discussion of three key standards for libraries in the electronic environment.

FORMAL STANDARDS

At the "top" in terms of formality and broad consultation are the standards developed by the American National Standards Institute (ANSI); by its affiliate in the information area, the National Information Standards Organization (NISO); and by the associated International Organization for Standardization (ISO). ANSI, NISO, and ISO standards are developed using formal procedures that include a consensus building process and careful validation of balloting, all controlled by published rules. These rules even allow participants to contest that the processing of a standard has not been properly carried out. The time for development is often long because of the requirements for consensus, wide review, and consultation. The documentation for the completed standards is of excellent quality and generally well edited and error free. The published standards can command strong trust by implementors.

The format *structure* used for MARC is an example of an ANSI (and ISO) standard, as are the information retrieval protocol, Z39.50, and the basic character set used daily in bibliographic work, ASCII. There are many other ANSI/NISO standards that are not as widely implemented by the community, but usefully could be, including standards for information to be included on the spines of items and on title pages, for expressing holdings, and for data to be included in references.

Other sources of relatively formal standards are various industry groups (and here libraries are classified as an "industry"). Industry groups use various procedures for developing and approving standards, usually with some formality but often not so strict as ANSI and ISO use. They establish review processes that vary in inclusiveness, but they often have faster development time. Many library standards are of this type, and they stand up well to use if they are developed with broad enough participation. The USMARC format is an industry standard. As mentioned above, the formal standards, ANSI/NISO Z39.2, *Information Interchange Format,* and its international version, ISO 2709, specify only a *structure* for the MARC format. Any user group must establish which options in the structure they want to use (e.g., field indicators will be 2 characters) and establish the content designation—the tags, subfield codes, coded values, and their meanings. That is what USMARC does. It defines the tags, subfields codes, and indicators for the bibliographic data application. The standard was developed with the participation of many library groups and endorsed by various U.S. library associations, in particular the American Library Association. Participation in maintenance of the format remains open and broad. Yet the development time for the first MARC format was relatively short because the procedures and balloting of the formal standards process were not involved.

Other examples of library industry standards are the set of Anglo-American Cataloguing Rules (AACR2) and the Dewey Decimal Classification (DDC). AACR2 was subjected to extensive review in the library community and is maintained by a national and international consensus committee, but did not go through a formal community-wide balloting process. While DDC was published in 1876 as a "personal" standard, for a number of years its development has been overseen by a national and now an international editorial committee. This does not diminish the relevance of these standards for bibliographic work.

INFORMAL STANDARDS

For formal standards, drafts are subjected to relatively broad-based development and maintenance processes and consensus is achieved before completion of the standard and implementation begins. The following development methods are also effective, however, for certain types of standards, such as those that (1) need a "jump start" to be applied before they are passed on to the more formal processes (e.g., Universal Character Set (UCS)), (2) require editorial processing for which it is difficult to achieve consensus in a large group (e.g., Library of Congress Rule Interpretations (LCRI)), (3) need constant, even daily, maintenance to be carried out (e.g., Library of Congress Subject Headings (LCSH)). Informal standards are usually developed by informal or semi-formal groups and often are developed in a very closed environment by individual companies. Some standards developed informally are made immediately available in products, thus becoming "standards" simply through their use and usefulness.

Informal group standards are usually developed by a closed circle of interested parties, quickly, with very limited review and approval sought. Often, if these standards fill a need and it is appropriate, they are taken on to a formal process to "validate" them for wider acceptance. An example of this is the UNICODE character set developed by a consortium of computer printer manufacturers. UNICODE is a single large character set with codes for many different scripts. The development was rapid and the review process was limited outside of a self-appointed group. However, UNICODE became the core of a Universal Character Set standard approved by ISO in the succeeding years. Informal standards frequently are catalysts for forcing faster development of more formal standards.

"Company" standards are also quite important to the bibliographic community. These are developed in an internal manner with no approval process required outside of the institution. Decisions can be rapid and use by the developing institution is the chief way they are propagated and become accepted standards. The LCRIs, which augment the AACR, are an example as are the LCSH and the Library of Congress Classification. For all these standards, there is often consultation today because of modern telecommunications, but the maintenance characteristics of the standards are such that "company" decisions are practically the only way they can be viably maintained.

Another example of a company effort that became a very effective standard is TCP/IP, the protocol that is central to Internet communication. Originally developed for the defense industry, its availability and effectiveness at the time the Internet was being planned made it the protocol of choice for the Internet, rather than the Open Systems Interconnection (OSI) standards that were at that time being laboriously put together by ISO.

Standards developed by the official organizations, ANSI, NISO, and ISO, and by industry groups that follow broad consensus and approval processes are generally referred to as *de jure* standards, while the various informal group and company standards are *de facto* standards. As can be seen from the many library community standards that are *de facto,* effective standards can be developed through very different channels, their acceptance and success being ultimately determined by their usefulness and their suitability to application needs.

RECENT DEVELOPMENTS

Bold new procedures are being used to formulate standards for the Internet by an industry group called the Internet Engineering Task Force (IETF). In the Internet community, the conventional wisdom has been that the formal standards processes, represented by ANSI and ISO, are too slow and bureaucratic. The charge is true in some respects as both organizations have focussed on assuring fairness and universal input over timeliness, with required processing steps becoming lengthy and complex. The Internet community has used its own medium to change this emphasis. Proposed Internet standards are made universally available for review over the Internet as soon as they are drafted and stakeholders are responsible for reviewing and responding in tight time frames, electronically. This increases timeliness and, while universal review is possible, the process does not demand proof of broad participation. This procedure has produced rapid finalization of standards, and also rapid approval of alterations to standards.

This revolutionary process was remarkably effective in the early days of the Internet development when experimentation was needed and rapid implementation was the norm. As the Internet matures, however, there are more players to be taken into account and investments have been made that may require more stability. Whether this development method can continue unaltered into this new era is an open question.

Another area in which the IETF process differs from the formal one is in the publication process for standards: standards are available free over the Internet. The ISO and ANSI bodies have traditionally derived a part of their income from the sale of standards. ISO requirements for the printing, translation, and editorial consistency of standards, plus their administrative overhead, has made the documents expensive. On the other hand, the casual editorial control of many free standards can pose a problem for implementors. In the experimental environment, such as the Internet has enjoyed, that was less problematic, but with maturity, the need for well-edited, clearly-written, error-free standards will increase. The support for formal standards-making organizations needs to be met in ways that enable them to offer their standards at little or no cost, as a free standard has a better chance of getting into the hands of implementors.

The IETF process is having positive effects on formal standards development. ISO and ANSI are moving as rapidly as they are able to streamline procedures and use electronic media in the development process, especially for computer and telecommunications standards. ISO is also forming relations with organizations such as IEEE in order to make possible the adoption of their standards, rather than duplicating them in labor intensive projects within ISO. The liberalization of ISO's procedures and tightening of those of the IETF may provide the eventual meeting ground for the ISO and the Internet standards groups, so that appropriate Internet standards can become ISO standards also.

Apart from the influence of the IETF procedures, the formal standards process has been trying to take advantage of the electronic communications now available. While ISO has an obligation to use communications mechanisms that enable all nations to participate in the work, the Internet has now become extensive enough for

ISO to begin to mandate electronic connectivity for some of its activities.

THREE KEY STANDARDS FOR LIBRARIES

Three major standards important to libraries today reflect this mix of provenance. These are the format standards for electronic bibliographic data, for electronic documents, and for document ordering transactions in electronic form. These three types of data are basic for library functions. All three have had a long history in printed form, through card catalogs, printed books and graphics, and "order slips." They also each have very different data content and handling characteristics. That is why there are three *formal* standards for the structure of formats for these in electronic form, namely, ISO 2709 (or ANSI/NISO Z39.2), *Format for Information Exchange,* for bibliographic data; ISO 8879, *Standard Generalized Markup Language (SGML),* for documents; and ISO 9735, *Electronic Data Interchange for Administration, Commerce and Transport (EDIFACT),* for the ordering of library materials.

ISO 2709 focusses on allowing detailed markup of variable length (but not extremely long) data elements to facilitate complex indexing and sorting requirements. It allows efficient access to the data in order to manipulate and access various subset combinations and to index selected parts. The field tags, indicators, subfields, and particularly the directory structure specified in ISO 2709 support these requirements.

ISO 8879 is targeted at encoding documents that may be any length, but will usually be very long. The documents need to maintain their linear order but hierarchies inherent in the data also need to be preserved. The method for establishing tags and attributes in ISO 8879 is supportive of these requirements. The absence of directory access to the data, as found in ISO 2709, is suitable for the often great (yet variable) length of the data segments and the emphasis in tagging on presentational characteristics rather than retrieval or sorting characteristics.

ISO 9735, on the other hand is structured for transaction type data, that requires relatively brief data elements and different groups of elements for each type of transaction. A major requirement for transaction data is to relate multiple short messages that are created and communicated at different times in response to each other. Yet they need to be clear enough to support critical activities like purchase orders and invoicing. ISO 9735 accordingly specifies a structure that is simple and supports easy segmentation and relationships among messages.

ISO 2709, ISO 8879, and ISO 9735 are all formal standards for data format structures. The formats based on those structures, that specify that the tags used for the data and the semantics for using them, must be established by the user communities. For ISO 2709, there is strong industry standardization on an implementation schema for cataloging and related data, the *USMARC Format for Bibliographic Data* and other USMARC formats. There are other formats used in some other countries, but USMARC dominates worldwide.

ISO 8879 is newer than ISO 2709 and is still in a period of proliferation of implementations for textual data. Two leading tagging schemes are ISO 12083 (informally called the AAP markup, which was originally an ANSI/NISO standard) and the Text Encoding Initiative (TEI) markup. ISO 12083 was targeted for modern publications, with fairly hierarchical structures, while the TEI was developed initially for conversion of older text into electronic form. Older documents often offer a bewildering array of structural characteristics that are not compatible with a hierarchical tagging schema.

There are a number of other document markups that were developed for special purposes, such as CALS, a U.S. Defense Department markup designed for manuals and other technical documentation; HTML, a very simple markup designed for use in marking documents for World Wide Web servers; and MAJOUR, a markup targeted at journal articles. Individual publishers that have adopted ISO 8879 structures for publications have tended to define their own proprietary tagging schemes. There are thus many unique ISO 8879-based markups due to differences in publications and viewpoints. The development of markup-creation tools has encouraged experimentation and invention.

ISO 9735 has struggled to make itself the preferred standard in an area where automation is far from universal and many simple in-house systems exist. The bibliographic community is developing its transaction sets (working from the formal standards already established for order data elements), but the total commercial community of EDIFACT users is much larger than the bibliographic. Work is underway to harmonize differences in the ANSI and ISO applications of EDIFACT. In this area ANSI/NISO has turned the format work over to industry groups, the Book Industry Study Advisory Committee (BISAC) and the Serial Industry Systems Advisory Committee (SISAC). NISO is establishing formal standards for the data elements for order transactions, but the industry groups are establishing the standards for the format encoding under ISO 9735.

These three formats, designed for different purposes and types of material, overlap regarding bibliographic data: a small amount of bibliographic data needs to be included on orders, and experiments with SGML indicate there may be a benefit to retrieval of full text if some bibliographic data is attached to documents. There is also the opportunity to pull off the bibliographic data for use in cataloging systems if it is appended to documents. At these boundaries, analysis is needed of the amount of bibliographic data required and how best to handle it.

There has been some experimentation with bibliographic data in SGML and EDIFACT formats. Experimentation with EDIFACT for bibliographic data found severe limitations imposed by the basic ISO 9735 structure, limitations that are not relevant and may be assets for transaction-based order data. Experimentation has also been carried out with bibliographic data in SGML. The Library of Congress is working with others to develop an SGML version of a MARC record that will allow roundtrip compatibility between the two record structures. The huge data bases of bibliographic data and the detail of searching strategies and different record views supported by MARC records do not operate efficiently off SGML records, however, even with full MARC markup. But there may be cases where standardized bibliographic data can certainly enhance full text retrieval on documents in SGML files.

FORMAT STANDARDIZATION

The bibliographic community has been fortunate—or farsighted—in its use of standards. The consistent use of MARC for bibliographic data is the key to the extensive sharing of data and the proliferation of vendor systems for library automation. It supported cost savings in the era of centralized automation of the 1970s and it continues to provide savings in today's mixture of central and local processing. The format makes possible the interchangeability of vendor systems, leading to competitive prices for systems. The standard MARC formats for bibliographic data enable libraries to move and mix records, from internal to external systems, among local system components, and from today's internal system to a new internal system.

Use of MARC is increasing worldwide as the Internet environment makes national boundaries irrelevant to data interchange. In a tape world, conversion of format when "loading" record sets seemed like a reasonable processing step, but it is a major barrier to interchange in the opportunities afforded by current telecommunications. In recent years agencies around the world have moved away from national formats, especially the establishment of new ones, and are adopting instead either USMARC or UNIMARC for their cataloging data. The bibliographic data and the systems available primarily use USMARC. In addition, the Library of Congress, National Library of Canada, and the British Library are working to completely align their formats, in order to eliminate troublesome—often minor—differences and to avoid the cost of duplicative format maintenance. UNIMARC still has considerable differences from USMARC, however, and there is a need to take steps to align those two formats.

Formats based on the SGML and EDIFACT structures have not reached the level of standardization of MARC, but there is increasing awareness of the benefits of bringing the diverse markups together. Establishing more standardization of the markup standards for electronic documents using the SGML structure and stabilizing the EDIFACT data elements in the same way that MARC has become universal for bibliographic data should be a target for the bibliographic community. Unfortunately, because of the inherent nature of the publishing industry, standardized tagging for SGML-structured documents may be elusive. The documents themselves are not standardized, as bibliographic data is. Also, diversity for commercial publishers is a form of competition to an extent; thus, there is not the same interest in standardization of tags that there is among librarians in standardizing tags for the bibliographic records. There may be groups of documents for which common tagging is established, however, e.g., TEI for older documents.

CONCLUSION

In summary, there are a number of methods for developing standards, each producing documents that may be useful; but potential users need to be mindful of the origins of standards so that that can be taken into account when evaluating the likelihood of widespread utilization, chances for stability, accuracy of documentation, and the soundness of the standard. MARC standardization is a major accomplishment of the community. There will be great benefits if at least partial standardization of electronic document and ordering formats can also be achieved.

AUTHOR NOTE

Responsibilities of the Network Development and MARC Standards Office include maintenance of USMARC and Z39.50, two key standards in the bibliographic community. Sally McCallum's office is also involved with the Library's implementations of SGML-based formats. Ms. McCallum has worked closely with the National Information Standards Organization (NISO), the affiliate of the American National Standards Institute (ANSI) that is responsible for standards in the area of information and publishing. She has represented ANSI internationally at meetings of the Information and Documentation Technical Committee of the International Organization for Standardization (ISO), chairing its automation standards section. She is also very active in the International Federation of Library Associations and Institutions (IFLA), and currently chairs the committee responsible for the maintenance of the IFLA UNIMARC format.

IFLA and International Standards in the Area of Bibliographic Control

Robert P. Holley

SUMMARY. The Division of Bibliographic Control of the International Federation of Library Associations and Institutions (IFLA) has taken an active role in standard setting to foster universal bibliographic control (UBC). UBC is built upon the assumption that a national cataloging agency will catalog national imprints and then share the records nationally and internationally. Standards in support of UBC include the International Standard Bibliographic Descriptions, UNIMARC, authority lists, and miscellaneous guidelines. The IFLA standard setting process requires consensus building and compromise among the various traditions of bibliographic control. The increasing importance of library networks and the internationalization of bibliographic control may reduce the importance of IFLA as a standard setting body. *[Article copies available from The Haworth Document Delivery Service: 1-800-342-9678.]*

INTRODUCTION

A discussion of international standards can take many forms even in the limited area of bibliographic control. As I pondered the directions for this paper, I considered several possible alternatives including a history of international standard setting, a listing of

Robert P. Holley is Director, Library and Information Science Program, Wayne State University, Detroit, MI 48202.

[Haworth co-indexing entry note]: "IFLA and International Standards in the Area of Bibliographic Control." Holley, Robert P. Co-published simultaneously in *Cataloging & Classification Quarterly* (The Haworth Press, Inc.) Vol. 21, No. 3/4, 1996, pp. 17-36; and: *Cataloging and Classification Standards and Rules* (ed: John J. Riemer) The Haworth Press, Inc., 1996, pp. 17-36. Single or multiple copies of this article are available from The Haworth Document Delivery Service [1-800-342-9678, 9:00 a.m. - 5:00 p.m. (EST)].

17

current standards, a comparison of standard setting activities among the international bodies with interests in this area, and an attempt to evaluate the success of various international standards. In the end, I decided that the best approach was to take advantage of my years of experience in the International Federation of Library Associations and Institutions (IFLA). Thus, this paper will give me an opportunity to collect my thoughts on standard setting in the area of bibliographic control within IFLA and on the role of standards within the international library community.

DEFINITION

The first issue is to define "standard." Among those found in *The Oxford Concise Dictionary,* the most appropriate definition is the very first one: "an object or quality or measure serving as a basis or example or principle to which others conform or should conform or by which the accuracy or quality of others is judged."[1] Before looking at the nature of standards in the area of international bibliographic control, I would like to eliminate several possible interpretations of this definition. First, these standards, except for those that deal with International MARC, are by their very nature different from most standards in technological areas because technical standards must be followed or the product will not work. This factor also limits debate about compliance with technical standards because the real-world test of workability provides immediate feedback on adherence to the standard. Second, I would also eliminate the concept of "standard" as an unobtainable objective that serves only as a goal. Many library-related "standards" are seldom reached goals that serve as arguments for increased funding. As a small example, I would cite the ACRL standard for student seating in college and university libraries. My institution has not been in compliance with this "standard" for years nor is there any real expectation that it ever will be.[2]

IFLA AND BIBLIOGRAPHIC CONTROL

IFLA has been involved in the area of standard setting for a long time, especially in the area of bibliographic control. Dorothy Anderson in her paper, "Reflections on Bibliographic Standards and the Processes of Standardization," considers the first efforts to have occurred in the early 1950's when an IFLA working group attempted to institute principles for establishing main entries for anonymous works and works of corporate authorship.[3] From this limited project arose the 1961 International Conference on Cataloguing Principles that endorsed the Paris Principles that became the philosophical basis for new cataloging rules formulated since then.[4]

To provide the organizational context within IFLA, the principal responsibility for bibliographic standards resides in the Division of Bibliographic Control that has three sections: Bibliography; Cataloguing; and Classification and Indexing.[5] The Division has a coordinating board made up of the two officers from each section. A Standing Committee of up to 20 members directs each section. These members go through the IFLA nomination process that is too complex to describe here. The members provide voluntary service to IFLA parallel to member service on American Library Association committees.

The Division has close ties with one of the IFLA core programmes, Universal Bibliographic Control and International MARC (UBCIM). The Universal Bibliographic Control office was established in 1971 within the British Museum. In 1987, the International MARC Project merged with it to form UBCIM.[6] This core programme, that moved at the beginning of 1987 to the Deutsche Bibliothek in Frankfurt, Germany, has a permanent paid staff with support both from IFLA and the host library. UBCIM, as its name indicates, seeks to foster universal bibliographic control and is also responsible for the International MARC format.

Perhaps the key to IFLA's interest in bibliographic standards is its acceptance of the goal of universal bibliographic control (UBC). In my opinion, IFLA, as represented by staff and committee members in the UBCIM Core Programme and in the Division of Bibliographic Control, does not regard UBC as an unreasonable goal.[7] While complete perfection in reaching this objective may not be attainable, much of the world's publishing output can be brought under effective bibliographic control by cataloging agencies and then shared with others on a national and international basis.

ASSUMPTIONS ON UNIVERSAL
BIBLIOGRAPHIC CONTROL

UBC, as conceived by IFLA, rests upon several key assumptions:

Each Work Should Be Cataloged Only Once

Human and fiscal resources for bibliographic control are too limited to duplicate effort by cataloging the same work several times. IFLA should work toward a system where catalog records are shared around the world.

Each Country Should Have Responsibility for Cataloging Its Own Imprints

IFLA considers the individual country as the building block in the realm of bibliographic control in keeping with several other assumptions that follow.[8]

The National Bibliographic Agency, Usually the National Library, Is the Most Appropriate Source for These Bibliographic Records or Should, at a Minimum, Gather Them from Other Cataloging Sources Within the Country

IFLA places great stress upon the role of national libraries in achieving universal bibliographic control, in part because the national library can assure some degree of standardization of bibliographic records within the country. While this centralized model does not always conform to reality including the United States where the Library of Congress is not officially a national library, I believe that this tenet has generally worked well in practice. My experience in IFLA has shown that the national library is often the most effective body to enforce standards within a country, to provide bibliographic records by cataloging materials for its own collection, and to collect bibliographic records from other national cataloging sources.

This assumption rests in part upon the concept of "legal deposit." IFLA supports legislation that requires all publishers to deposit one or more copies of their publications with the national library. In this way, the national library will have access to the bibliographic universe of the country at little or no cost. In practice, most countries lack appropriate sanctions to enforce legal deposit and are often not able to provide bibliographic records for all the materials that they receive.

Bibliographic Records Should Appear in the National Bibliography that Can Serve Both as a Record for National Imprints and as a Source of Bibliographic Records

The Division of Bibliographic Control's Section on Bibliography does not have a counterpart in American library practice. This Section is very concerned with national bibliographies, most often produced by the national cataloging agencies. The Section strongly supports the concept that a source should exist in each country that records the national publishing output. With the proliferation of online systems and databases, the utility of producing national bibliographies has come into question. In the United States, for example, large databases such as OCLC, RLIN, and WLN include national records; but they do not provide any systematic subset to reflect American publishing.

The Most Competent Authority for Attributing Authorship and for Determining the "Correct" Form for Access Points Is the National Library in the Country Where the Work Is Published

IFLA presumes that the national library in the country of publication has the best understanding of the publishing traditions, the concept of authorship, the languages used, and other cataloging concerns that depend upon the culture of that country.

The Records Created by the National Bibliographic Agency Will then Be Shared with the Rest of the World

To achieve universal bibliographic control, the national bibliographic agency must then share its records as appropriate with other agencies around the world. The next section develops another series of assumptions on this sharing process.

ASSUMPTIONS ON THE SHARING
OF BIBLIOGRAPHIC RECORDS

The Sharing of Bibliographic Records Requires the Establishment of Standards that Will Facilitate Their Transfer

As is true at the national level, the international transfer of records will not work if the receiving agency is forced to make so many changes that their modification requires the expenditure of more resources than simply creating a new record.

IFLA as an International Body Recognizes that the National Cataloging Agencies Cannot Be Required to Conform to a Standard from Another National Cataloging Agency or from a Group of Such Agencies

The followers of the Anglo-American cataloging tradition often have trouble understanding that other cataloging traditions exist and have equal weight within an international body such as IFLA. While the Anglo-American tradition with its *Anglo-American Cataloguing Rules* may be the most widely used cataloging standard in the world, France, Germany, and Russia, to name just the most obvious examples, have well developed codes for cataloging and bibliographic control. The argument that the rest of the world should simply adopt *AACR* as an international standard goes counter to the IFLA tradition of equal treatment of all national standards. General agreement on the Paris Principles has helped the cause of standardization by reducing the philosophical differences among cataloging codes, but fundamental variations among cataloging codes remain.[9]

Effective Transfer of Records Requires an Internationally Accepted Machine-Readable Format

The increased use of computer technology for record transfer and the ultimate use of bibliographic records in online catalogs makes it necessary to be able to transfer records in a machine-readable format.

*The Multiple Languages of Cataloging Records Is a Barrier
to Their Transfer and to Their Use and Interpretation Within
Different Linguistic Traditions*

This is perhaps the most difficult task that IFLA must face. I
believe that it is possible to make several points in this area.

THE ROLE OF LANGUAGE AND CULTURE
IN STANDARDS FOR BIBLIOGRAPHIC CONTROL

*Bibliographic Description Can Most Easily Cross Linguistic
Boundaries Because It Is Dependent on Data Elements that Will
Be Transcribed in the Language of the Title Page No Matter
what the Language of the Cataloging Agency*

While descriptive cataloging can differ according to various cataloging traditions,[10] its function is to transcribe accurately according
to established conventions the data elements inherent in the work.
Many parts of the descriptive record transcribe information in the
language of the work rather than in the language of the cataloging
agency. The parts of the descriptive record that depend in part on
the cataloging agency's language, notes for example, are usually
considered less important than the descriptive elements from the
chief source of information that appear in the body of the description. Furthermore, differing rules for descriptive cataloging including both major revisions in the cataloging rules and varying cataloging traditions can coexist in the same bibliographic finding tool.

*International Standards Can Be Established for Data Elements
and for Help in Interpreting Bibliographic Records*

One of IFLA's earliest attempts at international standardization
was the creation of International Standards for Bibliographic Description (ISBD). Besides creating a standard for including basic
data elements, the ISBD punctuation is, in many ways, an eye-readable equivalent of the MARC machine-readable code because it
allows the human reader to separate data elements according to

their bibliographic function without necessarily understanding the content of these data elements.

Choice of Access Points Is not Language Dependent and Has Become Less Critical in Online Catalogs

While the varying cataloging traditions include differing rules for the choice of access points and for the selection of main entry, this poses less of a problem for international standards now that online catalogs reduce the importance of main entry. In any case, these differences are not language dependent. As with description, varying rules for choice of access points and main entry can coexist in the same catalog though they can cause confusion for catalog users.

Form of Names and Authority Control

The form of name and authority control is also language independent if the principle of establishing the entry according to the most commonly used form is followed since most authors would be established by the cataloging agency of their native country. This principle is counterbalanced, however, by the competing goal of providing the form of name most recognizable to the users of the bibliographic record in the receiving country. On this question, IFLA has sought to draw upon the expertise of national cataloging agencies, especially in those countries whose naming conventions vary greatly from the North American/European tradition. Authority control is a critical area for standards because different forms for the same name undermine the collocating and identifying functions of the catalog.

Subject Access to Information

Subject access has been the most difficult area for IFLA standardization because the subject organization of knowledge is much more dependent upon culture and language than the other aspects of bibliographic control. In theory, classification is easier to share across linguistic boundaries because it is not language dependent. The Dewey Decimal Classification (DDC), the Universal Decimal

Classification (UDC), and increasingly the Library of Congress Classification (LCC) are accepted as international classification systems. While the classification notation may be easily shared, cultural differences often require local modifications to the underlying structure of the classification scheme to reflect a different organization of knowledge or a different level of detail for classification. For example, an Islamic country will not wish to give the same detailed treatment of Christianity as occurs in the standard edition of DDC. Verbal subject access is even more difficult to transfer because the same concepts are often expressed in different words even within various countries that share the same language.

IFLA AND INTERNATIONAL STANDARDS

Basic Technical Standards

IFLA has not been extensively involved in basic technical standards that are an underlying requirement for bibliographic control and the sharing of records. Among these standards, I would list the following as examples:

- the standards for character sets and for their conversion into machine readable form;
- transliteration standards; and
- the format of tapes for the transfer of machine-readable records.

These standards have implications far beyond bibliographic control and have generally been the responsibility of the International Organization for Standardization (ISO).[11]

UNIMARC

UNIMARC is the most technical international standard in the area of bibliographic control. It was devised to serve as a switching mechanism among the various national MARC formats though several countries including Portugal and Yugoslavia adopted it as their internal national format.[12] It also "can be applied amongst relatively small libraries through software developed for use on PCs."[13] The original purpose of UNIMARC was to simplify the sharing of bibliographic records by allowing each nation to create programs for the import and export of UNIMARC records without having to create programs for processing records in each individual national MARC format. Each national cataloging agency would export records in the UNIMARC format that could then be imported easily by the receiving agency. In this way, UNIMARC could serve as the Esperanto for bibliographic records.

Oversight for UNIMARC rests with the International MARC Network Committee that is appointed by the Conference of Directors of National Libraries. The UBCIM Programme maintains the format.[14] As a technical standard with practical implications for the transfer of bibliographic records, UNIMARC requires tighter control than would be possible within the voluntary committee structure of the Division of Bibliographic Control.[15]

International Standard Bibliographic Description

IFLA's development of International Standard Bibliographic Description (ISBD) has proved to be its most successful standard setting activity within the international arena. The various ISBDs define mandatory and optional data elements and format the bibliographic record in such a manner that it is possible to recognize the nature of each data element even without the necessary linguistic skills to understand the content. In some ways, the ISBDs were much more important in the card catalog with its fixed physical structure because the online catalog can use the MARC format machine-readable content designation to format the same records in multiple ways.

The first draft of the ISBD appeared as a recommendation of a working group in 1971. Even in this imperfect state, the concept was extremely successful to the point that various groups prepared draft ISBDs for other types of library materials. To maintain consistency among the various ISBDs, a meeting was held in Paris in 1975 to develop an ISBD(G) that would serve as a standard for all specialized versions. Currently, eight ISBDs are available as official IFLA standards (Antiquarian, Computer Files, Cartographic Materials, General, Monographic, Non-Book Materials, Printed Music, and Serials). In addition, *Guidelines for the Application of the ISBDs to the Description of Component Parts* provide help for using ISBD when creating records for parts of monographic publications such as individual articles or chapters in books.[16]

Even with the great success of the ISBD principle, there is a sense within IFLA that they have become less important.[17] As indicated above, the online catalog has made multiple display formats possible that can provide full headings for each data element. Furthermore, some national cataloging agencies in their efforts to reduce costs do not wish to include all the data elements required by the ISBD standards and want IFLA to develop a standard for minimal level catalog records.[18]

The IFLA Section on Cataloguing is facing this issue. Its Standing Committee has appointed the Functional Requirements for Bibliographic Records Study Group to look into the quality and function of bibliographic records to meet user needs in a changing cataloging environment.[19] The Section has delayed adoption of the Concise ISBDs until the Study Group completes its work. While the Section established a Maintenance Group at the 1993 IFLA Conference in Barcelona, this Group has also deferred needed revisions to the ISBD for computer files.[20] It thus appears that the time may have passed for major initiatives in the area of ISBDs, one of IFLA's most successful attempts at international standards' setting.

Authority Control

Efforts to institute a world-wide system of authority control have not been as successful as efforts in the area of descriptive cataloging. The goal was to have each national cataloging agency establish the authoritative form of name for personal authors, corporate authors, and uniform titles within its jurisdiction. The UBCIM Programme has published lists on: "(1) the treatment of national names; (2) names of legislative bodies; (3) the standardized forms of titles of anonymous classics; and (4) standardized liturgical headings."[21] While based upon national cataloging committees, these lists were not always wholly reliable; and most are very much out of date.[22] While efforts are underway to update the publication on *Anonymous Classics,*[23] this endeavor cannot totally succeed without greater participation from Third World countries where resources are often lacking for such projects. In the opinion of Winston Roberts, "it is not yet clear to what extent it would be economical to bring the old UBC uniform headings publications up to date–this would require a massive collaborative effort on the part of all national bibliographic services and national cataloguing commissions. . . . Such an effort would probably need to be co-ordinated by the UBCIM office and require more manpower than the office has presently available."[24]

Guidelines

Beyond the standards discussed above, IFLA has produced a number of guidelines in the area of bibliographic control. Guidelines are more flexible than standards and often give advice to libraries and other bibliographic agencies in the creation of local, regional, or national products so that these products can be more easily interpreted or shared across national and linguistic boundaries. Guidelines often appear in areas where differences are so great that a fixed standard is impossible.

Older guidelines exists in the following areas: "(1) national bibliographic agencies; (2) model agreements for exchange of MARC records; (3) recommended standards for national CIP programmes; and (4) union lists of serials."[25] Recent efforts have concentrated on the area of authority control with *Guidelines for Authority and Reference Entries (GARE)*, published in 1984, and *Guidelines for Subject Authority and Reference Entries (SGARE)*, published in 1993.

COMMENTARY

IFLA Is not a Standards Setting Body

The principal role of IFLA is not to set standards but "to promote international understanding, co-operation, discussion, research, and development in all fields of library activity . . . and to provide a body through which librarianship can be represented in matters of international interest."[26] Achieving universal bibliographic control is one way to promote co-operation, and standards foster UBC. As Winston Roberts states, "[IFLA] has a limited role in the production of certain types of standards. This role was forced upon it firstly by developments within the profession, and secondly by the very success of the standards produced."[27] In the world of printed catalog cards as the main type of bibliographic record, the impetus for record sharing was not so apparent as it is today. In its desire to increase this sharing, IFLA saw the need to create standards; but this was never its principal goal. The process then became self-generating as the various sections within the Division of Bibliographic Control followed the tradition by looking for areas within their charge where new standards would be useful.

Standards Are Difficult to Accomplish in a Voluntary International Association

Having served on a working group charged with developing a standard, I can attest to the difficulty of standard setting in a voluntary international association. The problems are many. IFLA meets only once a year, often in a distant location with travel costs so high that not all members can attend.[28] Our group split into North American and European contingents that either held special meetings or met in conjunction with other conferences such as those sponsored by the American Library Association. The chair of the working group attempted to act as a liaison by attending the meetings of both groups. We also did our best to share documents by mail to increase the efficiency of our meeting time, but much of the negotiation on differences of opinion required face-to-face encounters.

Language is another barrier. English and occasionally French are the working languages of almost all IFLA groups. Those without strong English-language skills find it more difficult to participate, especially since the official version of almost all IFLA standards appears first in English. This last fact puts an additional burden upon the English-speaking members of the group who often write most of the text or, at a minimum, revise the final product.

Group members also often have a steep learning curve since they must understand different cataloging traditions than their own. The first few meetings, that may span several years, require each member to understand the key factors that members from other traditions bring to the table.

The final complication is that the membership of any standard-setting group is likely to change as its participants move to new positions with different professional interests, come to the end of their IFLA committee appointments, or can no longer afford to attend IFLA conferences. If replacements are appointed to the standard-setting committee, any new members must then also go through the learning experience. Furthermore, they often reopen questions that have been settled during prior deliberations.

International Standards Require Compromise

The IFLA standard-setting process takes so long in part because the IFLA tradition requires that all members agree on the final product. Early on, I was advised by an experienced IFLA committee member that the American tradition of voting on disputed issues and then going along with the majority position did not happen at the international level. In my experience, any group discusses the issue until a compromise emerges that all can agree to.[29] This process can be arduous, but unanimous agreement is necessary before any standard can be sent out for review.

The review process further complicates matters because any proposed standard is widely distributed for comment by the appropriate national review bodies. While acceptance may not need to be completely unanimous, the standard-setting body must consider any significant criticisms and propose revisions. While comments often deal with minor matters or with questions of clarity, significant problems can arise at this point, especially if the country or cataloging tradition was not represented on the standard-setting committee.

Implementation of Any Standard Depends Upon the Members Who Devised the Standard

One of the reasons for reaching unanimity is that the members who propose the standard are often then charged with implementing it in their countries. Since IFLA does not have mechanisms to enforce the adoption of its standards, this step is critical. Without the tradition of unanimity and compromise, unhappy committee members would often have the power to sabotage acceptance of the standard in their countries. Acceptance by the IFLA standard-setting committee often guarantees the standard's success if the committee includes the national level decision makers.[30]

This tradition can cause problems within the United States with its decentralized decision making structure. In many countries, the national library sets policy that it has the means to enforce either directly through legislation or indirectly through its weight as the principal provider of bibliographic records. While the Library of Congress has great power in the area of bibliographic control, it is less than in many other parts of the world since the library associations, the networks, individual libraries, and the other national libraries (National Agricultural Library and the National Library of Medicine) also have their role to play. I also suspect that American librarians as a whole may have less interest in international standards.[31]

Yet another complicating factor is that the Americans who sit on standards-setting committees may often have little power to implement the standard within the United States. Americans have become the most active IFLA participants. They get nominated to standing committees and then get selected to serve on standard-setting groups for their prior service and individual expertise. During my years in IFLA, I have often encountered librarians from other countries who made the assumption that I could implement IFLA decisions in the United States. This assumption was reasonable, albeit inaccurate, because only the decision makers in their countries attend IFLA on a regular basis. I would hesitate to recommend that only highly placed librarians from the Library of Congress be allowed to serve on IFLA standard-setting committees, but such a strategy would probably foster the acceptance of IFLA standards within the United States.

IFLA May Lack Effective Mechanisms for Keeping Standards Up to Date

I am somewhat less sure about this observation, but I believe that this principle flows from several of my other points. Initial enthusiasm may energize a standard-setting body made up of voluntary

members, but it is more difficult to become excited about the pains-
taking process of revising and updating standards. Especially for
standards that are not tied to the accomplishment of specific tasks,[32]
the effort required may be too great in this period of rapidly changing technology in the area of bibliographic control and the use of
bibliographic records.[33]

Third World Countries Are Very Likely to Accept and to Implement IFLA Standards

I have great admiration for the efforts of many Third World
librarians to provide excellent library service in their countries. In
the Division of Bibliographic Control, they have participated as
actively as possible, given limited resources for travel, in the Standing Committees and on the various standards committees. I have
also frequently heard about their desire to implement IFLA standards to better serve users in their countries, to participate in the
global sharing of bibliographic records, and to give a tangible sign
of the importance that they attach to international cooperation.[34] In
turn, I believe that IFLA should continue to consider their needs
and capabilities in the formulation of standards. While computerization has become more accessible for Third World libraries with
the appearance of PC based systems for bibliographic control, the
paper format for bibliographic records remains important in much
of the world. Any new IFLA standards or revisions to current standards should continue to take this factor into account.

IFLA May Be Less Relevant as a Standard-Setting Body as Networks, Especially International Networks, Become More Important in Bibliographic Control

As stated above, IFLA has based its goal of universal bibliographic control upon record creation by a national cataloging
agency in each country. The increasing importance of networks,
especially networks that cross international boundaries, may lead to
the establishment of a new paradigm in which major networks set
de facto standards by accepting and redistributing bibliographic
records from many nations. In countries where they are not under

the direct control of the national cataloging agency, national networks may exert an increasing force through their importance as key players in the distribution process.

OCLC comes first to mind with member libraries in North America, Europe, Asia, Australia, and South America. REBUS (Réseau des Bibliothèques utilisant SIBIL) also transcends national boundaries by linking five networks in Switzerland, France, and Luxembourg. Moreover, even networks with a more limited national scope have the capability to exchange records directly among themselves without having to depend upon the national cataloging agencies as their only source.[35]

Since these networks have practical problems to solve that have fiscal consequences for their members, I am of the opinion that, like OCLC in the United States, they will become important players in the realm of international standards. How far they will displace or replace IFLA's role remains to be seen; but, as stated above, IFLA is not primarily a standards-setting agency and might welcome the shift to other agencies.

CONCLUSION

IFLA has played an important role in setting international standards in the area of bibliographic control. It has done so, not because it is basically a standards-setting body, but to foster the goal of universal bibliographic control. Its greatest accomplishment has been the series of International Standard Bibliographic Descriptions. UNIMARC has had some success as an international exchange format but has not reached its full potential. The efforts to develop an international system for authority control have not had a lasting effect.

I wish to stress the intangible benefits of standards setting. The various IFLA meetings, committees, and working groups have brought together librarians from all parts of the world. They have come away from the process with a greater understanding of varying traditions of bibliographic control and have often worked toward harmonization and toward the reduction of differences even when a fixed standard was not possible.

Events such as the growth of networks and the ease of sharing machine-readable records from many sources may diminish IFLA'S role in international standards since these events are reducing the importance of national libraries, the linchpin in IFLA's concept of UBC. Currently, the energy seems to be lacking to start a new round of standards setting according to the old model. Perhaps a new, more international model that takes less account of national boundaries is in order.

NOTES

1. *The Concise Oxford Dictionary of Current English,* 8th ed., ed. R. W. Allen (Oxford: Clarendon Press, 1990), 1888.

2. I believe that another IFLA objective, the universal availability of publications (UAP), fits more into the category of a desirable but unobtainable goal.

3. Dorothy Anderson, "Reflections on Bibliographic Standards and the Processes of Standardization," in *Standards for the International Exchange of Bibliographic Information,* ed. I. C. McIlwaine (London: The Library Association, 1991), 3.

4. See note 3 above, 3-4; Ross Bourne, "The IFLA UBCIM Programme: Standards in the Changing World," in *Standards for the International Exchange of Bibliographic Information,* ed. I. C. McIlwaine (London: The Library Association, 1991), 18.

5. The other principal IFLA sections with interest in bibliographic standards are Serial Publications; Information Technology; Rare Books and Manuscripts; and Government Information and Official Publications. Members of these sections are often asked to contribute to standards-setting activities of the Division of Bibliographic Control.

6. Winston Roberts, "The Role of IFLA in Framing and Promoting Bibliographic Standards" in *Standards for the International Exchange of Bibliographic Information,* ed. I. C. McIlwaine (London: The Library Association, 1991), 25-26.

7. "From the beginning the UBC programme was a practical one, albeit recognizing that it was idealistic and long term." See note 3 above, 6.

8. Dorothy Anderson gives this principle as one of the three strands of UBC philosophy: "the recognition that each country is best qualified to identify and record a publication of its own authors." Dorothy Anderson, "One Hundred and Eleven Years' Search for National Bibliographic Control," in *Eating the Menus: Essays in Honour of Peter Lewis,* ed. Ross Bourne (London: The British Library, 1989), 33.

9. "International standards in documentation and bibliographic matters, by contrast, were slow to develop, difficult to draft, and just as slow and difficult to win approval and acceptance. In part this was because there were already in existence many styles of standard practices considered satisfactory, and there were well-established and long-standing national traditions." See note 3 above, 3.

10. For a fuller discussion of my thoughts on this subject, see "Panel Discussion of First Day's Papers: Robert P. Holley," in *Seminar on Bibliographic Control: Proceedings of the Seminar Held in Stockholm, 15-16 August 1990, and Sponsored by the IFLA UBCIM Programme and the IFLA Division of Bibliographic Control,* ed. Ross Bourne (München: K. G. Saur, 1992), 61-67.

11. For a discussion of the relationship between ISO and IFLA, see Patricia R. Harris, "The Development of International Standards: Exploring the ISO/IFLA Relationship," in *IFLA Journal* 17, no. 4 (1991): 358-65. While a formal relationship exists between the two bodies that gives priority to each other's proposals, cooperative efforts between the ISO and IFLA are not significant in the area of bibliographic control.

For a discussion of cooperation between IFLA and other bodies in the area of standards, see note 6 above, 24-25.

12. See note 6 above, 29.

13. See note 4 above, 21.

14. See note 4 above, 21; see note 6 above, 26.

15. I have chosen not to discuss the competition between IFLA's UNIMARC and Unesco's MINISIS that eventually resulted in the Common Communication Format (CCF). For a discussion of the topic, see note 3 above, 7-8.

16. See note 3 above, 4-5. See note 4 above, 20. For a brief history of ISBDs and a list of current standards, see Jay H. Lambrecht, *Minimal Level Cataloging by National Bibliographic Agencies* (München: K. G. Saur, 1992) 12-15 and supporting references.

17. "The Programme of work on the ISBDs may not be seen to have quite the high priority it once had. . . . " See note 6 above, 31.

18. See note 16 above, 57-59.

19. This Study Group implements Resolution 2a, passed at the Seminar on Bibliographic Records in Stockholm, 15-16 August 1990. The text reads as follows: "That a study be commissioned to define the functional requirements for bibliographic records in relation to the variety of user needs and the variety of media." *Seminar on Bibliographic Control: Proceedings of the Seminar Held in Stockholm, 15-16 August 1990, and Sponsored by the IFLA UBCIM Programme and the IFLA Division of Bibliographic Control,* ed. Ross Bourne (München: K. G. Saur, 1992), 145.

20. Suzanne Jouguelet, "Section on Cataloguing: Review of the Work 1993/1994," (IFLA Document 040-BIBCO-4-E), IFLAI040.WP5 (as distributed by the Cuban Organizing Committee), 1.

21. See note 4 above, 20.

22. See note 4 above, 20; see note 6 above, 28.

23. See note 20 above, 2.

24. See note 6 above, 28.

25. See note 4 above, 21.

26. IFLA statutes as quoted in note 6 above, 23.

27. See note 6 above, 31.

28. The development of a standard "is a slow process, partly because of the necessarily detailed consultations that take place, but also because the work depends in most cases upon the dedication and enthusiasm of a few individuals, who are often unable to meet except at the annual conference of IFLA and who must undertake most of their work by correspondence." See note 6 above, 24.

29. For a discussion on the difficulty in reaching a compromise on the ISBD(G), see note 3 above, 5.

30. Anderson gives this as a reason for the rapid acceptance of ISBDs. "The ready acceptance of its stipulations by major organizations in a number of countries came about because of the composition of the working group, most of whom, in senior positions within their own national organizations, were able to agree to the adoption of the new descriptive rules." See note 3 above, 4.

31. In my research to prepare this paper, I noticed that virtually all publications, including many that I have not cited, were published either by IFLA or by British publishers.

32. I would make an exception here for UNIMARC and note that its maintenance has been entrusted to a standing committee made up of the participants who use the format.

33. "IFLA, as an international body of librarians coming together for meetings and discussions once a year, had not envisaged and was not prepared for a different role and in the years since it has not altogether accepted nor recognized its responsibilities; and as a non-governmental organization it has not the financial resources nor the status to sustain an effective initiating and maintenance role." See note 3 above, 9.

34. See the comments earlier in this paper on the adoption of UNIMARC.

35. For a discussion of international networks and networks outside North America, see: Robert P. Holley, "Cooperative Cataloging Outside North America: A Status Report 1993," in *Cataloging & Classification Quarterly* 17, no. 3-4 (1993): 201-36.

Internationalizing the Rules in AACR2: Adopting and Translating AACR2 for Use in Non-Anglo-American and Non-English-Speaking Cataloging Environments

Barbara Stern

INTRODUCTION

Many English-speaking and non-English-speaking countries have adopted the *Anglo-American Cataloguing Rules, 2nd Edition*[1] after both its 1978 publication and its 1988 revision. Indeed, it has been translated into fourteen languages.[2] This study examines some of the reasons why AACR2 has been internationally adopted and some of the problems encountered by various countries attempting to adapt it to a non-Anglo-American environment or translate it for a non-English-speaking environment. We examine whether AACR2 can be revised into a universal code or whether it must coexist with one or more other codes. We then examine the experiences of various countries that have adopted AACR2.

Barbara Stern is Catalog Librarian at the Los Angeles County Law Library, Los Angeles, CA 90012-3001.

[Haworth co-indexing entry note]: "Internationalizing the Rules in AACR2: Adopting and Translating AACR2 for Use in Non-Anglo-American and Non-English-Speaking Cataloging Environments." Stern, Barbara. Co-published simultaneously in *Cataloging & Classification Quarterly* (The Haworth Press, Inc.) Vol. 21, No. 3/4, 1996, pp. 37-60; and: *Cataloging and Classification Standards and Rules* (ed: John J. Riemer) The Haworth Press, Inc., 1996, pp. 37-60. Single or multiple copies of this article are available from The Haworth Document Delivery Service [1-800-342-9678, 9:00 a.m. - 5:00 p.m. (EST)].

37

Reasons for Wide-Spread Adoption of AACR2

The first edition of the *Anglo-American Cataloguing Rules*[3] was adopted by many Asian and African countries in English. Because of the wide international interest in AACR1, the Joint Steering Committee for the Revision of AACR sought to make AACR more suitable as an international cataloging code by setting forth several objectives:

1. Conform generally to the *Paris Principles* of 1961[4] already manifested in AACR;
2. Facilitate developments in machine processing of bibliographic records;
3. Incorporate the *International Standard for Bibliographic Description: Monographs (ISBD(M))*[5] as the basis for standardizing description of all materials; and
4. Revise the treatment of non book materials based on the rules of the Canadian Library Association, the British Library Association, the Association for Educational Communications and Technology, and the American Library Association revised Chapter 12 of *AACR1, North American edition.*[6]

Besides these objectives, the JSC's most important concern was to integrate the British and North American texts of AACR1 so that countries wishing to adopt AACR as their cataloging code would have a single text to use. The JSC was also asked to include more foreign language examples for the benefit of other countries.

General Problems with the International Adoption of AACR2

Those countries that adopted AACR1 and AACR2 faced problems stemming from inconsistencies and vagueness in the Paris Principles, as well as from discrepancies between the Paris Principles and both AACRs. Although AACR2 conforms generally to the Paris Principles and to the recommendations made at the International Meeting of Cataloguing Experts in Copenhagen, 1969,[7] there are some fundamental differences in AACR2 that make it more attractive for international use. For example, the Paris Principles and the International Meeting of Cataloguing Experts' recommendations emphasize "large general libraries,"[8] AACR2 is designed for "general libraries of all sizes,"[9] and attempts to encompass "all materials" (in AACR2R, "all library materials commonly collected at the present time"), rather than "printed books" only or "other library materials having similar characteristics."[10] (However, other libraries have recently noted that they prefer other codes to AACR2 when cataloging such non-book media as manuscripts, films, and computer software.)[11]

There are other areas, however, in which AACR2 is not as internationally oriented as the Paris Principles and the IMCE recommendations. For instance, both the Paris Principles, section 4.1 and AACR2 indicate that added entries should contain full descriptions at each entry, although AACR2 indicates that all entries will contain complete descriptions although different levels of description are permitted.[12] This caused problems for countries like Japan, which instituted the unit record where the full description is repeated with each added entry only in 1977, and which previously used single-entry listings only.[13]

Another problem is the confusion caused by the fuzzy manner in which AACR2 presents the main entry principle compared to the clearer description in the Paris Principles. The various criteria AACR2 lists for choice of main entry in cases other than single personal authorship can lead to differing decisions by different national cataloging agencies, especially where AACR2 uses the phrase "in case of doubt." The Paris Principles advocate going beyond using a single main entry, even for a standard citation for use in single-entry lists, to using multiple entries, allowing the user more access points. (Gredley suggests solving this problem by using the ISBDs as a standard citation format, since they are widely used by many countries who also use a variety of cataloging codes.)[14]

Along with main entry, the principle of corporate authorship found in the Paris Principles and in AACR1 was never accepted by many countries who were otherwise quite receptive to AACR1. AACR2 abandoned corporate authorship in favor of making main entry under corporate body in certain circumstances only, making AACR2 closer to many countries' practices and therefore more attractive. However, differences in the rules for corporate body main entry in AACR2 and in those of corporate authorship in the Paris Principles make it more difficult for countries to convert from the latter to the former. Specifically, AACR2 says that "in case of doubt" whether the work "emanates from a corporate body," do not make main entry under the body.[15] The Paris Principles, on the other hand, give specific instructions regarding whether one should choose a corporate body or personal name as the author, or should enter under title.[16]

Another area where AACR2 and the Paris Principles diverge is in geographic names. AACR2 rule 23.2[17] follows the Paris Principles section 9.44 in preferring the English forms of names. In contrast, the *AACR2* "General Introduction" states that "users of the rules who do not use English as their working language will replace the specified preference for English by a preference for their working language. Authorized translations will be allowed to do the same."[18] In other words, countries wishing to adopt AACR2 in English must either live with the preference for English names or break with AACR2 by substituting forms in their own languages.

Factors That Make AACR2 Attractive to International Use

Notwithstanding some of the problems attendant upon adopting AACR2, many countries have shown interest in using it as their cataloging code. What makes it amenable to international use?

First, the history and tradition behind AACR1 and its world-wide use set the stage for interest in AACR2. AACR2's basis in the ISBDs makes it a landmark tool for standardizing bibliographic description and facilitating international exchange of bibliographic data, especially in machine-readable form.

Second, AACR2's rejection of corporate authorship brings it more in line with other national codes which never used corporate authorship.

Third, AACR2's three levels of description permit libraries to include more or less descriptive detail in the catalog record, thereby serving the needs of both the national bibliographies and public libraries of many countries. This eliminates the need for separate sets of rules for research and public libraries, such as Germany has,[19] and Sweden had prior to adopting AACR2.[20]

Fourth, AACR2's greatest achievement, according to Gredley,

"is the extension of the ISBD framework to all materials."[21] Many countries who were dissatisfied with the rules for nonbook materials in AACR1 welcomed AACR2's integrated approach to all materials.

Is AACR2 a Truly International Code?

Is AACR2 adaptable enough to non-Anglo-American cataloging environments?

Anderson, in discussing the revision of AACR1,[22] spoke of interest in developing an internationally accepted cataloging code. AACR1, with its slant toward Anglo-American practices and culture, and its use of main entry and corporate authorship, was far from being an international standard, despite its broad adoption world wide. The editors of AACR2 were mindful of the objections to these aspects of AACR1 when they undertook the revision of AACR. Therefore, they sought to improve its international usefulness by incorporating the ISBDs as the basis for description of all materials, by rejecting corporate authorship, and by including more foreign language examples and rules for entry of foreign names.

Even with all these changes, the rules for choice and form of entry in Part II of AACR2 diverge too much from the practices of many countries to make AACR2 a universally acceptable code. For that matter, is an international code really desirable? It is doubtful that the conflicting needs and practices of so many countries could be reconciled well enough to construct such a code, even if the Paris Principles were thoroughly revised to facilitate truly standard international practices, especially with regard to choice and form of entries.[23] Also, the ability to exchange bibliographic data internationally via the MARC format, coupled with the flexibility of national codes in providing for local and national cataloging needs seem to make an international cataloging code unnecessary. Anderson has since reconsidered the idea of an international cataloging code, declaring "There is no one internationally accepted cataloguing code, nor are projects for the development of an international code underway or contemplated in the immediate future."[24]

There is always the possibility that an existing code, if widely adopted, could become a near-universal standard. AACR2, already translated into fourteen languages and adopted in English in many

Asian and African countries, appears to be the closest contender so far.

Experiences with Translating and Adopting AACR2

AACR2 has been translated into Arabic, Bahasa Malaysia, Chinese, Danish, Finnish, French, Italian, Japanese, Norwegian, Portuguese, Spanish, Swedish, Turkish, and Urdu.[25] To get an idea of the problems involved in adopting and translating AACR2, we briefly examine the experiences of Singapore, Malaysia and the People's Republic of China in their attempts to adopt the code. Then we look closely at Kenya's problems in using AACR2. Finally, we survey some of the translation difficulties faced by the Nordic countries and French-speaking Canada.

AACR2 IN THREE ASIAN COUNTRIES

Singapore and Malaysia

Singapore and Malaysia were already using AACR1 and therefore were accustomed to Anglo-American cataloging practices. Both countries timed their adoption of the code in 1981 to coincide with its implementation by the Library of Congress, the British Library, and the National Libraries of Canada and Australia because of interest in the bibliographic exchange of cataloging records and in AACR2's treatment of nonbook materials. Both Singapore and Malaysia made several recommendations to the Joint Steering Committee for the Revision of AACR as conditions for their adoption of AACR2:

1. That the JSC authorize the translation of AACR2 into Chinese and Bahasa Malaysia;
2. That Rule 22.27 for Malay names be adopted with a modification to 22.27D, allowing a title appearing in a father's name to be retained when used consistently by the author, to ensure compatible access points for Malay names in both Singapore and Malaysia; and

3. That the rules for Iban names developed by the National Library of Malaysia be accepted for inclusion in AACR2.[26]

China

The National Library of Beijing, China was using rules similar to the American Library Association 1908 rules until it decided to adopt AACR2. Just prior to making this decision, the Chinese were considering developing a new cataloging code compatible with the standards for description and the order of elements in the ISBDs. However, the Chinese were reluctant to introduce the unfamiliar prescribed punctuation symbols into their cataloging required by the ISBDs and AACR2. Before adopting AACR2, the China Society of Library Science studied the experiences of other countries using the ISBDs to describe non-roman publications, in particular UNESCO's documents on the application of the ISBDs in non-roman scripts, the report of the Working Party on Chinese Cataloguing of the Hong Kong Library Association, Chinese entries in the *Singapore National Bibliography* and the Japan Library Association's *Nippon Cataloguing Rules*.[27] The Chinese were especially interested in the Singapore Library Association's intentions to have AACR2 translated into Chinese.[28]

The Chinese finally opted to use the Singapore Chinese translation of AACR2 and the ISBDs between 1978 and 1983 in the absence of a true national cataloging code, despite the need these standards impose for punctuation. At this time, China was just emerging from the Cultural Revolution and had no national bibliographic agencies in place to spearhead the development of national bibliographic standards. Between 1979 and 1985, the China Scientific and Technical Information Society, the China Society of Library Science, and the China National Technical Committee for Standardization of Documentation were formed. They undertook the development of national cataloging standards incorporating the principles of various traditional Chinese cataloging rules, AACR2, and the ISBDs. Work began on these standards in 1983, and the final text of the Chinese *General Bibliographic Description* was approved by the China National Standard Bureau that same year.[29] Following the publication of the *General Bibliographic Descrip-*

tion, or *BD(G),* nine other *BD*s have been issued, closely patterned after the ISBDs.

However, there is a lack of standardization among the *BD*s because various agencies were responsible for creating them. For instance, there is a complex *BD* for General Material Designations, the *GB3469-83,* and a separate list of GMDs called "Name and Coded Characters of Media" to be used with non-book materials in Appendix A of the *BD(NBM) (Bibliographic Description (Non-Book Materials)).*[30] The GMDs sometimes conflict with the BD.

The Chinese standard that most closely approximates AACR2 is the *Descriptive Cataloguing Rules for Western Language Materials (DCR-WLM),* published in August 1985.[31] It retains the AACR2 main entry concept and principles for the construction of headings, although it contains more detailed instructions on corporate body and conference headings. It pares down the most frequently used AACR2 rules to six chapters and incorporates media-specific rules into the relevant areas of the elements of description. While the *DCR-WLM* has made Chinese bibliographic records for Western language materials easier to share internationally, it also causes non-Chinese-language materials to be entered according to different standards than Chinese-language materials. Differences between the *BD*s, ISBDs, and AACR2 also make international sharing of bibliographic records for Chinese-language materials more difficult. However, since the publication of *AACR2R* and the revised ISBDs, plans are under way to revise both the *BD*s and *DCR-WLM* to bring them more in line with both the ISBDs and AACR2R.[32]

AACR2 in Kenya

The Kenya National Library Service has mandated using AACR2 to catalog in Kenya's public libraries. Kenyan librarians are having great success using AACR2 to catalog the English publications constituting the majority of materials received by Kenyan libraries. However, the Kenyans have discovered a number of problems that make AACR2 difficult to apply to materials written in the dominant vernacular language, Kiswahili, and in the other seventy-odd languages and dialects spoken in Kenya.

For example, Kenyan publishers often do not include title pages in vernacular publications, which necessitates using the cover or another source as the chief source of information. When title pages *are* included, publishers often put different titles on the cover and on the title page, making many title added entries necessary. In addition, publishers often leave out important descriptive elements such as dates, particularly in such religious publications as those of Africa Herald Publishers of Kender Bay.[33] Another confusing practice is the interchangeable use of a variety of terms in Kiswahili for "edition," "reprint," "reimpression," and other imprint terms, making it difficult both to distinguish bibliographically between different versions of a publication and to choose the proper term to use in the edition area.[34]

Besides the descriptive problems in applying AACR2 to vernacular Kenyan publications, by far the biggest problem for Kenyan catalogers is the lack of instructions in AACR2's Chapter 22 for entering African names. The difficulty is to determine which part of a name constitutes the entry element. The Kenyan National Library Service came up with several methods for entering African names, but still encountered several cases that illustrate the problems caused by lack of guidelines.

First, the basic rule adopted by the Kenyan National Library Service was to enter an African name in direct order under the first element of the name, unless that element is of foreign origin. For example, the African author Flora Nwapa would be entered as "Nwapa, Flora" because the first element of her name is a foreign forename, not an African name.[35] The exception to this rule is when an author's preferred form for entering his or her name is known, in which case the author's preference should be respected. However, many times it is difficult to know or to verify the author's preference. This leads to differing entries in catalogs, as with the author Chinua Achebe, who is entered in the Kenyan national bibliography as "Chinua Achebe," but in the *British National Bibliography* as "Achebe, Chinua."

Another confusing case is that of African names with prefixes. AACR2's rule 22.5 and its subrules give detailed instructions for the entry of European names with prefixes, but no hint as to how to enter African names. For example, take a name such as "Stephen Sitoya ole Sankan." If the author chooses not to use his foreign first name, entry is simply under the first element, i.e., "Sitoya ole

Sankan." If the author uses "Stephen" as his first name, then the question is whether the prefix should be part of the entry element or not. Should entry be under "Sankan, Stephen Sitoya ole" or "Ole Sankan, Stephen Sitoya?"

Names of Africans who were *born* Muslims and of those who convert to Islam later in life also pose problems. When the person was born a Muslim, the Muslim name is a surname, and becomes the entry element.

> *Example: Name:* Said Abdalla Mohammed (born Muslim)
> *Entry:* Mohammed, Said Abdalla (Islamic name is surname and entry element)

If the person *converted* to Islam, the Islamic name is a given name, in which case the name follows the principle for vernacular African names and is entered in direct order.

> *Example: Name:* Mohammed Mbashiri Mbwana (converted Muslim)
> *Entry:* Mohammed Mbashiri Mbwana (direct entry)[36]

Yet another problem with entry of African names is the confusion about whether to enter African compound names with foreign elements using rule 22.4A (entry according to elements under which persons would be listed in authoritative lists in his or her own language or country) or 22.5C3 (under the first element in the compound surname).

The problems that Kenya and other English-speaking African countries are experiencing with AACR2 in dealing with vernacular publications could be remedied by several measures.

First, the national libraries of Kenya and other African countries could institute Cataloging-in-Publication programs to put pressure on publishers of Kenyan and other African vernacular materials to standardize title-page elements and edition statements.[37] Second, the African national libraries could send recommendations for changes in AACR2 through national cataloging committees to IFLA for forwarding to the Joint Steering Committee for the Revision of AACR. Third, the Kenyan National Library Service and other national African libraries or their national cataloging committees could draft provisional rules to supplement AACR2, covering such problems as entry elements for African names.

The Nordic Countries' Experiences with Translating AACR2

In the late 1960s, the Nordic countries decided to follow international cataloging standards because of the need for standardization and machine processing of bibliographic records. From 1970 to 1973, four meetings were held to harmonize the various Nordic rules with *AACR1, British edition*; the Paris Principles; the proposed ISBD(M); and the MARC-II format.[38] Denmark issued its new joint rules for research and public libraries in 1974 but did not begin using them immediately. Sweden also issued new rules in 1974, which were initially also used only in research libraries but were later used in preparing the *Swedish National Bibliography.* Norway had published new rules in 1970 based on the ISBDs, which have been used for description in its research libraries since 1972. Norway and Sweden, however, did not translate the ISBDs, but based their rules on the English versions.[39]

Denmark, Finland, Norway, and Sweden all adopted the *AACR1, British edition* principle of corporate authorship, but none of them were completely comfortable with it. Norway's and Sweden's rules were closest to AACR1 and these countries were the most at home with corporate authorship. Denmark and Finland, however, did not adopt corporate authorship completely, especially not for entry of serials, which continued to be entered under title. When AACR2 abandoned corporate authorship for corporate body main entry under certain circumstances, the Nordic countries were most relieved, and this was a primary consideration in their decision to adopt their own versions of the new code. However, abandoning main entry was not without its problems, especially for Norway and Sweden, who then had to do massive recataloging of their serials and make large-scale changes in their online databases.[40]

When the Nordic countries decided to adopt and translate AACR2 they took differing approaches, depending upon how extensive their translations of the ISBDs were. We will examine each country's approach to translating and adopting AACR2 and the problems each encountered in the process.

Denmark

Denmark had translated the ISBDs in 1979, and its 1974 cataloging rules had already incorporated some of the forthcoming changes in AACR2, such as abandoning main entry under editor and corporate author and retaining title main entry for serials.[41] Denmark began using *AACR2* in 1984, beginning with the publication of an integrated manual for serials cataloging which combined the general descriptive rules in Chapter 1 with the Chapter 12 rules for serials and the Chapter 25 rules for serial uniform titles. The manual also included an appendix to the previous Danish rules on choice and form of access points and the revised rules for entry under corporate body. The rules for other materials would follow the AACR2 structure and were due to be drafted by the summer of 1986. The translation of Part II of AACR2 would be limited to general rules for choice of access points in rule 21.0, rule 21.1B for entry under corporate body, and Chapter 25 rules for uniform titles, especially rule 25.5B for serial uniform titles.[42]

Denmark had to make a number of modifications in translating AACR2. First, since Denmark takes a more restrictive approach to entry under corporate body than AACR2 does, it developed a more detailed version of 21.1B1 for determining when a corporate body is named, which it published in the serials manual. In this version of 21.1B1, main entry under corporate body can be made only if the body is prominently named in all cases, not in the case of conferences and exhibitions only, as in 21.1B2d.[43]

The Danes changed sources of information for certain types of material. For instance, they decided that accompanying material could serve as a chief source of information for cartographic materials if the items themselves did not provide adequate information. Also, the chief source for microforms in the case where title frames are lacking or contain incomplete information would be the source that contains the most detailed information, whether it is eye-readable text found on the microform or accompanying material.[44]

There were also changes in some general material designations. For instance, the term "multi-media" would be used for items containing more than three types of materials only. Items with two or three types would list all the general material designations, rather than choosing one only.

Uniform titles have been used rarely in Denmark except as added entries for anonymous classics. Uniform titles would be omitted for treaties and liturgical works, but used restrictively for printed music and sound recordings of classical music.[45]

Finland

Since Finland had already translated the ISBDs, it decided that these were sufficient for its descriptive rules, with the exception of an extension of AACR2's Chapter 13 on analysis for multi-level descriptions of multi-part items. Finland concentrated mostly on translating Part II of AACR2.

Most of Finland's translation problems were due to the long, complicated British sentences, which often had to be rearranged in order to avoid anglicisms. One example of the difficulty of translating AACR2 was the wording of rule 21.1B1, main entry under corporate body. Finland had just instituted corporate authorship successfully in 1977, only to have to abandon it when it decided to switch to AACR2. The term "corporate body" comes out as "corporate corpse" in a literal Finnish translation, so the Finns had to substitute the term "corporation responsible" in 21.1B1. Another difficulty arose in translating the rules for nonbook materials, since the Finns had had little experience with these outside of microforms and sound recordings. An interesting sidelight to Finland's approach to translating AACR2 was its decision to put the code into the passive voice to match the Finnish translation of the ISBDs. Apparently, the Finns don't like to be told what to do.[46]

Finland also had to rewrite the rules for making main entry under names of spirits, churches, religious denominations, liturgical works, and persons or corporate bodies associated with serials, to allow making added entries for them instead. The Finns don't use these types of entities as access points.

Besides problems with translating rules for main entry and corporate bodies, the Finns had some difficulties with the ISBDs, particularly the instructions for transcribing parallel titles and series statements. Finland has two national languages, Finnish and Swedish, and most publications appear with titles not only in these languages but in three or four others as well. Transcribing all those parallel statements creates very long records. The Finns decided simply to mention parallel titles in languages other than Swedish or Finnish in a note.[47]

Another difficult concept for the Finns was the Anglo-American idea of collocating "works," especially with regard to translations, since a large number of these are published in Finland each year. The Finns treat translations as "publications" and make no attempt to collocate them using uniform titles, except for anonymous classics, for which they make uniform title added entries. The original title for translations of other types of works is given in a note.[48]

The Finns welcomed AACR2 Chapter 22, which allows use of national forms of personal names, so that they could use names found in Finnish reference works for such classical authors as Homer. Geographic names posed problems in adopting Chapter 23 because the Finns use two forms of names for a place, one in the nominative, such as "Helsinki," which is generally better known internationally, and one in the genitive, such as "Helsingin Kaupunki," which is better known in Finland.[49]

Norway

Unlike Denmark, Finland, and Iceland, Norway and Sweden had not translated the ISBDs, and both countries were therefore interested in translating the complete AACR2. The Norwegian translation is more literal than Finland's because Norway was accustomed to AACR1 and wanted to stay as close to the English version of AACR2 as possible. Norway too, however, had to make modifications in its translation.

Like Denmark and Finland, Norway had the greatest problems with the translation and interpretation of Chapter 21, especially rules 21.1B1, 21.1B2, and 21.13 for entry of texts with commentary. The principle of corporate authorship was more entrenched in Norway's and Sweden's cataloging practices because they adopted AACR1 earlier than Finland did. In the face of AACR2's abandonment of corporate authorship for corporate main entry under the conditions of 21.1B1 and 21.1B2, the Norwegians felt a strong need for rule interpretations, especially when trying to decide if a corporate body is named or not. They had particular trouble with such statements as "Libraries in the Eighties" (a conference) and "Making an Exhibition: an Exhibition on Exhibitions," where the words "Conference on" and "Exhibition on" do not precede the titles, but the statements look as though they might be named entities. The Library of Congress rule interpretations for the 21.1B2 rules helped straighten out some of the confusion in the United States, but the Norwegian cataloging committee couldn't find any examples in AACR2 to back up the LC interpretations, and were concerned that the interpretations might be local to the United States only.[50]

The Norwegians had to modify Chapter 24's rule 24.18 for subordinate entry of government bodies to include all local agencies using the Norwegian word for "Council" in their names. In the English edition of AACR2, bodies with "Council" in the name are often entered directly.[51]

The Norwegians also added much new material to their edition of AACR2. First, they were dissatisfied with the incomplete descriptions and insufficient number of the examples in the English edition. They added many new examples in Norwegian, making it much larger than the English edition. Next, they enlarged the glossary with 160 new definitions of unfamiliar terms.

The Norwegians, as well as the Danes and the Swedes, make heavy use of multi-level descriptions for multi-part items, particularly in the national bibliography. They extended Chapter 13 rule 13.6 to include more instructions for multi-level descriptions.

The Norwegians decided that to minimize unnecessary confusion and decision-making, numerical designations for serials in Chapter 12 of the Norwegian AACR2 were always to be transcribed as designation followed by numbering, e.g., "v. 1," "Jahrg. 1," etc., rather than as they occur in the item, as in the English AACR2.

Another necessary change involved rearranging certain sections, such as Chapter 8 rules 8.5C and 8.5D for physical details of visual materials and Appendix A.35 through A.53, to conform to Norwegian alphabetical order.

A number of changes in the Norwegian edition pertained to choice and form of names. For instance, entries for classical Greek and Roman names would be made in Greek and Latin rather than in Norwegian, according to older cataloging practice. The English AACR2 prefers a common vernacular form of a classical name if there is one. The Norwegians also added sections to Chapter 22 for the treatment of Pakistani and Vietnamese names, as these two immigrant groups are heavily represented in their user population. Both the Norwegians and the Swedes needed to add a rule to their versions of Chapter 23 called "Places in Scandinavia" in order to deal adequately with local place names.[52]

Sweden

The Swedes adopted AACR2 primarily to consolidate different sets of rules for research and public libraries into one code. The Swedes, like the Norwegians, aimed to stay as close as possible to the English edition of AACR2, but also had to make changes and additions to suit their needs.

The Swedes made several changes in their edition of AACR2 for the benefit of their public libraries. One of these was to add a note to rule 1.0D, levels of description, to allow public libraries to treat works of fiction as "works" rather than as publications. This would allow a title to be cataloged once, with an added note to indicate the date of the first edition, and would eliminate the need to catalog subsequent editions. Another change was to rule 0.13 to allow research and public libraries to use different romanization systems, although examples in the Swedish text of AACR2 show only one system.

The English AACR2 section on entry of legal publications was replaced with two simple sections on laws, stating basically that laws emanating from a corporate body should be entered under that body, and that added entries be made for other persons or bodies involved. Next, the number of examples was reduced, rather than increased as the Norwegians did.

The Swedes also added several appendices to their edition of AACR2. They added extra terms to Appendix B, "Abbreviations," and rewrote Appendix D, the "Glossary," to include sixty new definitions for terms such as "prominently," "government agency," "related work," and "title page substitute." They also added "Appendix E," for uniform titles for works created before 1501, sacred scriptures and anonymous works, and "Appendix F," for names of states in Swedish.

Three changes were made to allow the Swedes to continue certain existing practices. The Swedes rewrote rule 21.1C3, entry under title if a work does not fall into the categories in 21.1B2 and no personal author is involved, to ignore rule 21.1B2 and enter serials under title except in cases of personal authorship.

The Swedes also rewrote Rule 22.2C for choice between variant forms of pseudonyms. Originally, Swedish libraries chose between variant pseudonyms based on forms found in reference sources, on the most recent name, or on the fullest form. In 1974, they began using the form of name found in the item, which led to massive changing of records in databases and remarking of materials. In order to avoid forcing libraries to make even more changes and to spend time tracking down pseudonyms and variant names of an author, the Swedes simply opted to continue to use the form found in the item.[53]

The third change was to the rules for music uniform titles. Rule 25.25 was changed to allow the Swedes to continue the existing practice of using uniform titles in Swedish and Danish. A new rule, 25.27AS, allows an established Swedish uniform title to be used instead of the title in the composer's original language.[54]

The development and now wide-spread use of the LIBRIS automated system for cataloging, acquisitions, and interlibrary loan in Sweden and the other Nordic countries has entrenched *AACR2* as the preferred cataloging code. The adherence to AACR2 as an international standard has allowed Swedish academic libraries to make use of catalog records for British and American materials as well as for Swedish materials. Around 90% of the new English titles included in the *British National Bibliography* and from the Library of Congress database are also loaded in LIBRIS.[55] The Swedish Committee for Cataloguing and Classification published the second edition of the *National Cataloguing Rules* based on AACR2R in 1990.[56]

Despite the problems with translating and adopting AACR2, the Nordic countries have been generally receptive to it because it offers one integrated set of rules for different types of libraries, incorporates rules for all materials into one sequence, and facilitates international exchange of bibliographic data by standardizing description of catalog records.

French-Speaking Canada

Although one would think that cataloging rules adopted from France or French-speaking African countries might be more useful, French-Canadian libraries decided to translate first the American Library Association's 1941 cataloging rules, then the 1950 Vatican rules, and finally AACR1 because of the need to share cataloging with their English-speaking neighbors. After the British and North American texts of AACR1 were published in 1967, the École de bibliothéconomie de l'Université de Montréal made an agreement with the American Library Association to translate AACR1 into French.[57] *AACR1* had not been conceived with international use in mind, so that many changes had to be made in translation to adapt the rules for bilingual French and English catalogs.

The editors of AACR2, mindful of the international adoption of AACR1, were more aware of the problems of adoption from the experience gained in translating AACR1 into French, and therefore set about making the revised edition of AACR more flexible for international use. Rule 0.12 in AACR2, allowing for authorized translations and the replacement of the specified preference for English by a preference for the working language of a country is a direct outgrowth of this awareness.

In order to continue to share bibliographic data with the English-speaking Canadian and American library communities, the French-Canadians decided to translate AACR2 also and to make any necessary modifications for use with French-language cataloging. The code was translated by Paule Rolland-Thomas, professor of library science at the École de bibliothéconomie de l'Université de Montréal.[58]

Some of the problems in translating the code into French centered on matters of French usage and style, while others dealt with problems of main entry under corporate body, uniform titles, and the slant towards British and American culture inherent in certain rules in Chapters 22 through 25.

Differences in French usage and spelling caused the French Canadians to omit rule 0.2, which gives instructions for English usage and spelling only. Also, translator's notes had to be added instructing French Canadian users to ignore a number of rules, such as

Appendix A rules A.18D for lowercase names of political and economic systems, and A.26, for geologic terms. In addition, the order of items in Appendix A had to be rearranged to put the rules for French capitalization first and to list the rules for other languages in French alphabetical order. The Appendix B.9 general abbreviations list was supplemented with a list of terms taken from the Association française de normalisation (AFNOR) standards. Another translator's note was required telling French Canadian catalogers to ignore the English list of abbreviations for countries, provinces, and states in B.14 and to use a short substitute list, since few geographical names are abbreviated in French.[59]

Translating Part II of AACR2 into French presented more problems than did Part I, as with the Nordic language translations. First, the abandonment of corporate authorship in AACR2 caused some difficulty translating 21.1B2, since the phrase "if it originated with that body" could be rendered in French only as "if the body is the author" ("si la collectivité en est l'auteur").[60] Rolland-Thomas speculates that the idea of corporate body as originator of a work came from Verona's work on corporate headings, in which she translates the German "Urheber" as "originator," because the word "Verfasser" (author) can be used for persons only.[61] Rolland-Thomas concludes that the translation problem in 21.1B2 really comes from the lack of a strict theoretical concept of the ideas of "authorship" and "responsibility" in AACR2.[62]

Certain biases toward English and American language and culture and Anglo-American cataloging practices created problems in translating parts of Chapters 22 through 25. Rules 22.6 A1-A3 give instructions for entering names of nobility, but most of the examples are for British names, with few for French or other nationalities. Chapter 23 gives specific rules for geographic names of areas in the United States, Canada, the United Kingdom, and Australia, but not for names in French-speaking Canada. The rules for entry of legal publications and for government headings in Chapter 24 favor the British and American legal and governmental systems. Additions to headings as well as subheadings for uniform titles must be given in English in the original edition of AACR2. This created problems in translating such rules as 25.18A3, uniform titles for the individual books of the Bible, which must be based on the *Authorized Version,* for which there is no French equivalent.[63]

Despite these problems of translating AACR2 into French, Rolland-Thomas sums up the finished product in these words: "As far as we know, the *Règles de catalogage anglo-américaines, Deuxième édition* serve the French-language Canadian cataloguing community rather well; we might now question their appropriateness for other French language cataloguing agencies. The 'internationalization' of AACR2 could offer a challenging endeavour for years to come."[64]

Evidently, since the translation of AACR2, French Canadian libraries have continued to use the code successfully. AACR2R was translated into French in 1989 by the Association pour l'avancement des sciences et des techniques de la documentation (ASTED).[65]

CONCLUSION

We have seen that a number of countries were induced to adopt AACR2 as their cataloging code by such factors as the wide-spread respect for and international adoption of AACR1, the incorporation of the ISBDs into the revised AACR, the need for standardization, especially of machine-readable records, and provisions to allow authorized translations of the code and substitution of "working languages" other than English.

In addition, we saw that most of the countries that have adopted or translated AACR2 have encountered problems with the difficult concepts of main entry, entry of serials, and entry under corporate body. The abandonment of corporate authorship in Part II of the English edition of AACR2 also caused problems. Lesser problems stemming from idiomatic differences hampered the translation of the rules for description in Part I of AACR2.

Despite all the troubles encountered in translating AACR2, those countries now using it either in English or in their own languages appear to find it satisfactory for most, if not all, of their needs. Since cataloging needs differ so across countries, it seems unlikely that one international code could serve them all.

AACR2 and the ISBDs have gone a long way toward standardizing bibliographic description, and the MARC formats, particularly

UNIMARC, have made international exchange of bibliographic information much easier. Indeed, there is now a move afoot by the Library of Congress and the British Library to harmonize the differences between the USMARC and UKMARC formats, creating one common MARC format for Anglo-American materials. On June 24, 1994, LC and the British Library met to discuss this topic and to explore the possibility of preparing a discussion paper to examine the links between AACR2 and the MARC format, possibly leading to a simplified and less costly cataloging record.[66]

It remains to be seen whether it is possible or desirable to standardize choice and form of access points, since users in different cultures search for personal, corporate, and geographic names in different ways, and since national libraries will generally standardize authoritative forms of names in their respective countries. Also, the publication of the International Federation of Library Associations and Institutions' *Guidelines for Authorities and Reference Entries* in 1984 makes it possible to develop a UNIMARC authorities format and an international authority file that links variant national forms of headings.[67]

The IFLA Sections on Information Technology and Library Services to Multicultural Populations have advocated including all scripts and languages in cataloging rules and in future catalogs.[68] For now, since AACR2 is the most widely-used body of cataloging rules, it is the closest thing we have to an international code.

NOTES

1. Michael Gorman and Paul W. Winkler, eds. *Anglo-American Cataloguing Rules, 2nd Edition.* (Chicago: American Library Association, 1978).
   Michael Gorman and Paul W. Winkler, eds. *Anglo-American Cataloguing Rules, 2nd Edition, Revised.* (Chicago: American Library Association, 1988).
   Hereafter cited as *AACR2* and *AACR2R,* respectively.
2. Telephone conversation between Richard P. Smiraglia and Karen Muller, Executive Director, Resources and Technical Services Division, Oct. 19, 1987; supplemented by telephone conversations with Helen F. Schmierer, ALA representative to the Joint Steering Committee for the Revision of AACR, Oct. 22, 1987, and with Evelyn Schavel, Director of Marketing, ALA Publishing, June 3, 1991. *Referenced In*: Richard P. Smiraglia, ed. *Origins, Content and Future of AACR2 Revised.* ALCTS Papers on Library Technical Services and Collections, no. 2. (Chicago: American Library Association, 1992), p. xii.

Hereafter cited as *Smiraglia*.

3. *Anglo-American Cataloguing Rules*. (London: Library Association, 1967).

Anglo-American Cataloguing Rules. (Chicago: American Library Association, 1967).

Hereafter cited as *AACR1* and/or *AACR1, British edition* and *AACR1, North American edition*, respectively.

4. *Statement of Principles Adopted at the International Conference on Cataloguing Principles, Paris, October 1961*. Annotated ed., with commentary and examples by Eva Verona. (London: IFLA Committee on Cataloguing, 1971).

Hereafter cited as the *Paris Principles*.

5. *ISBD(M): International Standard Bibliographic Descriptions for Monographic Publications*. 1st standard ed. (London: IFLA Committee on Cataloguing, 1974).

6. Ellen J. Gredley. "Standardizing Bibliographic Data: AACR2 and International Exchange." *Journal of Librarianship* v. 12, no. 2 (April 1980): 84.

Hereafter known as *Gredley*.

7. "IFLA International Meeting of Cataloguing Experts, Copenhagen, 1969." *Library Resources and Technical Services* v. 14, no. 2 (Spring 1970): 292-96.

Hereafter cited as *IMCE*.

8. *IMCE*, p. 292.

9. *AACR2*, p. *1*.

AACR2R, p. 1

10. *AACR2*, p. 2.

AACR2R, p. 14.

11. Alan Jeffrey. "The *Anglo-American Cataloguing Rules, 2nd edition (AACR2)*: Now and in Europe." *In* Lorcan Dempsey, ed. *Bibliographic Access in Europe: First International Conference* [proceedings, University of Bath, 14-17 September 1989]. (Aldershot, Hants.: Gower, 1990), p. 265.

12. *AACR2*, p. 2.

AACR2R, p. 14.

13. Shojiro Maruyama. "Descriptive Cataloguing and the Cataloguing Rules in Japan." *International Cataloguing* v. 15, no. 3 (July-Sept. 1986): 28-29.

14. *Gredley*, p. 86.

15. *AACR2*, rule 21.1B2, p. 285.

AACR2R, rule 21.1B2, p. 314.

16. *Gredley*, p. 87.

17. *AACR2*, rule 23.2, p. 395.

18. *AACR2 and AACR2R*, rule 0.12, p. 3.

19. Christoph Kirchner. "AACR2, RAK und ihre problematischen Anwendungsstufen: auf der Suche nach RAK-WB und RAK-ÖB." *Buch und Bibliothek* v. 32, no. 3 (1980): 262.

20. Inger Cathrine Spangen. "Implementation of AACR2 in the Nordic Countries." *Catalogue & Index* no. 81 (Summer 1986): 2-3.

Hereafter cited as *Spangen*.

21. *Gredley*, p. 93-94.

22. Dorothy Anderson. "The Future of the Anglo-American Cataloguing Rules (AACR) in the Light of Universal Bibliographic Control (UBC)." *Library Resources and Technical Services* v. 20, no. 1 (Winter 1976): 7.

23. *Gredley*, p. 98.

24. Dorothy Anderson. *Standard Practices in the Preparation of Bibliographic Records*. Rev. ed. (Paris: IFLA UBCIM Programme, 1989). *Referenced in:* Alan Jeffreys. "The *Anglo-American Cataloguing Rules 2nd Edition, (AACR2)*: Now and in Europe." *Lorcan Dempsey, ed. Bibliographic Access in Europe: First International Conference*. (Aldershot, Hants.: Gower, 1990). p. 262.

25. *Smiraglia*, p. xii.

Citations to the publication titles of AACR2 in the various translations are not provided in *Smiraglia* and they are beyond the scope of this paper. Compilation of such a bibliography is left to the author of another, future paper. Additional information may be obtained from the publishers of AACR2.

26. "IFLA activities: Singapore: LAS/PPM Joint Cataloguing Seminar 8-10 December 1980." *International Cataloguing* v. 10, no. 1 (Jan.-Mar. 1981): 4-5.

27. "IFLA Activities: People's Republic of China: Notes on Cataloguing Activities." *International Cataloguing* v. 10, no. 3 (July-Sept. 1981): 28.

28. Ibid.

29. Yan Yi-Qiao and He Yun. "Recent Development of Descriptive Cataloguing in China, 1980-1990." *International Cataloguing & Bibliographic Control* v. 20, no. 4 (Oct./Dec. 1991): 60-61.

Hereafter cited as *Yi-Qiao*.

30. *Yi-Qiao*, p. 62.

31. Ibid.

32. *Yi-Qiao*, p. 64.

33. Monica R. S. Nyabundi. "Local Cataloguing Problems in Public Libraries in Kenya: With Special Reference to the Kenya National Library Service." *International Cataloguing* v. 13, no. 4 (July-Sept. 1984): 33-34.

Hereafter cited as *Nyabundi*.

34. Ibid.

35. *Nyabundi*, p. 33.

36. *Nyabundi*, p. 34.

37. Tirong K. arap Tanui. "Cataloguing Problems and Multilingualism in Kenya." *International Cataloguing* v. 13, no. 3 (July-Sept. 1984): 35-36.

38. Karen Lunde Christensen. "AACR2 and the Nordic Countries." In: Graham Roe, ed. *Seminar on AACR2: proceedings of a seminar organized by the Cataloguing and Indexing Group of the Library Association at the University of Nottingham, 20-22, 1979*. (London: Library Association, 1980), p. 32.

Hereafter cited as *Christensen*.

39. Ibid.

40. *Spangen*, p. 1.

41. *Christensen*, p. 34.

42. Ibid.

43. *Spangen*, p. 2.

44. *Spangen,* p. 5.

45. Ibid.

46. Thea Aulo. "Translating ISBD and AACR2 into Finnish." *International Cataloguing* v. 15, no. 2 (Apr.-June 1986): 21.

47. Ibid.

48. *Spangen,* p. 3.

49. *Spangen,* p. 4.

50. *Spangen,* p. 3.

51. *Ibid.*

52. *Spangen,* p. 3-5.

53. Ibid.

54. Ibid.

55. Ingrid Cantwell. "The Swedish Bibliographic Scene." *International Cataloguing & Bibliographic Control* v. 19, no. 2 (Apr./June 1990): 20-21.

56. "Sweden: New Edition of Cataloguing Rules." *International Cataloguing & Bibliographic Control* v. 19, no. 4 (Oct./Dec. 1990): 64.

57. Paule Rolland-Thomas. "An Examination of the International Status of AACR2 Through the Translation Process: the French Version." *International Cataloguing* v. 15, no. 2 (Apr.-June 1986): 19-20.

Hereafter cited as *Rolland-Thomas.* The translation of the French version of AACR appeared in 1973 as the *Règles de catalogage anglo-américaines* (abbreviated RCAA).

58. Lise Lavigne. "Le catalogage au Canada francophone." *International Cataloging* v. 11, no. 3 (July-Sept. 1982): 30.

59. *Rolland-Thomas,* p. 20.

60. Ibid.

61. Eva Verona. *Corporate Headings: Their Use in Library Catalogues and National Bibliographies: A Comparative and Critical Study.* (London: IFLA Committee on Cataloguing, 1975), p. 15.

62. *Rolland-Thomas,* p. 20.

63. Ibid.

64. Ibid.

65. "French translation of AACR2 (1988 revision)." *International Cataloguing & Bibliographic Control* v. 18, no. 1 (Jan./Mar. 1989): 2.

66. "Toward a Common MARC Format." *LC Cataloging Newsline* v. 2, no. 6 (Aug. 1994): Item no. 4 [online newsletter]; available from listserv@lccn.loc.gov; INTERNET.

67. Tom Delsey. "Authority Control in an International Context." *Cataloguing & Classification Quarterly* v. 9, no. 3 (1989): 20-23.

68. Eeva Murtomaa. "Second IFLA Satellite Meeting on Automated Systems for Access to Multilingual and Multiscript Library Materials, Madrid, 18 & 19 August 1993." *International Cataloguing & Bibliographic Control* v. 23, no. 1 (Jan./Mar. 1994): 10-11.

The Evolution of LCRIs–
From *De Facto* Standard to ?

Kay Guiles
Robert Ewald
Barbara Tillett

SUMMARY. This paper describes the evolution of *Library of Congress Rule Interpretations (LCRIs)* from what initially was internal documentation prepared for the use of descriptive catalogers at the Library of Congress to their status as a *de facto* national cataloging standard today and explores the role they may play in the cataloging of the future. *[Article copies available from The Haworth Document Delivery Service: 1-800-342-9678.]*

INTRODUCTION

Descriptive cataloging, which collocates works, describes items, and provides non-subject access, is governed by the *Anglo-American Cataloguing Rules,* 2nd ed., 1988 Revision (*AACR2R*). The rules embody internationally agreed upon conventions and standards, namely the Paris Principles and the *International Standard Bibliographic Description,* used for the bibliographic control of a wide

Kay Guiles and Robert Ewald are Senior Cataloging Policy Specialists, Cataloging Policy and Support Office, Library of Congress, Washington, DC 20540-4305. Barbara Tillett is Chief of the Cataloging Policy and Support Office, Library of Congress, Washington, DC 20540-4305.

[Haworth co-indexing entry note]: "The Evolution of LCRIs–From *De Facto* Standard to ?" Guiles, Kay, Robert Ewald, and Barbara Tillett. Co-published simultaneously in *Cataloging & Classification Quarterly* (The Haworth Press, Inc.) Vol. 21, No. 3/4, 1996, pp. 61-74; and: *Cataloging and Classification Standards and Rules* (ed: John J. Riemer) The Haworth Press, Inc., 1996, pp. 61-74. Single or multiple copies of this article are available from The Haworth Document Delivery Service [1-800-342-9678, 9:00 a.m. - 5:00 p.m. (EST)].

variety of materials issued in various media and according to various patterns. While the rules themselves are extensive, they include options and alternative rules, which cataloging agencies are to decide upon and then to record as binding decisions (*AACR2R* rule 0.7). In addition, clarification is sometimes needed when rules are worded ambiguously or are silent regarding particular situations. Therefore, the rules are supplemented by rule interpretations issued at the national level by some of the national agencies that are themselves the authors of the *Anglo-American Cataloguing Rules*. The *Library of Congress Rule Interpretations* (*LCRIs*) are those rule interpretations issued by the Library of Congress for its own guidance and for libraries in the United States.

Rule interpretations are stimulated by a combination of factors, some relating to the nature of the rules themselves (e.g., the characteristics of their design, their completeness, their intelligibility) and others relating to extra-rule considerations. Given the breadth of coverage of materials, the changeability of publishing/issuing practices, the variability of online library systems, and the broad range of users to be served, it is likely that any set of widely-applied rules will require rule interpretations. Rule interpretations can serve as a common frame of reference in approaching cataloging problems for the U.S. library community, a means of exchanging information, and a method for supporting an overall consistency, thus making it easier to share records.

BACKGROUND

The development of documentation in support of descriptive cataloging at the Library of Congress has itself been an evolutionary undertaking. Catalogers seemingly always have kept notes for themselves on solutions to particular problems and documented rules. Cataloging rules for the Library of Congress existed in handwritten form in the 19th century. Even after the availability of printed cataloging rules, such as the *A.L.A. Rules-Advance Edition* issued by the Library of Congress in 1902 and again in 1904, LC's catalogers had their "Rules on cards" typed on 3 × 5 inch card stock and kept in shoe boxes at their desks. The rules on cards were created and distributed among LC's catalogers from approximately

1899 through about 1941 when the *A.L.A. Catalog Rules, Author and Title Entries* was published by the American Library Association.

In 1949, LC's publication, *Rules for Descriptive Cataloging,* was published as a complementary volume to the 1949 *A.L.A. Cataloging Rules for Author and Title Entries.* In the late 1950's through the 1960's there were attempts to distribute further documentation of some of LC's decisions regarding descriptive cataloging, for example decisions of the meetings of section heads were recorded and distributed, but for the most part catalogers developed their own means of "documentation" such as annotating their copies of the rules, inserting notes on cards or paper at the appropriate place in the rules, or continuing their own separate files of 3 × 5 cards recording decisions, examples, etc. Much of this information was recorded by new catalogers during the course of their training as they worked closely with an experienced advisor. Ben Tucker reported:

> As long as the neophyte was under revision there was a good deal of coordination of these answers, etc., between the personal apparatus of the reviser and that of the trainee. There was no comparable attempt at coordination among members of a section, or indeed among the various sections—at least not normally. Of course in the case of major disagreements or the discovery of really major decisions, word was passed around a section by the section head or to all the section heads by the principal descriptive cataloger.[1]

In June 1960 the Library of Congress introduced the antecedent to the current *LCRIs.* The announcement of this significant decision appeared in *Cataloging Service,* Bulletin 55, June 1960:

> A new series of memoranda, called "Cataloging Memoranda," has been inaugurated by the Chief of the Descriptive Cataloging Division as a vehicle for conveying directives dealing with the cataloging policies and interpretations of cataloging rules to be followed by the staff of the Descriptive Cataloging Division. Insofar as they are deemed to have some

general interest to readers of *Cataloging Service* they will be reproduced herein. Several of these memoranda appear below.

Material from these decisions appeared from time to time through December 1964. After a hiatus, a combination of factors, including the expansion and rearrangement of some of the cataloging staff at LC in 1966 and the adoption of the *Anglo-American Cataloging Rules (AACR1)* in 1967, led to another series of documentation, this time called "Cataloging Decisions," as announced in *Cataloging Service,* Bulletin 96, November 1970:

> In June 1968 the Library of Congress began to make its cataloging decisions available in processed form for the use of its descriptive catalogers but not for general distribution. By this means the catalogers are informed of official LC interpretations and decisions relating to the application of the *Anglo-American Cataloging Rules* together with directives relating to cataloging routines. With the thought that some of this material may be of considerable interest to other libraries, the following excerpts are published in virtually unedited form. The decisions are arranged according to the number of the pertinent Anglo-American rule, with several which do not fit neatly under a rule at the end, arranged alphabetically by topic.

As an interesting aside, prior to the adoption of *AACR1,* the chief of the Descriptive Cataloging Division had attempted to discourage the "personal documentation" noted above by asking catalogers to turn in their copies of the rules and begin "afresh" with "clean" copies.[2] This was a transition period of moving from individual practice among LC's catalogers to more widespread standardization of practice described in shared documentation.

Note that the mood in the late 1960s was still somewhat relaxed ("With the thought that some of this material may be of considerable interest to other libraries . . . "). Although the development of MARC (MAchine-Readable Cataloging) had taken place and the Library of Congress had begun issuing catalog records in machine-readable form in 1968, the infrastructure to support the nearly century-long effort at shared cataloging was only beginning to be developed. Sharing online records revealed an even greater need for standardization of an "acceptable" record.

The "official LC interpretations" announced in 1970 continued to be published, with the caption "Rule Interpretations" first appearing in bulletin 123, Fall 1977 (the title of *Cataloging Service* having meanwhile changed to *Cataloging Service Bulletin* (*CSB*) beginning with number 1, Summer 1978). While Rule Interpretations to *AACR1* continued to be issued, information pertaining to the *Anglo-American Cataloguing Rules,* second edition, 1978 (*AACR2*) first began appearing in *CSB* number 2, Fall 1978. The caption "Rule Interpretations for AACR 2" first appeared in *CSB* number 6, Fall 1979 as the result of the Library of Congress' early application of chapters 22-25 of *AACR2*:

> to provide some extra information in the automated name authority file. (This application of *AACR 2* has no effect on currently used headings, which must continue to be formulated under *AACR 1* and the Library's policy of superimposition.) We have developed a number of rule interpretations for the guidance of our catalogers working with *AACR 2,* chapters 22-25, and these statements are being reproduced here.

This application was in anticipation of adopting *AACR2* in 1981. Rule interpretations for *AACR1* continued, but now under the caption "AACR 1 Rule Interpretations" and the first formal rule interpretations for *AACR2* appeared in *CSB* number 10, Fall 1980. The very next issue, number 11, Winter 1981, p. 2, contains the following notice:

> *Library of Congress Rule Interpretations.* As a convenience to the library community the Library of Congress rule interpretations to be applied beginning January 2, 1981, are being republished in their entirety. Although many of the statements have appeared in the last few issues of *Cataloging Service Bulletin,* additional interpretations have been developed or brought over from pre-*AACR 2* interpretations. It seems preferable to have a single series of documents to which to refer.

This point might be regarded as the formal birth of the *LCRIs* as we know them today.

A final step in increasing their accessibility was taken in January 1988 when they became available through subscription from the Library's Cataloging Distribution Service. The subscription service included the basic set of *LCRIs,* with updates issued quarterly. That pattern of publication continues today, as well as the continued publication of *LCRIs* in *CSB.* (The internally issued documentation series "Rule Interpretations" continued simultaneously with the CDS issued *Library of Congress Rule Interpretations* until 1989.)

CURRENT STATE OF AFFAIRS

As the *LCRIs* continued to be issued in the 1980s, other well-known developments, such as the increased application of auto-mated techniques to bibliographic control, the development of bib-liographic utilities, the development of library networks, reductions in cataloging staff, and increased budgetary constraints throughout the library community, served to mandate an increased use of shared catalog records, now made possible by the technological developments mentioned above. These activities in turn began to transform the environment of bibliographic control from one in which relatively disparate agencies "did their own thing" in rela-tive isolation, except perhaps for the bibliographic services pro-vided by the Library of Congress, to one in which copy cataloging (use of a common record over and over by many libraries) began to assume increasing importance as a means of addressing some of the serious budgetary problems experienced by libraries. At the same time the emphasis on common practice to minimize the need to change records used in copy cataloging began to focus on the *LCRIs* as the basis for a common standard–albeit one in which there was increasing concern over the cost their application might entail.

The various bibliographic utilities (e.g., OCLC, RLIN, WLN) recommended following the *LCRIs* along with the *Anglo-American Cataloguing Rules* as the national standard for descriptive catalog-ing to be followed by their members in preparing new online rec-ords added to their databases.[3] This expanded the use of *LCRIs* to a much wider audience than before. As more libraries began using *LCRIs,* the number of rule interpretations was perceived to be ex-cessive and the presence of LC-specific requirements was called to question. Cries against LC-centric rules were heard. This contributed to the Cooperative Cataloging Council's call in 1994 for re-examination of the *LCRIs* to seek more generalized rule interpretations.

In 1977, at about the same time as the bibliographic utilities were expanding their membership, selected libraries participated with the Library of Congress in a major cooperative endeavor that established the Name Authority Co-Operative Project (NACO) to create a common name authority database. The premise of the project was that participants follow the cataloging policies of the Library of Congress. Indeed, participants became contributors in formulating that policy by responding to *LCRI* proposals and by requesting that special needs be addressed in the *LCRIs*. The early to mid-1980s saw various developments with respect to the contribution of bibliographic records (the Government Printing Office began a cooperative cataloging program with LC in 1981; Harvard began to input records via LC in 1983; the National Library of Medicine began in 1984 to cooperate with LC in preparing records relating to medicine through the Cataloging In Publication (CIP) program; the University of Chicago began to input records via LC in 1985 as the result of a major project to incorporate the holdings of the John Crerar Library; the University of Illinois began to contribute records for Slavic materials in 1986).

These efforts at cooperative cataloging programs utilizing online bibliographic and authority files culminated in 1988 in a more formal program, the National Coordinated Cataloging Program (NCCP). The NCCP participants, stimulated by a need to bring down the costs of cataloging, convened a meeting in July 1989 to discuss cataloging "simplification." Part of that effort involved identifying those *LCRIs* that should be changed to make them easier to apply. A follow-up effort, called cataloging "modification," was initiated in 1991 by the National Agricultural Library and the National Library of Medicine. By now the attempts at cooperative cataloging had led to a major concern about policy and its ultimate effect on standards and cooperative cataloging. The calls for cataloging "simplification," the need to rely more heavily on solutions in technology, and the continued concern about the cost of bibliographic control led to new initiatives in seeking remedies for these concerns. The NCCP was judged as being in need of substantial change and revitalization.[4]

The new initiative was begun in November 1992 at a meeting of representatives from NCCP, the CONSER Policy Committee, the Library of Congress, and others with a stake in cooperative cataloging. The group of almost 50 participants reaffirmed its support for sharing in the creation of mutually acceptable records that followed agreed upon standards, and decided to propose the next steps towards their goal during the midwinter conference of the American Library Association in January 1993. Subsequently, the Cooperative Cataloging Council (CCC) was established in April 1993.[5] The CCC attempted to address a variety of issues related to cooperative cataloging, and to that end established a series of task groups to address them.[6] One of the task groups is the CCC/CPSO Task Group on LC-Issued Descriptive Cataloging Documentation whose charge is to:

1. Identify RIs that exist because of inadequacies in the cataloging code. Notify Barbara Tillett's CCC task group on code revision of suggested rule revisions.
2. Prior to the 1994 ALA Annual Conference, develop a statement outlining the philosophy, purpose, and rationale for creating RIs. Create a comprehensive list of conditions requiring an RI; e.g., local options, accommodation of special interest groups, system requirements, etc.
3. Examine each RI and indicate the conditions from the above list that apply to it, and develop an action plan to implement an efficient revision of the RIs. Complete the revision process in the shortest practicable time period.[7]

In the course of its work the Task Group took a census of the LCRIs to ascertain their current state. As part of that census the Task Group counted what it called "rule statements" in *AACR2R* (directions/ statements that contain actual text exclusive of headers without text or those that contain only examples but no text) and "direction statements" in the RIs (sections/paragraphs on a common theme or topic), there being 2065 of the former and 710 of the latter. Of the total number of direction statements in the RIs, 12.11% fall into the category of what the Task Group judged "explanation," 8.87% are in the category of *AACR2R* being "incomplete," and 27.61% are in the category of *AACR2R* requiring "amplification." Seventy-seven (10.8%) of the direction statements were stimulated by special interests. Of those 77 direction statements, 25 (32.4% (3.5% of the total)) relate to issues of interest to law librarians; 23 (29.8% (3.2% of the total)) relate to issues of interest to music librarians. The remaining 29 direction statements (37.8% (4.1% of the total)) relate to issues originating from a variety of other special interest groups.

In its statement on the results of the LCRI census that accompanies the Task Group's *Interim report,* the Task Group categorized the rule interpretations as follows:

1. **Option decisions**. There are several options and alternative rules in *AACR2*. Rule 0.7 instructs cataloging agencies to make decisions about these options and to keep a record of these decisions.

2. **Rule change implementation announcements**. The Joint Steering Committee for Revision of *AACR* (JSC) continuously revises *AACR2* but only publishes updates to the code on an infrequent basis. If the JSC chooses to sanction implementation of a rule change before it is issued formally as a rule change, the rule change can appear in an RI.

3. **Rule replacement decisions**. In exceptional circumstances, LC decides not to follow the rules as written. Such decisions are based on an assessment of the impact of the rule were it to be followed and a judgment, after consultation with other interested agencies, with respect to whether the impact is a desirable one or not. An RI is provided for each rule that LC does not follow.

4. **Rule explications**. *AACR2* does not explicitly cover all situations that exist in the bibliographic universe. Neither is it always adequate to the needs of current bibliographic control without supplementary clarification. Thus an RI is provided when consistency is desirable or when the RI can help shorten the decision-making process (or both). RIs address rule explications in the following situations:

   a. *AACR2 is silent. AACR2* does not include a provision to cover the situation.

   b. *AACR2 needs explanation.* The *AACR2* provision is not self-evident as to its intent.

   c. *AACR2 is incomplete.* The *AACR2* provision does not go far enough in dealing with the situation.

   d. *AACR2 needs amplification. AACR2* provides a basic general principle that requires additional development work to implement the principle in a manner that supports standard bibliographic control, particularly in an environment in which records are increasingly shared.

   e. *AACR2 needs correction.* Something in the text itself needs correction.

   f. *LC procedures.* Library of Congress procedures developed for its cataloging operation.

5. **Inter-code policies.** *AACR2* is written as if all bibliographic and authority records in the catalog are constructed according to *AACR2.* In our practical world, *AACR2* records mingle with records created according to *AACR 1,* the ALA rules, and other conventions. An RI is provided when consistency is desirable when dealing with records of different heritages or when the RI can help shorten the decision-making process or when significant time or money can be saved.[8]

The Task Group's report also identified the following optimal characteristics of rule interpretations, which will also govern their revision in the future:

1. **Environment.** After the adoption of *AACR2* in 1981, many of the RIs were stimulated by conditions encountered in day-to-day cataloging activities. Although the application of automated techniques to bibliographic control had been introduced many years prior to the adoption of *AACR2,* there were still many libraries that did not yet make extensive use of automation either directly or indirectly. Thus in creating RIs, it was necessary to take into account both manual and machine modes of bibliographic control. This introduced a kind of ambiguity of purpose in the RIs in that some of the conventions in support of a manual mode were no longer needed in a machine mode and vice versa. With the increasing and extensive

technological developments of the last several years, it now appears that enough time has elapsed to permit the focus of RIs to be bibliographic control in a machine environment.

2. **Language**. Because to utilize the RIs to their fullest advantage all users must understand them in the same way and because many subtleties are lost in textual translation, the RIs are written in English.

3. **Content**. RIs will embody the following characteristics when practicable:

    1. the terminology used is that of, or is consistent with, *AACR2*;
    2. terminology specific to 3 × 5 images of bibliographic data is not used;
    3. examples are used liberally; whenever meaningful, an attempt is made to include an English-language example, especially when an understanding of the RI is dependent upon a clear understanding of the sense of the example;
    4. examples that are complete USMARC fields are shown with USMARC content designation; and
    5. each RI is as self-contained as possible.

4. **Presentation**. Many of the RIs are seen as being too "dense," i.e., essentially a lot of text without any structural conventions that might be used to elicit or highlight key factors. It is not clear that this can be easily corrected, since in some cases the RI emulates the layout of the rule in an attempt to provide structural assistance in that manner. Nevertheless, exploring the design of a model RI is a worthwhile enterprise. Some of the possible issues to explore are:

    1. design a standard means of orienting the RI; such an orientation might include the scope of the rule, the scope of the RI, the purpose of the RI, and the context of the RI;
    2. develop a standard design, with appropriate use of typography and layout; provide, as needed, a bridge from one page to the next;
    3. label made-up examples as such;

4. put examples in context;
5. use a standard monospaced font; and
6. use a standard means of indicating matter applicable within LC only.[9]

5. **Limitations.** The RIs supplement the rules; they are not seen as a stand-alone tool. They are not designed for training or performance evaluation purposes. Their use assumes a basic knowledge of cataloging and some experience with the conventions of bibliographic control. Other documentation is much more suitable for training and other purposes. Some examples are: *CONSER Cataloging Manual*; LC's *Cataloging Concepts: Descriptive Cataloging*.[10]

THE FUTURE

The work of the Task Group on the LCRIs will take many months to complete and should result in rule interpretations that will clarify and standardize practices for all participants in our shared cataloging efforts. A new model for the rule interpretations prescribes the use of MARC content designation in examples, an improvement which was frequently requested by respondents to various CCC surveys.

The CCC itself has now evolved into the Program for Cooperative Cataloging (PCC), which will include governing members from the British Library and the National Library of Canada in addition to a group of standing representatives and elected representatives from U.S. libraries. This is just one of several converging activities that lead us to formulating changes to the *LCRIs*. International cooperation with the other major players in the *Anglo-American Cataloguing Rules* and the proposed development of an Anglo-American Authority File (AAAF) is resulting in efforts to further standardize our cataloging practices and converge the various MARC formats we use to share bibliographic and authority records. There are many issues to be resolved in these international efforts, not the least of which is the governance for future management and maintenance of cataloging rules and rule interpretations. The PCC's Standing Committee on Standards will be addressing many of these important issues. Rule interpretations will remain as a method of documenting standard practices that are not incorporated in the cataloging rules themselves, although it is hoped that many of the rule interpretations will find their way into revised rules in the *Anglo-American Cataloguing Rules.*

Moreover, there will continue to be a need for institution-specific instructions to accommodate the individual characteristics of local systems' retrieval, display, and normalization capabilities. It is hoped that local systems will evolve with the best features rising to become standard, but that may take many years, if not decades, to accomplish. It has proven useful for the Library of Congress to document and share its practices with other libraries in order to facilitate their interpreting LC's bibliographic and authority records found in shared databases. As LC's own computer systems evolve, the rule interpretations and other documentation of cataloging practices will change accordingly.

The availability of the *LCRIs* is also evolving. Once as internal memoranda, then as notices in the *CSB,* and currently as an LC publication from the Cataloging Distribution Service, the *LCRIs* are also available on the CDS product, the Cataloger's DeskTop. This online product includes hypertext links among the various documents in its database and can be loaded into a local area network environment to allow for shared annotations. We can expect further links to other online LC cataloging documentation in the future, possibly including access through the Internet.

NOTES

1. Ben R. Tucker, "Ask Me No Questions and I'll Write You No RIs," in *The Conceptual Foundations of Descriptive Cataloging* (San Diego : Academic Press, 1989), pp. 46-47.

2. *Ibid,* p. 47.

3. For example, in OCLC's current documentation, member libraries are instructed to apply AACR2R and additional tools are also listed, the *LCRIs* being the first listed as useful in interpreting the cataloging rules. (*Bibliographic Formats and Standards.* Dublin, Ohio: OCLC, 1993, p. 6). See also *R.L.G. Bibliographic Standards,* 1981, p. 2.

4. Susan Rosenblatt, "The National Coordinated Cataloging Program from the Participant's Perspective," in *Cataloging & Classification Quarterly,* v. 17, nos. 3/4 (1993): pp. 189-99.

5. David W. Reser, comp., *Towards a New Beginning in Cooperative Cataloging* (Washington, D.C.: Library of Congress Cataloging Distribution Service for the Regional & Cooperative Cataloging Division, 1994), pp. 6-10.

6. *Ibid,* pp. 10-11.

7. Letter to Kay Guiles from Sarah Thomas, May 2, 1994.

8. CPSO/CCC Task Group on LC-Issued Descriptive Cataloging Documentation. *Interim report.* Memorandum, June 21, 1994. Accompanied by *Results of RI Census–Explanatory Statement,* pp. 1-2.

9. Note that in the original text numbers 4) and 5) are numbered as 4) and number 6) is numbered as 5).

10. *Ibid.,* pp. 4-5.

The Development of the MARC Format

Karen M. Spicher

SUMMARY. Use of machine-readable cataloging data requires a commitment to the standardization of data elements and record formats. Early machine-readable formats were initiated by several research libraries to serve the needs of particular university systems. In developing MARC, the Library of Congress drew on the experiences of these libraries in establishing a standard acceptable to the research library community for the interchange of bibliographic data. This article discusses early machine-readable formats influencing MARC, the origins of the MARC Pilot Project, and design factors influencing the evolution of the format through MARC II. Research was based on primary sources documenting the early history of MARC, including unpublished documents in the Library of Congress Archives. *[Article copies available from The Haworth Document Delivery Service: 1-800-342-9678.]*

INTRODUCTION

Conversion of bibliographic data to machine-readable form was basic to the automated systems projected by research libraries in the 1960s. When the Library of Congress reported in 1963 on the feasibility of automating its own operations,[1] a number of Ameri-

---

Karen M. Spicher holds an MLS from the College of Library and Information Services, University of Maryland. While studying at the University of Maryland, she was a Graduate Assistant for music cataloging. Ms. Spicher was selected as a 1995 Junior Fellow by the Library of Congress Manuscript Division.

[Haworth co-indexing entry note]: "The Development of the MARC Format." Spicher, Karen M. Co-published simultaneously in *Cataloging & Classification Quarterly* (The Haworth Press, Inc.) Vol. 21, No. 3/4, 1996, pp. 75-90; and: *Cataloging and Classification Standards and Rules* (ed: John J. Riemer) The Haworth Press, Inc., 1996, pp. 75-90. Single or multiple copies of this article are available from The Haworth Document Delivery Service [1-800-342-9678, 9:00 a.m. - 5:00 p.m. (EST)].

75

can research libraries were experimenting with computer-assisted catalog production and document retrieval. The machine-readable records developed for these projects shared features later adopted in MARC design: transcription of text elements, such as main entry, title, and imprint, into tagged variable fields and use of fixed fields for coding information implicit to human readers, such as language or intellectual level.

The differences among early formats reflected the scope and purpose of each university's project; in each case the experiment was justifiable to the extent that it proved feasible a projected application of automation within its institution. In all cases the influence of the catalog card format was evident in the use of existing cards as conversion copy and in the expectation that the new systems would be used to produce card and book catalogs. As the Library of Congress's transition to automation unfolded, its interests lay in the establishment of a standardized format that would be widely accepted for interlibrary communication and would support centralized cataloging services.

EARLY MACHINE-READABLE CATALOGING

In creating a format which would serve as standard both within and without its own environment, LC expected to draw on the experience of earlier experiments.[2] Theoretical work at the University of Illinois Chicago Library had defined the machine-readable catalog entry as a single sequentially transcribed string.[3] The small size of random access memory then available in library experimentation would not accommodate large bibliographic databases; the necessity of tape as a storage medium confirmed the concept of a sequential string. Elements within the bibliographic string were accessible to computer programs only if individually delimited. This implied the subdivision of text elements in a manner analogous to the use of punctuation in manual cataloging. A computer could distinguish place of publication from publisher, for example, only if the position of each element was defined. The variable lengths of text elements favored delimitation by coded characters within the text rather than by assignment of a fixed location for each element. Standardization of these elements was clearly needed to contain the complexity of computer programs used to identify them. There was some doubt that computers could manipulate text data at both an acceptable level of accuracy and an acceptable cost: computer manipulation of text elements, as opposed to text blocks or numeric data, was untried and promised complexities greater than those yet unsolved in manual description and filing. Researchers at the University of Illinois stressed identification of bibliographic elements as prerequisite to feasible machine-readable cataloging.[4]

Florida Atlantic University conferred with the University of Illinois in creation of an automated library system for the opening of FAU in 1964. FAU's machine-readable format differed from that implemented in Chicago in the use of fields delimited by maximum lengths rather than by interspersed codes. Lengths were not necessarily fixed: the length of one field could be extended with the unused space of another. The text contained in each field was accessed as a unit, simplifying the input procedure by a graphic blocking of text on the input worksheet. Selected imprint and collation elements were then coded as single characters or Boolean values and reentered in additional fields for quick retrieval. FAU credited Louis Schultheiss, of the University of Illinois, for suggestions leading to this use of fixed fields.[5] FAU defined its system as one of document, rather than information, retrieval; the format facilitated production of bibliographies and lists defined by coded information without the additional complexity of text searching.[6]

The Ontario New Universities Library Project, begun in 1963 at the University of Toronto Library, created an automated system to serve the libraries of five new Ontario colleges and universities. In assembling collections for the new libraries, ONULP developed an integrated system of bibliographic control in which one record format would yield acquisition, circulation, and technical services output, as well as catalogs and bibliographies. The format included fixed and variable fields; elements of variable fields were rigidly defined and delimited within subfields for selection or exclusion in various applications. Designed for cooperative use among five institutions, the ONULP system indicated a potential for wider cooperation based on a standardized record structure.[7]

Experiments in library automation distinguished between document and information retrieval. Projects such as those above determined the former attainable within relatively small environments and urged further research with larger and more complex databases. Automated document retrieval was dependent on machine access of the individual elements of records: precision increased with standardization of the definition and encoding of elements. The possibilities for application of automated techniques to information retrieval were not as clearly defined or as readily supported by existing technology. Some systems, such as that designed for the Columbia-Harvard-Yale Medical Libraries, supported real time searching and retrieval of records by subject matter.[8] These capabilities were, however, immediately feasible for few other libraries, while standardization of descriptive elements had a wide base in both experimentation and potential users.

AUTOMATING BIBLIOGRAPHIC DATA AT THE LIBRARY OF CONGRESS

In 1963, the Library of Congress published the results of a study, funded by the Council on Library Resources, on future automation of its operations. In evaluating the benefits of computerized techniques applied on a large scale, this report recommended automation of LC's bibliographic processing operations. Automation of cataloging, indexing, and document retrieval were recommended as immediately feasible and necessary for future information retrieval and library networks.[9] These recommendations were to be implemented through LC's Office of the Information Systems Specialist, renamed Information Systems Office in 1965.

Samuel Snyder, appointed Information Systems Specialist in 1964, established contacts between his office and representatives of current library automation projects, including Columbia-Harvard-Yale Medical Libraries, Florida Atlantic University, University of Toronto, and information retrieval experimentation at Massachusetts Institute of Technology.[10] In exploring the need for a national pool of authoritative bibliographic data, Snyder and Barbara Markuson, Assistant to the Information Systems Specialist, met with Mortimer Taube, of Documentation, Inc.

Taube's experience in automated production of book catalogs for public libraries had shown that the costs of the library community's conversion to machine-readable cataloging could be contained only through the pooling and distribution of machine-readable data. This idea became an objective of LC's emerging system.[11]

The Council on Library Resources awarded a contract in 1964 to Lawrence Buckland to study the conversion of LC catalog card data to machine-readable form. Buckland, of Inforonics, Inc., had already consulted with LC on conversion hardware and had recommended punched paper tape as an input medium. His 1964 report was to demonstrate a method for conversion of the bibliographic and typographic content of LC cards to a machine-readable form which would support automated selection and printing of catalog products in multiple formats. The report presented two methods of encoding data elements: in block form, interpreted by the computer according to row and column position of individual elements, or in segments delimited by coded symbols. Detailed discussion addressed the need for explicit coding for machines of information usually left implicit for humans, such as the language of a work, country of publication, and distinction between personal and corporate names. The report concluded that although computer controlled printing of familiar catalog products was now possible, development of future uses for machine-readable data would depend on further study of the data and of methods for explicit coding.[12]

Buckland's work was based on implementation of a trial system. His report discussed this system in general terms and included examples of data preparation, a listing of LC card elements for encoding, and sample inputs and outputs. Documentation of programs and system operation, however, was not included. The Library of Congress had anticipated that Buckland's findings would be immediately applicable to catalog card production. That the report lacked programs and flowcharts necessary for implementation was surprising to L. Quincy Mumford, Librarian of Congress, who had expected documentation suitable for adaptation by U.S. Government Printing Office programmers.[13] Lack of this documentation prompted discussion within LC of the delegation of technical support, with the result that the technical development of machine-readable cataloging was supervised directly by LC rather than through the GPO.[14]

As a result of the Buckland report, LC decided to proceed with development of a machine-readable format and to seek funding for a conversion project.[15] LC first sought to consolidate support for its course of action by conferring with members of the library profession. Though the benefits of LC's leadership were undoubted, the amount of unstandardized machine-readable cataloging already underway indicated that a continuity of leadership would not be easily maintained during the transition from the centralized production of catalog cards to that of machine-readable records. In spite of reservations that the Buckland report alone was an insubstantial basis on which to assert leadership,[16] LC sponsored a Conference on Machine-Readable Catalog Copy in January, 1965, with the report as a framework for discussion. The conference was attended by representatives of university libraries, government agencies, and private research and industry. Recommendations included the following:

> Early availability from the Library of Congress, by subscription, of machine-readable bibliographical data for current materials, as a by-product of L.C.'s cataloging operations, is desirable and will help individual libraries as they face the question of whether or not to automate . . .
>
> The basic requirements of a machine-readable bibliographic record will differ according to the type of library using the record. Perhaps the Library of Congress should include in its machine-readable record all of the data now on the card plus some additional information . . . Most participants favored coding as much data as possible to assure maximum retrieval in the future. . . It would seem desirable for L.C. to go ahead with what it needs for its own purposes and other libraries can use as much or as little from the L.C. machine-readable record as they wish . . .
>
> The machine-readable record will be used for production of card and/or book catalogs . . . for information retrieval, bibliographies and lists, circulation control, for acquisitions work, and for information about trends and other data needed by management . . .
>
> Agreement on form of input is desirable, and standardization should be more nearly attainable in a machine system. If L.C. makes the decision on the form of all bibliographical

information, this could become the best single source of standardization . . .[17]

THE MARC PILOT PROJECT

As a database of machine-readable records was now crucial to action on the Conference's recommendations, the Office of the Information Systems Specialist created a three-member task force to develop a proposed format. Henriette Avram began her work at LC, in March, 1965, as a member of this task force. A systems analyst formerly with the National Security Agency, the American Research Bureau, and Datatrol Corporation, Avram had gained experience in cataloging while responsible for Datatrol's corporate library.[18] She was joined on the task force by descriptive cataloger Kay Guiles and reference librarian Ruth Freitag, both from LC staff. This configuration of systems analyst, cataloger, and reference librarian provided combined computer and library expertise, an intention of the Information Systems Office in both its systems development and data representation activity.

The Office of the Information Systems Specialist summarized the goals of the task force in a memorandum to the Librarian of Congress:

> Since it is the intent to set an LC standard for a computer-based bibliographic record, it is necessary to provide an input format that is reasonable to produce, function codes to explicitly define those elements that cannot be recognized by machine today, and programming rules to define those elements implicitly defined. Each decision made must be justified in terms of ease of punching versus machine storage versus machine running time/cost. The computer specialist must be aware of the possibilities of future developments both in the fields of library science and machine hardware, and the design of the machine-readable bibliographic record should include the concept of "openendedness," that is, the ability to make additions and changes without costly redesign.[19]

Libraries which had laid groundwork in machine conversion had an interest in LC's success: experimentation in relatively small environments had made clear the benefits of the cooperative work which would be made possible by standardization. Documentation of earlier projects, including those at Yale and Toronto, were available to the task force.[20] The Library of Congress benefitted in particular from the experience of the University of Toronto; Assistant Librarian Ritvars Bregzis met with Avram at LC during work on the proposed format.[21] LC differed from other institutions in the large scale and complexity of its internal bibliographic control system and distribution services: precedent projects had incorporated limitations of detail and flexibility acceptable within a limited scope of data.

The task force's proposed format, outlined in a June, 1965, report, was based on several pragmatic assumptions. Record content would conform to current LC cataloging practices so that existing work patterns could be appropriated for the preparation of conversion copy. The primary purpose of the machine-readable record would be its information content; catalog card production would be important but secondary. Accordingly, typographic features would not be coded explicitly in the record but could be assigned in programming for the printing of fields. The format would temporarily disregard filing rules and initially would not accommodate non-roman characters. Upper and lower case characters, however, were desirable and could be differentiated when input on punched paper tape.[22]

The proposed format contained numerically tagged variable fields and coded fixed fields. Variable fields served to organize catalog card text for machine access. Numeric tagging was favored by the task force as a means of maintaining accurate definition of text elements in a large database. Further experimentation by Lawrence Buckland with delimitation implied in text formatting had shown error increasing with the complexity of the data.[23] The variable content of the record was supplemented by fixed fields in which data implicit in the text, such as language, intellectual level, or choice of entry, could be encoded. Fixed fields were also assigned for elements encoded for fast searching, such as publication date or place or the presence of illustrative material, bibliographies, or indexes. The body of each record in the proposed format was preceded by two control fields describing record length and followed by a series of control fields comprising a table of the relative locations of the record's variable fields.[24]

The report on the proposed format was circulated for review within LC and among other libraries. Although presented as a preliminary draft, the report was welcomed as a demonstration of the practicality of LC's plans and means of moving from discussion to action. The proposed format was the subject of a second Conference on Machine-Readable Catalog Copy, sponsored by LC in November, 1965,[25] at which conferees representing university, public, and special libraries expressed interest in receiving machine-readable records distributed by LC. It was felt that remaining uncertainties about the processing of machine-readable data should not delay a start in conversion of records: a database of records was needed immediately as a basis for continued experimentation.

Following this conference, in December, 1965, LC received a grant from the Council on Library Resources for a pilot project in the creation and distribution of LC cataloging data in machine-readable form. The MARC Pilot Project, under the direction of Henriette Avram, was formed to test a system for the distribution of records to a sample group of libraries. These libraries would define uses for the data and report to LC on the adaptation of records for local use and the efficiency of the distribution system. The sixteen libraries selected to participate met at LC for a third Conference on Machine-Readable Catalog Copy in February, 1966.[26]

During the planning phase of the MARC Pilot Project, the proposed format was reevaluated and revised, a process which benefitted from current studies by LC and by the American National Standards Institute (then called the United States of America Standards Institute). ANSI's Subcommittee on Machine Input Records, of which Henriette Avram was chairman, defined a standardized list of data elements used in bibliographic records. The findings of this study were published in 1967[27] but were in use at LC during the previous year.[28] At the Library of Congress, a sample of recent LC catalog cards was statistically analyzed to determine the frequency of descriptive characteristics affecting complexity in machine conversion, such as choice of main entry and number of languages, dates, and publication places per entry. This report,[29] also authored in part by Avram, discussed efficient coding of fixed fields, a subject of much previous speculation.

Each variable field in the MARC I format consisted of a three-character field length and a three-character tag, followed by the data content. Fields might incorporate subfields delimited by a pound or dollar sign, symbols considered unlikely to conflict with data. The field length specified the number of positions to be traversed from the beginning of one variable field to the beginning of the next; this value was used in the location of positions within a record. The tag was a numeric code identifying the data element in that field. The assignment of tags followed the arrangement of data elements on a catalog card, with tags of at least two digits needed to account for the twenty-four variable fields used. Tags were not strictly sequential but grouped so that multiple fields within a single area, such as title, physical description, or series, would share the same first digit. In a few of these areas, extended subdivision already indicated the use of a third digit, although in most MARC I tags the third position remained blank. Reservation of all three numeric characters for each field's tag allowed for future expansion while ensuring that the number of control characters remained constant between fields. This simplified machine processing by uniformly defining the first six positions in each field as control data.[30]

THE MARC II FORMAT

The Pilot Project operated from November, 1966, through October, 1967. During the following interim period, the MARC I format continued in use while the MARC II format was developed in preparation for implementation with LC's Distribution Service in October, 1968. Time constraints in the preparation of the MARC Pilot System had dictated limitations in the first format: the necessity of completing the format before beginning programming had resulted in a decision to limit the scope of materials to English-language monographs.[31] MARC II was to be adaptable for all types of material: the record was designed as a single structure which could accommodate tagging schemes for different materials, such as monographs, serials, maps, or music. The first tagging scheme, for monographs, was completed for the initiation of the Distribution Service.

Each MARC II record included a leader which specified the type of material described by the record. As the configuration of fixed fields was different for each type of material, the length of the fixed field area was constant for each type but variable between types; the fixed field area was therefore tagged as a single variable field. Tag and length information in MARC II were removed from the variable fields themselves to a directory following the record leader. This enabled the record to be searched by means of the directory rather than by processing of the entire record. The use of single character indicators as adjunct to tags was introduced in the MARC II monographs format, as was expanded use of subfields delimited by symbols qualified with alphabetic characters. MARC II tagging schemes utilized three digits in all variable field tags; tags were coded to reflect both the function and type of the information contained in the field. The first digit continued to group fields by function, such as title, physical description, or series, while the second digit identified, where appropriate, the type of information, such as personal, corporate, or uniform title.[32]

The possibility of international interchange of records had guided LC's reevaluation of the MARC I format.[33] The interest of the British National Bibliography in the Pilot Project had resulted in a UK/MARC Pilot Project and in cooperation between BNB and LC staff on the design of MARC II.

> Both agencies recognized the future implications of an inter-change format and the importance of two major publishing countries agreeing on a standard. Not only would it be possible to exchange machine-readable records between the U.S. and the U.K., but the way would be open for other countries to follow the lead and develop their own MARC projects.[34]

The distinction between structure and content in MARC II design enabled the establishment of standards for the interchange of machine-readable records even as systems of content designation continued to develop. MARC II specifications for record leader, directory, and variable field control data comprised the standard record structure proposed to the American National Standards Institute, the British Standards Institute, and eventually to the International Organization for Standardization.

MARC development had been closely tied to continuing work by ANSI in information communications standards. MARC II incorporated character set, tape, and tape label standards approved by ANSI. Under the chairmanship of Henriette Avram, ANSI's Subcommittee on Machine Input Records approved the MARC II record structure as a national standard in 1970. Documentation defined the American National Standard for Bibliographic Information Interchange on Magnetic Tape as

> a format which is intended for the *interchange* of bibliographic records on magnetic tape. It has not been designed as a record format for retention within the files of any specific organization. Nor has it been the intent of the subcommittee to define the content of individual records. Rather it has attempted to describe a generalized structure which can be used to transmit, between systems, records describing all forms of material capable of bibliographic descriptions as well as related records such as authority records for authors and subject headings.[35]

This standard of interchange, later revised for general application to other storage media,[36] established common ground necessary for the widespread use of machine-readable bibliographic data. The availability of MARC records facilitated data exchange among large institutions and made automation feasible for libraries in which conversion would have been precluded by the costs of local record creation. The Library of Congress's efforts in standardization were well supported by the advice and participation of other libraries: MARC development benefitted from a convergence of library automation experience. As a means of interlibrary communication, MARC has redefined access to bibliographic information.

NOTES

1. Gilbert W. King et. al., *Automation and the Library of Congress* (Washington, D.C.: Library of Congress, 1963).

2. Henriette D. Avram, *The MARC Pilot Project: Final Report on a Project Sponsored by the Council on Library Resources, Inc.* (Washington, D.C.: Library of Congress, 1968), 4.

3. Louis A. Schultheiss, Don S. Culbertson, and Edward M. Heiliger, *Advanced Data Processing in the University Library* (New York: Scarecrow Press, 1962), 121.

4. Ibid., 122.

5. Format design and sample input documents are discussed in Jean M. Perreault, "The Computerized Book Catalog at Florida Atlantic University," *College and Research Libraries* 25 (May 1964): 185-95.

6. Clayton D. Highum, "Cataloging for Document Retrieval at Florida Atlantic University," *College and Research Libraries* 25 (May 1964): 199.

7. A preliminary discussion of the ONULP system is found in Ritvars Bregzis, "The Ontario New Universities Library Project–An Automated Bibliographic Control System," *College and Research Libraries* 26 (November 1965): 495-508.

8. Ritvars Bregzis, *The Columbia-Harvard-Yale Medical Libraries Computerization Project* (Toronto; Springfield, Va.: distributed by Clearinghouse for Federal Scientific and Technical Information, 1966). Frederick G. Kilgour, principal investigator of the Project, invited Bregzis to review the Project's first phase.

9. King, *Automation and the Library of Congress*, 2-3.

10. Samuel S. Snyder, "ISS Progress Report," 22 September 1964, MARC Records, Library of Congress Archives, Manuscript Division, Library of Congress.

11. Barbara Markuson, "MARC–Its History, Development, and Use," in *Proceedings of the MARC II Seminar* (Kensington: University of New South Wales, 1973), 1-2.

12. Lawrence F. Buckland, *Recording of Library of Congress Bibliographical Data in Machine Form,* Rev. 1965 (Washington, D.C.: Council on Library Resources, 1965). Buckland's earlier consultation is discussed in the foreword, page v.

13. Samuel S. Snyder, Memorandum to L. Quincy Mumford, 21 December 1964, MARC Records.

14. Samuel S. Snyder, Memorandum to L. Quincy Mumford, 17 December 1964, MARC Records.

15. Ibid.

16. Snyder, Memorandum, 21 December 1964.

17. Buckland, *Recording of Library of Congress Bibliographical Data in Machine Form,* vii-x.

18. Josephine S. Pulsifer, "Henriette D. Avram," *Library Resources & Technical Services* 15 (fall 1971): 526.

19. Henriette Avram, "Defining the Fields of Data for the LC Machine-Readable Bibliographic Record," Memorandum to L. Quincy Mumford, 2 April 1965, MARC Records.

20. Documents and communications are found in the MARC Records.

21. Ritvars Bregzis, Letter to L. Quincy Mumford, 2 June 1965, MARC Records.

22. Henriette D. Avram, "The Philosophy Behind the Proposed Format for a Library of Congress Machine-Readable Record," in *Institute on Information and Storage Retrieval with Special Reference to the Biomedical Sciences* (Minneapolis: Nolte Center for Continuing Education, Univ. of Minn., 1966), 156-9.

23. Ibid., 158.

24. The proposed format is described in Conference on Machine-Readable Catalog Copy, *Proceedings of the Second Conference on Machine-Readable Catalog Copy* (Washington, D.C.: Library of Congress, 1965), 30-3.

25. Ibid.

26. Conference on Machine-Readable Catalog Copy, *Proceedings of the Third Conference* (Washington, D.C.: Library of Congress, 1966).

27. Ann T. Curran and Henriette D. Avram, *The Identification of Data Elements in Bibliographic Records* (New York: United States of America Standards Institute, 1967).

28. Joan Stockard, "A Selective Survey of MARC Literature," *Library Resources & Technical Services* 15 (summer 1971): 280-1.

29. Henriette D. Avram, Kay Guiles, and Guthrie T. Meade, "Fields of Information on LC Catalog Cards: Analysis of a Random Sample, 1950-1964," *Library Quarterly* 37 (April 1967): 180-92.

30. MARC I and MARC II formats are discussed in John F. Knapp, "Design Considerations for the MARC Magnetic Tape Formats," *Library Resources & Technical Services* 12 (summer 1968): 279-81.

31. Henriette D. Avram, *MARC: Its History and Implications* (Washington, D.C.: Library of Congress, 1975), 5.

32. Knapp, "Design Considerations for the MARC Magnetic Tape Formats," 282-4.

33. Avram, *MARC: Its History and Implications,* 21-2.

34. Ibid., 21.

35. American National Standards Institute, *American National Standard for Bibliographic Information Interchange on Magnetic Tape,* ANSI Z39.2-1971 (New York: American National Standards Institute, 1971), 7.

36. ANSI, *American National Standard for Bibliographic Information Interchange on Magnetic Tape,* ANSI Z39.2-1979 (New York: American National Standards Institute, 1979); ANSI, *American National Standard for Information Sciences–Bibliographic Information Interchange,* ANSI Z39.2-1985 (New York: American National Standards Institute, 1986).

SOURCES CONSULTED

Unpublished

MARC Records, Library of Congress Archives, Manuscript Division, Library of Congress.

An Oral History of MARC. Sound recordings and transcripts, presented to the Library of Congress by the MARC XX Committee, 1990, Library of Congress Archives, Manuscript Division, Library of Congress.

Published

American National Standards Institute. *American National Standard for Bibliographic Information Interchange on Magnetic Tape.* ANSI Z39.2-1971. New York: American National Standards Institute, 1971.

_____. *American National Standard for Bibliographic Information Interchange on Magnetic Tape*. ANSI Z39.2-1979. New York: American National Standards Institute, 1979.

_____. *American National Standard for Information Sciences–Bibliographic Information Interchange*. ANSI Z39.2-1985. New York: American National Standards Institute, 1986.

Avram, Henriette D. "MARC Is a Four Letter Word: A Report on the First Year and a Half of LC's Machine-Readable Cataloging Pilot Project." *Library Journal* 93 (July 1968): 2601-5.

_____. *MARC: Its History and Implications*. Washington, D.C.: Library of Congress, 1975.

_____. *The MARC Pilot Project: Final Report on a Project Sponsored by the Council on Library Resources, Inc.* Washington, D.C.: Library of Congress, 1968.

_____. "MARC: the First Two Years." Library Resources & Technical Services 12 (summer 1968): 245-50.

_____. "The Philosophy Behind the Proposed Format for a Library of Congress Machine-Readable Record." In *Institute on Information and Storage Retrieval with Special Reference to the Biomedical Sciences*. Minneapolis: Nolte Center for Continuing Education, University of Minn., 1966, 155-74.

Avram, Henriette D., and Ann T. Curran. "New Developments in an Information Interchange of Data Elements in Machine Readable Format for Bibliographic Data." In *The Bowker Annual of Library and Book Trade Information, 1971*. New York: Bowker, 1971, 104-6.

Avram, Henriette D., Kay Guiles, and Guthrie T. Meade. "Fields of Information on LC Catalog Cards: Analysis of a Random Sample, 1950-1964." *Library Quarterly* 37 (April 1967): 180-92.

Bregzis, Ritvars. *The Columbia-Harvard-Yale Medical Libraries Computerization Project*. Toronto; Springfield, Va.: Distributed by Clearinghouse for Federal Scientific and Technical Information, 1966.

_____. "The Ontario New Universities Library Project–An Automated Bibliographic Control System." *College and Research Libraries* 26 (November 1965): 495-508.

Buckland, Lawrence F. *Recording of Library of Congress Bibliographical Data in Machine Form*. Rev. 1965. Washington, D.C.: Council on Library Resources, 1965.

Conference on Machine-Readable Catalog Copy. *Proceedings of the Second Conference on Machine-Readable Catalog Copy*. Washington, D.C.: Library of Congress, 1965.

_____. *Proceedings of the Third Conference on Machine-Readable Catalog Copy: Discussion of MARC Pilot Project*. Washington, D.C.: Library of Congress, 1966.

_____. *Proceedings of the Fourth Conference on Machine-Readable Catalog Copy*. Washington, D.C.: Library of Congress, 1967.

Curran, Ann T., and Henriette D. Avram. *The Identification of Data Elements in*

Bibliographic Records. New York: United States of America Standards Institute, 1967.

Fineberg, Gail. "Portrait of a Pioneer: Henriette Avram Left Indelible Mark on Library Profession." *LC Information Bulletin* 51 (9 March 1992): 99-104.

Highum, Clayton D. "Cataloging for Document Retrieval at Florida Atlantic University." *College and Research Libraries* 25 (May 1964): 197-9.

King, Gilbert W. et. al. *Automation and the Library of Congress.* Washington, D.C.: Library of Congress, 1963.

Knapp, John F. "Design Considerations for the MARC Magnetic Tape Formats." *Library Resources & Technical Services* 12 (summer 1968): 275-85.

Leach, Thomas E. "Compendium of the MARC System." *Library Resources & Technical Services* 12: (summer 1968): 250-75.

Library of Congress. *Preliminary Report on MARC (MAchine-Readable Catalog) Pilot Project.* Washington, D.C.: Library of Congress, 1966.

Markuson, Barbara. "MARC–Its History, Development, and Use." In *Proceedings of the MARC II Seminar.* Kensington: University of New South Wales, 1973, 1-13.

Parker, Patricia E. "Preparation of MARC Bibliographic Data for Machine Input." *Library Resources & Technical Services* 12 (summer 1968): 311-9.

Perreault, Jean M. "The Computerized Book Catalog at Florida Atlantic University." *College and Research Libraries* 25 (May 1964): 185-95.

Pulsifer, Josephine S. "Henriette D. Avram." *Library Resources & Technical Services* 15 (fall 1971): 525-31.

Schultheiss, Louis A., Don S. Culbertson, and Edward M. Heiliger. *Advanced Data Processing in the University Library.* New York: Scarecrow Press, 1962.

Stockard, Joan. "A Selective Survey of MARC Literature." *Library Resources & Technical Services* 15 (summer 1971): 279-89.

The Core Bibliographic Record
and the Program for Cooperative Cataloging

Sarah E. Thomas

SUMMARY. The Program for Cooperative Cataloging seeks to increase the availability of unique records created in a decentralized fashion by a network of libraries according to mutually acceptable standards. A critical element in achieving its mission is the core bibliographic record, a cataloging record that embodies the principles of usefulness, cost-effectiveness, and dynamism. The PCC intends that Program records, full or core, represent acceptable bibliographic control such that record "tweaking" at the local level is minimized. Emphasis is on essential description and on the development of trust in others' bibliographic records, obviating the need for expensive revision and leveraging scarce cataloging resources for grappling with an expanding universe of challenges. *[Article copies available from The Haworth Document Delivery Service: 1-800-342-9678.]*

INTRODUCTION

Over the past few decades libraries accumulated sizable backlogs of bibliographic materials awaiting cataloging. A combination of practices and circumstances conspired to bring about a state of dissatisfaction with cataloging and its resulting products. Libraries faced zero growth in budgets for cataloging or even contracting

Sarah E. Thomas, PhD, is Director for Cataloging at the Library of Congress in Washington, DC.

[Haworth co-indexing entry note]: "The Core Bibliographic Record and the Program for Cooperative Cataloging." Thomas, Sarah E. Co-published simultaneously in *Cataloging & Classification Quarterly* (The Haworth Press, Inc.) Vol. 21, No. 3/4, 1996, pp. 91-108; and: *Cataloging and Classification Standards and Rules* (ed: John J. Riemer) The Haworth Press, Inc., 1996, pp. 91-108. Single or multiple copies of this article are available from The Haworth Document Delivery Service [1-800-342-9678, 9:00 a.m. - 5:00 p.m. (EST)].

resources, and administrators increasingly tended to invest in automation or to support inflationary materials budgets at the expense of technical services. Original catalogers especially were an endangered species. Managers questioned the high cost of cataloging, a labor-intensive process that seemed to them to yield little output for the investment. Carol Mandel, Deputy University Librarian at Columbia University, identified one of the causes for the growth of backlogs as the shift from original cataloging to copy cataloging.[1] As librarians played the game of bibliographic chicken, waiting to see if someone else would catalog an item first, enabling them to save by copying or adapting the record, rather than creating it, significant holdings of uncataloged materials developed. These backlogs were on a collision course with the rising expectation of readers that they would have access to current publications in online public access catalogs (OPACs). Mandel, in a November 1992 meeting that would prove seminal for the Program for Cooperative Cataloging, evoked the image of the golden goose when describing the decline of original catalogers. As libraries shifted resources away from original cataloging to other, higher priority areas, there were fewer institutions capable of supporting the need for high quality initial bibliographic control, and the golden eggs produced by each cataloging department became fewer. Copy cataloging was indeed economical, and it was sound policy on the part of technical services directors to avoid duplication of effort by using copy, but the overall impact was to concentrate original cataloging in a few institutions. Most catalog departments elected to give priority for copy cataloging to Library of Congress (LC) records, which they increasingly accepted with little or no modification because of the predictable high standard and uniformity of the work. If LC copy were unavailable, they held books for a period of six months, one year, or even longer, waiting for LC's record. At the Library of Congress, where the emphasis lay on original cataloging, and use of records by other agencies was marginal, the Library developed an arrearage of almost 1,000,000 monographs as a result of an imbalance of staff and cataloging procedures.

THE NEED FOR COOPERATIVE CATALOGING

Librarians have proposed various answers to these problems over the years. Dorothy Gregor and Carol Mandel, in their 1990 *Library Journal* article "Cataloging Must Change," advocated expansion of cataloger judgment and a relaxation of absolute consistency in the application of subject headings and other areas where rigid uniformity has exacted a costly price for uncertain value.[2] Others have sought improvements in automation as a means of increasing productivity. A recurring theme, however, was a need for cooperation. The history of cooperative cataloging has been well-documented.[3] In the 1990's, there were three major national programs administered by the Library of Congress: CONSER (Cooperative Online Serials), NACO (Name Authorities Cooperative Program, later National Coordinated Cataloging Operations), and NCCP (National Coordinated Cataloging Program). The three programs differed in their management and thrust. CONSER is a 22-year-old program with 23 members; CONSER members establish policy and the Library of Congress serves as the coordinator of the program. OCLC provides material support for CONSER, and maintains the master copy of CONSER records in its database, making copies of CONSER records available for tapeloading. NACO, begun in 1977, focuses on the contribution of name authorities to a common database that is maintained in mirror image formerly through the use of the linked systems protocol (LSP) and now file transfer protocol (FTP) in databases at LC, OCLC, and the Research Libraries Group. The Library of Congress established policy unilaterally, since the national authority file was also its own local authority file. NCCP was a heavily subsidized program in which, at its inception, eight university libraries cataloged monographs according to LC standards directly into LC's catalog. Despite extensive financial support by the Council on Library Resources (CLR), NCCP remained disappointing in quantity of output, and program participants chafed at the restrictions imposed on them to achieve consistency with LC practice. From the LC perspective, the program was valuable, however, because the Library of Congress realized substantial savings through the use of NCCP records, which it treated as though they were its own bibliographic products. With the prospect of CLR funding coming to an end, the NCCP program faltered. Although the Library expanded the program, several of the original participants suspended or curtailed their activity, so the net effect was a decline in growth in actual number of records created.

It was at this point that the Library of Congress initiated an informal evaluation of NCCP. Since some participants favored the so-called CONSER model, in which partners established policy cooperatively, and in which LC played a coordinating, rather than dominant role, LC proposed a joint meeting of NCCP representatives and the CONSER Policy Committee. The alternatives in November 1992, when the meeting took place, appeared to be cessation of NCCP or reconstitution along CONSER lines. The meeting that spawned the Program for Cooperative Cataloging offered stimulating discussion and varied opinion on the nature of cooperative programs, but it failed to offer a clear-cut vision for the future of cooperative cataloging of monographs. Several hours of debate culminated in a mission statement "to provide broad bibliographic access to materials in research libraries collections and other information resources."[4]

RECONSTRUCTING NCCP

After an intense beginning in which the path to cooperation seemed so uncertain, the Cooperative Cataloging Council (CCC), the precursor of the Program for Cooperative Cataloging (PCC), nevertheless emerged. The CCC has paved the way for the PCC, which officially came into being in 1995, following the election of an Executive Council. What distinguishes the PCC from its predecessors is the extent to which it is largely a grass roots enterprise, formed out of the recognition that the environment in which catalogers conduct their business today calls for a sharp departure from past practice. In less than a year, the CCC transformed the possibilities for the present and the pressing future. Representing a broad spectrum of the U. S. bibliographic cataloging scene, the CCC sought to be inclusive, in contrast to the more elitist NCCP. The Council consisted of eight volunteers: Liz Bishoff, OCLC, and Karen Smith Yoshimura, RLG, supplying the perspectives of two major bibliographic utilities; Sue Phillips, University of Texas at

Austin and Linda West, Harvard University, the former representing a NCCP participant with active OCLC participation; the latter representing a NCCP participant with RLIN experience; Patricia Thomas of the Stockton San Joaquin County Public Library, identified as voicing the concerns of public libraries; Carol Mandel, Columbia University, who served as an authority on cooperative cataloging programs, having evaluated NCCP for the Council on Library Resources and authored papers on the history of cooperative cataloging; John Byrum, the manager of NACO and NCCP programs at LC, and Sarah Thomas, Director for Cataloging at LC. The diversity of viewpoints was a hallmark of the CCC, yet it did not prevent the group from achieving consensus on a variety of topics.

In April 1993 members of the CCC convened at the Library of Congress and outlined five goals they conceived as supporting the mission of the program, developed out of the one which they had defined with others at the joint NCCP/CONSER meeting in November 1992. The revised mission read: "to work together to increase the availability of unique records under mutually acceptable standards, to facilitate the creation and use of these records; and to provide leadership for the bibliographic community."

The CCC developed a strategy to formulate the objectives that would lead to the successful achievement of the goals. Grouping the issues that predominated in the goals, they charged six experts in the field of cataloging with conducting a rapid analysis of actions needed to advance the mission and goals of the program. The Council asked each expert to lead a small team that would swiftly examine issues, solicit ideas and comments from a broad segment of librarians, and would prepare a succinct statement of issues and recommendations. The task groups aligned themselves along the following lines: (1) How to encourage the creation of more records cataloged in a timely fashion according to cost-effective means. (2) How to define the mutually accepted standard according to which records might be created in a cooperative environment. (3) How to establish the level of authority control and foster the addition of authoritative headings to a common database. (4) How to satisfy the need to make the cooperatively-created records widely available. (5) How to provide the training and education for an effective cooperative program, and (6) How to enable catalogers to make better use of records created outside the United States.

REVISITING STANDARDS UNDERLYING CATALOGING RECORDS

With their broad charges in hand and an element of fervor to investigate the needs and requirements that would be necessary for libraries to engage in a successful cooperative endeavor, the task groups conducted their business briskly. Using the powerful and democratic network of the Internet, the task groups collected ideas from a variety of sources and called on their peers to vet their draft reports before submitting them in final form to the CCC. The PCC rests on the simple premise that cooperative cataloging, done in a standard and cost-effective manner, will result in a sufficient output of bibliographic records that will enable most cataloging entities to find a high proportion of reliable, quality bibliographic records available at the time of receipt. This abundant source of cataloging records will facilitate timely, inexpensive processing of materials. Participants in the PCC would benefit from the reduced cost of providing access to the majority of their materials, and the savings realized in this area would enable them to devote a small proportion of their resources to the creation of original cataloging to sustain the common good. The system distributes the load more evenly across libraries, permitting retention of a limited number of experts in individual institutions to describe and analyze important, unique items. The cooperative cataloging model of the PCC is an alternative or supplement to two other approaches: depending solely on LC or outsourcing. In the first, libraries rely heavily on the Library of Congress for cataloging. LC bibliographic records have the advantage of being reasonably priced high-quality cataloging that is amenable to check-in cataloging performed by low-level staff or even subject to machine-assisted loading in an online cataloging environment. Relying solely on the Library of Congress led to the buildup of backlogs, however, for several reasons. First, the Library of Congress's policy, practices, and staffing levels created LC's own arrearage, meaning that bibliographic records in their final, full-cataloging state often appeared in databases months or years after receipt of books in the library. As awareness of the importance of timely services grew in libraries, library administrators began a drive to end the backlogs.

Libraries could have moved to combat this unfortunate circumstance by advocating an increase in appropriation to the Library of Congress to support centralized cataloging. LC's position as a supplier through the infusion of added funding would benefit all libraries using the cataloging. In fact, LC calculates the savings to the nation at exceeding $336 million annually for the records it provides that would otherwise require original cataloging by libraries. Several reasons mitigated against increased centralization at LC. One was that some librarians thought that the kind of catalog the Library of Congress was attempting to create and maintain was out of proportion to the resources required to sustain it, particularly in view of the increasing disparity between the number of items to be cataloged and the number of records available for use. In their view, the Library was becoming somewhat out of touch with the harsh realities facing library administrators across the country. The cataloging it was doing offered high quality but at a high cost to production with unnecessary precision and consistency. Hampered by its aging automated system, the Library of Congress invests more of its staff resources in database maintenance than other institutions with state-of-the-art computer systems. In addition, LC's collections themselves are not comprehensive, and other libraries often find they hold specialized materials not duplicated at the Library of Congress. Many studies of collections at research institutions confirmed that even universities collecting at a level 4 (the collection level supporting graduate research) in the RLG conspectus held disparate titles. There remained a need for original cataloging at local institutions to provide access to these unique materials.

Just as computers reinforced a trend towards a decentralized, network model for databases and other critical library functions, they also made possible and practical the model of decentralized cataloging. Recently, the concept of outsourcing has furthered the reduction of cataloging staff by the displacement of processing activities to outside agencies. Outsourcing allows libraries to receive bibliographic records for loading into their OPACs conjunctive with receipt of materials. In some cases this builds on the tradition of outsourcing collection development through approval plans, and in some cases it relies on the reasonably-priced labor and predictability a bibliographic service can provide. For the most part, however, the success of contractors in supplying their customers with inexpensive ready-to-use bibliographic records is dependent on the vendors' access to cataloging for copy. In Michigan State's 1993 test of OCLC's Promptcat Service prototype, for example, over 90% of their needs were met by LC records.[5] For other libraries, most items in their collections are represented either by an LC record or by member copy in a national bibliographic database. A cooperative cataloging program enlarges the pool of records for libraries to draw on, whether the method is a local solution involving copy cataloging or delegation of that function to an outside agency.

What the PCC represents is a program of cost containment or even cost reduction. At the same time, it is a paean to the principle of the bibliographic "commons" advanced by K. Wayne Smith, CEO and President of OCLC. Smith posits that the commons (today, a database maintained by multiple contributors; two centuries ago, a communal grazing area that supported livestock) is an essential element for a successful society. Each library should contribute in order to reap the larger benefits for the whole. Nourishing the database by expanding the store of original cataloging is necessary for the system to succeed. Distributed over many institutions, the burden lessens, and the advantage to the majority increases. The very simple concept of the PCC is that many institutions, working cooperatively, generate a rich, sustaining source of bibliographic records for all to use.

To make the results even more cost-effective, the PCC will provide training and documentation leading to the creation of a standard record, a record that libraries can introduce into their catalog as seamlessly as they can now add LC bibliographic records. Rather than concentrating on a few selected universities, as did NCCP, the PCC strives to be inclusive, inviting participation from a wide variety of libraries: public, special, small, large. Although those institutions that produce a substantial output of original cataloging offer potentially the greatest benefits to the Program, in terms of requiring the least amount of overhead to support the Program, relative to number of records produced, even those with only a small number of units can still make a valuable contribution. What matters chiefly is that each PCC record conforms to a standard and users of PCC records can readily identify them as such.

A NEW STANDARD AND ITS RATIONALE

To achieve a commonly held standard, the PCC has espoused a mutually reinforcing program of a core bibliographic record, authority control, and training. The core bibliographic record is a record that falls between minimum-level-cataloging (MLC) and full-level-cataloging. Developed by a CCC task group that then surveyed public and technical services librarians on its viability using listservs, the core bibliographic record seeks to capture key elements in bibliographic records, omitting fields deemed non-essential. According to the task group's report, the core record must or can contain the following fixed and variable fields:

"FIXED FIELD VALUES": Code fully.

DISCUSSION: These fields may be used as primary or secondary (i.e., limiting) access devices in OPACs and in the utilities; they may be used for record sorting, potentially they may be used to generate notes (e.g., bibliography or index notes)

020,$a (ISBN): If present on item
040 (Cataloging source)
042 (Authentication code)
050, 082, 086, etc.: Assign at least one classification number from an established classification system recognized by USMARC.

DISCUSSION: This specification must necessarily be stated in the broadest terms to accommodate a wide variety of needs. The Task Group recognizes that assignment in some cases will constitute solely classification while in others it will consist of a full call number. While this fact, as well as the use of any of a variety of classification systems may mitigate against the availability of records that can be used without modification, it is in support of the need to accommodate the broad spectrum of the library community in soliciting as wide a pool of records as possible.

1XX (Main entry): If applicable

240 (Uniform title): If known or readily inferred from material being cataloged.

245-300 (Title page transcription through physical description): Describe fully, using all data elements appropriate to the item described.

4XX (Series area): Transcribe series if present.

Other aspects of series treatment (classification (together or individually), analysis, tracing) are local in nature. If, however, a participant chooses to trace a series, it must be in an authoritative form (440/8XX) as appropriate) supported either by an existing national-level authority record or one that is supplied by the participants if an authority record does not already exist.

5XX (Note fields): Minimally, include the following if appropriate:

500: Note for source of title if not from t.p.
505 (Contents note): For multi-part items with separate titles
533 (Reproduction note)

DISCUSSION: The basis for the recommendation is that only those notes that support identification of an item need be included. No doubt these criteria will vary from one form of material to another. With respect to justification of added entries, that function may be provided alternatively in some cases through other data elements, e.g., the tagging itself or use of relators.

6XX (Subject headings):

If appropriate, assign from an established thesaurus or subject heading system recognized by USMARC at least one or two subject headings at the appropriate level of specificity.

DISCUSSION: The recommendation is cast in the form of "one or two" to convey the idea that one is not an absolute limit, to preclude any agonizing that might be stimulated by the limit to one, and to accommodate certain situations in which multiple subject headings are called for. The inclusion of the phrase "at least" is intended to indicate that the stipulation, while describing a sufficiency for the core record, is not necessarily a strict upper limit.

7XX (Added entries): Using judgment and assessing each item on a case by case basis, assign:

1. a complement of added entries that covers at least the primary relationships associated with a work (e.g., joint authors);
2. added entries to bring out title access information judged to be important.

DISCUSSION: For both (1) and (2) above, determination of primary relationships and of the relative importance of title access information are intended to reflect either individual catalogers' judgment or the institutional policy of the participant.

8XX (Established form of series if different from that in 490 field): If series is traced, use as appropriate.[6]

RELATION TO EXISTING STANDARDS

The core record differs from the MLC record, primarily in that it includes classification (but a particular classification is not specified), and at least one subject heading as appropriate. The architects of the PCC considered subject analysis an essential aspect of providing access to library materials. Catalogers must also code fixed fields fully, because of their potential for system manipulation and substitution or inclusion of more text in the bibliographic record. Descriptive elements in the core record exceed those of the minimal cataloging record, but there are fewer note fields, for example, than for a full level record. In general, the sense of those creating the standard for the core bibliographic record was that the minimal level record was inadequate in terms of access for many types of materials, and that the core bibliographic record would represent a substantial improvement over MLC. Also, because the PCC specified that all headings must be under authority control, the core record, with authoritative headings, could serve as a solid foundation for bibliographic access. The core record could function as an adequate standard cataloging record that libraries could use without modification. They could trust the data in the record and eliminate the costly revision and upgrading associated with MLC at many institutions.

The core record differs from a full record in that it carries less information. Essentially, its descriptive elements duplicate that of the full record except in the notes area, where there are fewer mandatory notes. Only those notes essential for identification are required. As noted above, the core record must have *at least* one subject heading if subject access is appropriate; full bibliographic records would receive all appropriate subject headings, without limitation.

Another critical aspect of any core bibliographic or full bibliographic record created under PCC auspices is that every access point is under control in the shared resource authority files. Authority control of headings ensures that all records introduced into catalogs maintained in concert with the Anglo-American Authority File (AAAF) are in harmony, thereby guaranteeing that searchers can retrieve all the titles by a given author or on a specific topic.

One of the underlying ideas behind the core bibliographic record is that it is economical to create, yet sufficiently detailed to provide adequate access and reliable retrieval. It should be cheaper to produce, and yield a bibliographic record in less time than it takes to create a full bibliographic record. In an experiment at Cornell University, Christian Boissonnas reported that catalogers creating core bibliographic records were 25% faster than a control group creating full records for similar types of materials provided they did not take time to create or assure national level authority records for all access points. Based on this experience, Cornell is proceeding to catalog some items using the core record, and UCLA and Cornell will participate in a study endorsed by the CCC on the application of the core bibliographic record to a select group of records. Both institutions will examine further the cost-effectiveness of the core bibliographic record, as well as attempt to establish more soundly the proposition that omitting fields such as notes and cutting back on subject headings does not, in any significant way, impoverish the majority of information seekers. As outlined in a paper prepared by Brian Schottlaender for the Cooperative Cataloging Council in November 1994, the pilot project at UCLA will confine itself to monographs in roman script with no corresponding full cataloging records in OCLC (for UCLA) or in RLIN (for Cornell). UCLA will use only experienced NACO catalogers in the experiment, as the CCC core record calls for authoritative headings established in the resource authority files. Belle lettres are out of scope for the pilot, because they are already very efficient to catalog. Since the encoding level for core records has not yet been implemented in the MARC format, the CCC recommended coding half the records in the experiment as minimal and half as full, using the 040 subfield e to label them as core.

In the future, the 042 field will include the label "PCC Core," an important aspect of the Program, since it is the stamp of approval that enables subsequent users of the record to import the record into their local system with few, if any, modifications. With the certainty of its adherence to known standards, libraries holding a copy of the item represented by the record can minimize review and modification, thereby achieving savings over traditional copy cataloging involving non-standard records.

UCLA plans to track the extent to which other institutions upgrade minimal level records to full in order to explore the degree to which others view core records themselves as sufficient for access and to ascertain the validity of the dynamism of the core record. The primary objective of the pilot would be to quantify the potential savings in time required to create core bibliographic records compared with the time required to create full-level cataloging records for similar items.

Some librarians believe the core bibliographic record should be the sole record, replacing both MLC and full-level cataloging. Others are unwilling to relinquish full level, maintaining that they need to supply their clients with a richer set of data than the core record offers. Yet, the core record offers these institutions the potential for savings, too. Its creators designed it to be flexible and dynamic. Since catalogers create it to a standard, there is no need for a library performing copy cataloging to tweak or modify any information contained in the record. If they wish, they can augment the record with notes or additional access points, but they do not need to duplicate any of the work done by others that manifests itself in the original, core bibliographic record.

For a more complete account of the core bibliographic record, its inception and issues surrounding its use, consult Willy Cromwell's excellent article in the November 1994 issue of *Library Resources & Technical Services.*[7]

OTHER NEEDED CHANGES

Hand in glove with the creation of the core bibliographic record according to a prescribed set of standards is the training for the catalogers, who will produce the records, and their revisors and administrators. The training, to be supported by user-friendly documentation, will include both a review of technical considerations and a focus on nourishing a cataloger value system that encourages application of professional judgment. The *Anglo-American Cataloguing Rules,* second edition (AACR2), published in 1978 and implemented in 1981, offered a more user-centered approach by emphasizing the importance of the data presented on the item being cataloged. AACR2 also offered more flexibility through the use of options and alternative rules. Since this was the first cataloging standard to be implemented simultaneously by the national libraries of Australia, Canada, Great Britain, and the U.S., it was an AACR2 requirement that the national libraries make an application decision on the AACR2 options and alternative rules. In preparation for the implementation of AACR2, LC issued cataloging policy statements on situations which were not covered by AACR2 but which were important enough to ensure consistent application by all participants contributing to a shared database, e.g., unique identifiers for serials with the same title. In addition, there were LC cataloging management decisions, partially stimulated by large research libraries, related to bridging the gap between the pre-AACR2 catalog and its successor. Although applicable to LC, the widespread distribution of LC records mandated the dissemination of LC policy. The Library of Congress issued its cataloging policy decisions through *Cataloging Service Bulletin* and *Library of Congress Rule Interpretations* (LCRIs). Since actual implementation of AACR2, new LCRIs have been issued primarily in response to the special cataloging needs of certain materials (law, music, serials) and to cover gaps in AACR2 (e.g., initial articles in geographic names) not addressed in the RIs issued prior to implementation.

Although originally issued to meet the needs of LC as well as a wider audience, critics seized on the RIs as exemplifying "LC centrism" (because they addressed some of LC's unique local considerations, including systems limitations). Furthermore, the sheer number of LCRIs was evidence to these critics that, again, LC was attempting to create and maintain a catalog that was out of proportion to the resources required to sustain it. As a result of CCC involvement, LC is reexamining the rule interpretations with a view to determining which material to recommend moving to AACR2, which to remove altogether, which to retain, which to retain but revise to clarify or simplify, and which to label explicitly as LC practice.

More significantly, the PCC advocates the exercise of judgment by catalogers in lieu of the formulation of complex policies and interpretations. Understanding the principles of access, particularly access in online catalogs, is thought to be more productive than the memorization of or consultation of detailed written instructions that cover every possible case. Catalogers should use their professional expertise to be decisive, and risk the loss of absolute consistency, where consistency is not essential. The emphasis on slavish consistency robs the cataloger of flexibility and can be a barrier to timely record creation. Consistency in headings is highly valued, as is accuracy, but consistency in the formulation of notes, or the inclusion of some notes altogether is seen as "nice to have" but non-essential. At a certain point, catalogers encounter the law of diminishing returns when adhering to the principle of consistency.

To achieve balance between the advantage offered the user through consistency in bibliographic records and the flexibility that allows for exercise of judgment and cost-effective cataloging, the

Program for Cooperative Cataloging places a premium on clear, succinct, and unencumbered documentation coupled with training that focuses on values as much as it does technical competency. The Cooperative Cataloging Council, in planning for training, makes the assumption that PCC catalogers already possess a high degree of technical knowledge about cataloging, but that they would benefit from "values" training that promotes goals supporting the mission of this cooperative endeavor. This training would not see the individual bibliographic record as an end unto itself, but would seek to underscore its connection to the user. Timeliness and cost-effectiveness will figure in cataloging decisions. In addition, the PCC intends to provide education for catalogers to give them the necessary foundation on which to base their decisions. They will be better equipped to evaluate the level of treatment various bibliographic materials deserve, to understand the cost to scholars and researchers of institutional backlogs, or to determine if a particular bibliographic element warrants further research, and how much research is reasonable. By clarifying values for catalogers that are appropriate for this era of rapid transmission of information and high user expectations, the PCC strives to develop new sources of pride for cataloging staff. As they adapt to be more in tune with the goals of their organizations, they will grow in esteem and be increasingly respected for the service they provide. Adherence to mutually agreed upon standards for bibliographic and authority records will ensure the creation of records that will provide reasonable access to bibliographic materials. Set in the framework of a value system that promotes efficiency, accuracy, dependability, and accessibility, the PCC records will enable libraries to eliminate backlogs and meet the needs of their clients.

BENEFITS TO BE PROVIDED

Past experience in cooperative endeavors has demonstrated that to be truly successful, a cooperative activity must be one in which all participants can identify tangible benefits. Altruism fades under economic pressures, so cooperating institutions must be certain that collaboration is a significant improvement over local independence. The more participants contribute to the determination of the principles and governance of the cooperative enterprise, the more likely the entity is to reflect their needs, and therefore, to be of greater value for them. The Program for Cooperative Cataloging offers several advantages to its partners. Members become part of a network in which their investment pays a high return. The PCC has a goal of achieving 200 Program members by the year 2000. If each partner contributed just 500 original records annually, they would produce 100,000 standard bibliographic records; an average of 1000 original records per participating institution would result in 200,000 bibliographic records. For most libraries, this would mean a much higher percentage of records of dependable quality accessible for copy cataloging than they have available for their use today. This would stabilize the size and expertise of cataloging departments, contain costs for provision of bibliographic access, and result in a more uniform product. The success of any cooperative program depends on the support of the participants, each doing their part to share the workload of record creation and maintenance.

Since libraries would find more useful copy, they could process new acquisitions more efficiently, getting those materials to readers more swiftly. Part of the savings resulting from this improvement could be directed to a more modest level of original cataloging for the Program contribution, but again, because there would be fewer titles needing original cataloging, there would be less likelihood of a backlog. Items requiring original cataloging would also be represented in OPACs promptly, offering improved service to users.

Another benefit to participation in the PCC would be the opportunity to influence the development of national and international standards. To date, the CCC has approved the core bibliographic record for monographs. A core record for music and for JACKPHY (Japanese, Arabic, Chinese, Korean, Persian, Hebrew, and Yiddish) materials has been drafted, and there are requests to create core records for audiovisual materials. Members have the chance to play an important part in determining policy and procedures for global interaction in the cataloging arena. The PCC will communicate through its representatives with standards setting organizations such as the Joint Steering Committee for the Revision of AACR and the American Library Association Committee on Machine-Readable Bibliographic Information (MARBI), and will serve as a focused body to communicate with library systems vendors and others. By virtue of the composition of PCC it is linked to bibliographic utilities, the Association for Library Collections & Technical Services (ALCTS), and national libraries such as the British Library and the National Library of Canada. These links increase the possibility that its unified voice will be heard when decisions affecting cataloging are made. It is this potential for increased communication leading to increased understanding that is a valuable aspect of the PCC. Lastly, by collectively embracing common standards and approaches to bibliographic control, PCC members will conserve resources to devote to new endeavors. This additional capacity, extracted from developing more efficient modes of cataloging, will enable catalogers to turn their organizational talents to the challenges of structuring information on the Internet, establishing connections with materials not traditionally included in online catalogs, and making the transition to the future.

NOTES

1. Carol Mandel, "Cooperative Cataloging," presented at the Library of Congress Nov. 4, 1992.

2. Dorothy Gregor and Carol Mandel, "Cataloging Must Change," *Library Journal* 116, no. 6 (April 1, 1991): 42-7.

3. Carol Mandel, "Cooperative Cataloging: Models, Issues, Prospects," *Advances in Librarianship* 16 (1992): 33-82.

4. Sarah E. Thomas, "Rethinking Cooperative Cataloging," *ARL* 165 (November 1992): p. 5-6.

5. Nancy Campbell, "Michigan State Tested PromptCat Prototype in Fall 1993." *OCLC Newsletter* No. 212, (Nov./Dec. 1994): p. 22.

6. Cooperative Cataloging Council Task Group 4: Standards, "*Final Report.* October 29, 1993."

7. Willy Cromwell, "The Core Bibliographic Record: A New Bibliographic Standard," *Library Resources & Technical Services* 38 (October 1994): 415-24.

Meta-Information Structures
for Networked Information Resources

Casey Palowitch
Lisa Horowitz

SUMMARY. This article develops a model of meta-information architectures (header, local index, and directory) and presents three current or proposed meta-information structures for networked information resources with applicability to organization and access in libraries and networked information environments. Special emphasis is given to the Text Encoding Initiative's TEI Header and Independent Header as a model for meta-information for academic and library needs. Recommendation is made for the specification of a generalized SGML meta-information header based on the principles of the TEI Independent Header, to address the needs of cataloging, automatic processing, and serving of networked information resources. *[Article copies available from The Haworth Document Delivery Service: 1-800-342-9678.]*

Casey Palowitch is Electronic Text Librarian at the University of Pittsburgh Library System, and manages the Electronic Text Project there. He holds an MS in Information Science from the University of Pittsburgh. He can be reached via e-mail to cjp+@pitt.edu. Lisa Horowitz is Reference Librarian Fellow, Van Pelt Library, University of Pennsylvania, where she is a graduate student in comparative literature. Prior to this she worked as Project Librarian at the Center for Electronic Text in the Humanities at Rutgers University and Princeton University. She holds an MLS from Rutgers University. She can be reached via e-mail to lrhorowi@sas.upenn.edu.

[Haworth co-indexing entry note]: "Meta-Information Structures for Networked Information Resources." Palowitch, Casey, and Lisa Horowitz. Co-published simultaneously in *Cataloging & Classification Quarterly* (The Haworth Press, Inc.) Vol. 21, No. 3/4, 1996, pp. 109-130; and: *Cataloging and Classification Standards and Rules* (ed: John J. Riemer) The Haworth Press, Inc., 1996, pp. 109-130. Single or multiple copies of this article are available from The Haworth Document Delivery Service [1-800-342-9678, 9:00 a.m. - 5:00 p.m. (EST)].

INTRODUCTION

As the use of networked information resources increases (networked information resources here defined as electronically encoded and primarily, but not exclusively textual information), so does the need for libraries to catalog, archive, preserve, and make them accessible. Libraries are increasingly faced with demand for networked information services from patrons, are pressured to reap the cost efficiencies of automation by administrators, and are being asked to support remote access to materials as never before. The library's traditional cataloging role has been to collect and produce meta-information about its textual collections (meta-information defined as that information not found within the text, e.g., bibliographic data, subject or keyword analysis, formatting information, revision status), through which use of their collections is facilitated. Meta-information is also generated and used by other network information producers and access agents, such as publishers and maintainers of archives, and common formats for meta-information are desirable and a prerequisite for the development of library support procedures for their use.

Over the past two years, there have been several pilot studies and research projects on cataloging Internet resources (for example Bowman 1994; Jul 1994; Monroe 1994). Workshops have been held on cataloging of digital documents with AACR2 and the relationship between Standard Generalized Markup Language (SGML) text (Goldfarb 1990), the TEI Header, and the MARC cataloging record (Library of Congress 1994a; Horowitz 1994). But as of yet there has not been wide agreement on standard cataloging structures and methods, nor on procedures for providing bibliographic control of networked information resources. This may be in part due to little communication between the library community and the networking community. But because the meta-information problem also affects other areas of the information and internetworking industry than the library, and because the library community is increasingly affected by standards developed in these other areas, we will present models and structures for meta-information originating from both communities. The utility of these meta-information structures with respect to library and network information applications will be explored. Finally, some desirable characteristics for a generalized SGML meta-information structure for networked information resources based on the TEI Header will be suggested.

CATALOGING OF ELECTRONIC TEXT AND NETWORK RESOURCES

For the most part, the cataloging of electronic resources in the library context has meant the cataloging of software or data files stored on portable magnetic or optical media, owned or licensed by the cataloging library. The cataloging procedure entailed the application of AACR2 description rules for Computer Files (Gorman and Winkler 1988, chap. 9), the preparation of a bibliographic record following a standard such as the USMARC Computer Files Format (Library of Congress 1994b), the assigning of subject designations based on content, then call number assignation and shelflisting. The resulting catalog records are stored in a database and patrons pointed to the resources by the catalog records. This architecture can be termed "many to many" (many records in library catalogs pointing to many physical instances of a given resource in libraries). This model still holds in most library environments. Enhancements such as the encoding of mode-of-access, such as URI information (Universal Resource Identifier) (Berners-Lee 1993) in specific fields in the MARC record are being adopted to allow for extension of the model to resources that may lie outside the given library. As more and more electronic documents reside only in virtual space, there is currently no guarantee that they are ever cataloged and made available to library patrons. Attempts to create an exhaustive catalog of all electronic texts must eventually circumscribe their scope (Hoogcarspel 1994). Questions also arise as to whether any given electronic document on the network is published or not. Some electronic resource cataloging guidelines consider documents as published only if they carry "a formal statement of publication similar to the statement found on the title page of a book" (OCLC 1992). These ambiguities and trends in network publishing and network resource management call for new structures and methods for organizing and facilitating access to networked information resources.

In the current distributed network environment of the Internet, the physical location of resources has a lessened importance, given network reliability. Unique information resources may be located at any point on the network, yet need to be reliably described and accessed by many users, through library catalogs or individually. In this architecture, the relationship can be described as many to one (many library catalogs and users pointing to one or a small number of copies of a resource). Electronic resources in the networked environment present certain additional characteristics: (1) Mutability—they are easily copied and altered, and revision and edition tracking becomes an issue, (2) Mobility—locations of resources may change frequently, and (3) Distributed components—a given resource may encompass many individual files, on many machines, spread over great distances. These characteristics make even more difficult the task of bibliographic control, identification and access, and address/pointer reliability. The establishment of standards for reliable addressing of resources is being addressed through the URI protocols of the Internet Engineering Task Force (IETF); it is the authors' opinion that the establishment of meta-information standards for bibliographic control, location, and access points is best carried out within the library community, which has a long tradition in the establishment of such standards (for more on the IETF and its mission, see IETF 1994; Malkin 1994). Currently, the most widely used meta-information standard for bibliographic control, location, and access points is the MARC record. MARC, however, does not satisfy many of the needs for meta-information in the network environment. The most significant reason for this is that it cannot be flexibly applied to information other than that for which it was designed (which, technically, was to produce printed cards for library catalogs). For example, MARC cannot be intuitively manipulated by users. In the other architectures defined below, user-defined tags or labels are possible, so that users can, for instance, declare a math notation set and put a math equation in a notes field, or create a label useful to them (but as yet undefined in the standard) with an explanation of that label so that others can still understand it. MARC is machine-readable only, not machine- and human-readable, because of its numeric codes and single-letter subfield designations which require a codebook for understanding. The architectures defined below are more user-friendly in this regard as well, because users can understand most labels intuitively. As it stands now, MARC does not allow for any hypertextual linking, a possible demand in a future meta-information architecture. MARC has some procedural, rather than descriptive, fields, meaning that a program reading a MARC record must understand the procedural requests. Below, we describe three existing architectures which solve some of these problems, and then we propose a meta-information architecture which combines some of the best features of MARC with the best features of the network architectures.

META-INFORMATION ARCHITECTURES

The characteristics of meta-information architectures may be assessed at two levels. At a systemic level, the salient issues are the location of the meta-information with respect to the resources being described, and the linking mechanism for location and access. Architectures for meta-information can be organized into four non-exclusive systemic models (approaches can be taken that combine models). They are: (1) Meta-information records redundantly held by all users (this is the current model, the term "users" here includes libraries); (2) Meta-information held with the resource in a header structure or accompanying file (header model); (3) Meta-information maintained by the publisher on the network, in a collection in the same location as the resource, but separate from the resource itself (the local index model); or (4) Meta-information held in a third location, with users identifying resources and accessing them indirectly (directory model). The second level of analysis of meta-information architectures is the descriptive, in which the salient issues are the extent to which the meta-information record allows for a sufficient description of the resource as needed by a given application, and the level of structure implicit in the record. For example in library applications, the level of description is greater in archival finding aids, but more structured in MARC bibliographic records. But for most any library application, the level of meta-information needed is greater than that found for most resources currently accessed through the Internet.

The mobility problem described in section II above is best addressed by the directory model; mobile resources need only update their meta-information once, with the directory. It is this problem that has driven much of the meta-information work to date within the networking community. The directory model is not surprisingly used for many types of network addressing and directory schemes, such as Internet hostname resolution and the draft standard for the Uniform Resource Name (Berners-Lee 1993). The mutability problem lends itself to solution by the header model, at least while human intervention is required for updating; the closer the meta-information to the resource, the more likely it is to be updated to match the file. And as copies are made and modified, new copies of the meta-information are made as well. The distributed components problem also lends itself to the header model; a header containing linking information can be checked and updated more consistently and easily if proximate to the documents in question. The latter two problems have been important to meta-information efforts within the electronic text and humanities computing community. The header model, with meta-information kept with the resource, is not a new idea either; the idea of prefacing an electronic file or tape block with a section of meta-information has been used in many file- or block-oriented information systems, such as the MARC format itself (meta-meta-information).

Although it is not possible in the space provided here to analyze all existing meta-information structures field-by-field and application-by-application, the three examples given below illustrate the models, and evaluation is left to another forum. The choice of the three meta-information structures presented is not an attempt to compare them against each other or to champion one against the others; not only are two of the three still in draft stage, but different design considerations led to different scopes and extents of their approach. Their presentation is intended only to provide a stimulus for a discussion of the future course of the effort to organize network resources and electronic texts and to illustrate the different system-level and descriptive-level strategies being employed for meta-information. It is hoped that this discussion prompts more communication and cooperation in the development of meta-information standards between the library and networking communities.

UNIFORM RESOURCE CHARACTERISTICS (URCs)

The proposed Uniform Resource Characteristics (URC) Specification (Daniel and Mealling 1995) of the IETF is designed with several characteristics in mind. The intent of the URC is to provide meta-information for documents published to the Internet without regard to their location or access protocol, with specific design elements for compatibility with World Wide Web server software. The URC specification is consistent with the directory model outlined above, and is expected to be used with special applications, such as WWW clients, to access servers with URC records containing URI addresses which point to the network resources. Older efforts using the URC did not utilize SGML encoding of data, but rather used attribute/value pairs separated by the colon character, following the practice of other network systems, such as RFC822-compliant e-mail headers (Crocker 1982). Part of the design requirements was explicit backward compatibility with existing network systems, and this forced a rather minimalistic approach. Whereas this approach made the URC specification easily incorporated into the design of information retrieval applications, it was at the expense of its descriptive capability. However, a new proposal to use URCs to embed SGML-encoded meta-information into URC entries (Daniel 1995) is a promising step in the direction this article points.

The current minimal set of attributes defined for a URC are:

URN	Uniform Resource Name
URL	Uniform Resource Locator
LIFN	Location Independent File Name (a future IETF standard)
Author	Author of the Document
TTL	Sets a time limit on the validity of the immediately prior attribute in the URC record

Several other attributes are proposed, such as:

Collection	URIs for other resources considered part of a collection with this resource

> Authoritative   Identifies an authoritative URC server for
>   the URN

. . . and additional attributes possibly included from the IAFA Template discussed below, and attributes for compatibility with the http server protocol.

At the systemic level, the URC system describes a distributed network of meta-information directories, each pointing to a certain set of resources existing on the network. A URC server may be sent a query containing an author's name or keywords, and would return a list of URLs or URNs for resources with matching authors or with the keywords found in the abstracts. A URC server may also be sent a URL, and return a URC record profiling the resource in question, on any of the attributes associated with the resource in the database record. The URC system is one approach to meta-information provision that while brief in scope, leverages existing network protocols to serve meta-information about resources in arbitrary locations to queries from arbitrary locations.

At the descriptive level, the URC design is meant "to provide a vehicle or structure for the representation of URIs and their associated meta-information" (Daniel and Mealling 1995), and provides for a minimally acceptable level of data to be associated for informational purposes with a URI, although no specific data set is required for a valid record. The intent of the URC is to provide a means through which a user, unsure of the content of a resource at, say, the other end of a WWW anchor, can query meta-information associated with the URL and retrieve content, size, and perhaps cost information and a digital signature (insuring against fraud) associated with the resource. The URC's scope covers bibliographic information, and is designed to facilitate web-wide bibliographic searching, similar to the mechanism employed with the Arc hie facility (Bunyip Information Systems 1994). One of the more interesting ideas proposed with the URC is the inclusion of "Seals Of APproval" (SOAPS) (Roscheisen, Mogensen, and Winograd 1995), with which a digitally-signed review or rating (given by a reputable learned society or reviewer) can be included with the resource, and used by the bibliographic searcher to filter the results. The specification also stresses extensibility, such that any new attribute/value pair can be represented in a URC. In terms of structuring, the URC specification as currently configured does meet its design criteria of machine parsability, transport friendliness, searchability and related criteria (Daniel and Mealling 1995), but if used outside the context of RFC822 and RFC 1590 ("Media Types"–see Postel 1994), the attribute/value structure may prove less generalizable and translatable than a structure with a specifiable syntax, nestable and predictable components.

IAFA TEMPLATES

The Internet Anonymous FTP Archives (IAFA) working group, also of the IETF, has developed another meta-information structure, IAFA Templates (Deutsch et al. 1995), to provide description and access to network-resident resources, in this case specifically those located on anonymous-FTP sites. The intent of this initiative is to provide, in one or a few files, a set of records describing the resources located on a site, so as to present a complete site catalog suitable for both automated searching and processing and human reading. The intent is also to create a structured meta-information package that can be used for automated retrieval applications. The IAFA template system is a local index architecture, as defined above. Meta-information is specified in a similar manner to URCs, through attribute/value pairs. The current specification of the IAFA Templates suggests the following attribute/value pairs, but does not limit the record to them:

(Note: The following is a simplification of the record structure. For an authoritative specification, please consult ibid.)

Template-Type:	One of a list of resource types such as DOCUMENT, IMAGE, SOUND, VIDEO, SOFTWARE, etc.
Category:	Type of object, for instance "User manual"
Title:	Complete title of the object
URI:	Uniform Resource Identifier
Short-Title:	Summary title
Author:	Description/contact information about the author

Admin: Description/contact information about the maintainer of the resource
Source: Information as to the source of original
Requirements: Hardware or software requirements for use
Description: Description, such as an abstract
Bibliography: Bibliographic entry for the resource
Citation: The citation when quoted in other works
Publication-Status: Current publication status (draft, etc.)
Publisher: Description/contact information about the publisher
Copyright: The copyright statement
Creation-Date: The creation date
Discussion: Free text description of possible discussion forums appropriate for this resource
Keywords: Appropriate keywords for the resource
Version: A version designator for the resource
Format: Data formats in which the resource is available
Size: Size of resource
Language: Language of resource (examples Russian, C++)
Character-Set: The character set standard used in the resource
ISBN: International Standard Book Number of the resource
ISSN: International Standard Serial Number of the resource
Last-Revision-Date: Last revision date of the resource
Library-Catalog: Library cataloging information

An IAFA index would be constructed as a file containing line separated records (one attribute/value pair per line), each of which had some subset of the attributes listed above. In contrast to meta-information practice utilizing the MARC record, though, the IAFA spec does not "mandate or require that any particular class of information be offered" (ibid.) but leaves the choice and extent of encoding up to the author, or more likely, the maintainer of the resource. At the descriptive level, then, both the URC and the IAFA can be seen as differing in practice from a cataloging approach, which ensures at least a minimal set of access points where that information exists. In terms of structure, the same considerations apply as with the URC scheme above, which utilizes the attribute/value pair encoding.

SGML AND THE TEXT ENCODING INITIATIVE

Academic computing and librarianship have benefitted greatly by the flurry of information technology standardization occurring in the last 10 years. Advances in networking, multilingual character encoding, and database standards have had direct payoffs to academic enterprise. Text structuring standards such as SGML have found immediate application in the humanities, where textual resources are one of the primary tools. Over the past two years, trends in the fields of networked information and internetworking protocols point toward the increased use of SGML for broad classes of networked information. These trends are: (1) The increased use of textual resources over the Internet due to the popularity of the World Wide Web and the availability of low- or no-cost client interface software; which is closely linked to (2) The use of HTML (Hypertext Markup Language, one particular SGML DTD, or Document Type Definition) as the standard encoding for World Wide Web documents; (3) The ongoing changes being made in the specification of HTML and the WWW clients to produce stricter SGML compliance, as can be seen in the HTML3 DTD specifications (Raggett 1995); (4) The increased acceptance and use of online publishing using structured text standards, including SGML, by a wide range of publishers; and (5) Developments such as the extensible Mosaic Common Client Interface (CCI) (NCSA 1994) with the potential to allow clients to view more richly encoded text, such as arbitrary-DTD SGML data, from the Web, through low- or no-cost products like SoftQuad Corporation's announced Panorama[TM] client software (SoftQuad 1994). For various reasons SGML's potential is only now being proven as a general text-structuring convention for networked use, and it is through the unlikely help of the World Wide Web.

Although not immediately utilized by the networking community, SGML was embraced early on by the humanities computing community, which recognized its utility and established guidelines for its use in the Text Encoding Initiative (hereafter TEI). The TEI is an international project whose goal has been to develop, disseminate, and advocate guidelines for the "encoding and interchange of machine-readable texts intended for use in literary, linguistic, historical, or other textual research" (Sperberg-McQueen and Burnard 1991, 20). The focus of the project has been to produce guidelines for the transcription into electronic form of primary source materials in the humanities, including but not limited to literary texts, historical primary source materials, and written transcripts of speech. The project's initiators also felt that electronic texts were not being consistently or well-documented, in terms of bibliographic information as well as specific encoding information and revision histories, resulting in electronic texts of varying quality, in disparate levels of usefulness for scholars other than the text's creator, with inconsistent documentation, and often with proprietary encoding schemes. The benefits of the TEI guidelines' basis in SGML are multiple for humanities texts. First and most important, the use of SGML means that the TEI guidelines established a standard for encoding documents that is system- and application-independent. This allows interchange of electronic texts (for research or for display) across any platform and/or software understanding SGML. Second, the choice of SGML as the mark-up language means that the guidelines are already rooted in a national and international standard, lowering the acceptance curve for many users of the guidelines, and lowering the cost and production time for developers writing browsers and search engines, who can leverage on the economies of the government and commercial markets and the quality work done on public-domain SGML parsers. Finally, the choice of SGML also means that encoding of humanities texts is descriptive and not procedural, a vital characteristic for use in humanities research, where it may be less important to create a page break at a certain point than to know that a page break existed in the original document transcribed.

The TEI guidelines' design as a standard for the transcription of print humanities materials into electronic form raises the question of their application in libraries for encoding other kinds of electronic texts, such as journal articles, raw data files, or technical manuals. Indeed, the guidelines are intended to be broad enough to encourage people to use them when creating a text, with few enough minimum requirements not to be burdensome, yet with enough information to ensure that the text can be used easily by others. The minimum requirements impose a skeletal mark-up which is general enough to use for differing electronic texts. The guidelines also allow a very rich encoding for the complicated sorts of textual analysis desired by humanities scholars, or any level of encoding between these two extremes. The minimum requirements within the TEI guidelines allow for a minimal level of encoding in varying texts and the guidelines could be used for a standard encoding scheme for electronic texts. But in addition to specification of minimum encodings for the texts, the TEI guidelines also specified the TEI Header, which has more immediate uses in the library context, and in fact, was designed in consultation with librarians as the likely users of the standard.

THE TEI HEADER AND INDEPENDENT HEADER

One of the main problems encountered in the current model of cataloging computer files (AACR2 Chapter 9) is the difficulty in identifying a chief source of information according to the guidelines. This was one of several considerations informing the design of the TEI Header, which although only a small part of the TEI Guidelines, is important in terms of its comprehensive design for the documentation and description of electronic texts. The TEI Header contains tags for information on the text's source and bibliographic citation, as well as a place for description of the encoding scheme and revision history. It comprises four parts, only one of which is required. The others are optional, but highly recommended. The TEI Header can either be attached to the electronic file directly, or it can be a separate file which points to the electronic text (called an Independent Header). The basic structure of either of these headers is the same; however the TEI considers certain elements "recommended" for the independent header, where they are merely "optional" for the attached header, because of the text's separation from the independent header (Sperberg-McQueen and Burnard 1994, chap. 5, chap. 24; Horowitz 1994).

In all four sections of the header, syntax is very flexible. Header creators can make the choice of encoding information as free text within broad catch-all tags, for example:

> <titleStmt>Two stories by Edgar Allan Poe: electronic version, by Edgar Allan Poe, compiled by James D. Benson</titleStmt>

On the other hand, the TEI guidelines also permit, and recommend, making the header highly structured, using nested elements that isolate atomic meta-information units:

```
<titleStmt>
    <title>Two stories by Edgar Allan Poe: electronic ver-
        sion</title>
    <author>Edgar Allan Poe</author>
    <respStmt><resp>compiled by</resp>
    <name>James D. Benson</name></respStmt>
</titleStmt>
```

(Note: These examples are taken from Sperberg-McQueen and Burnard 1994, 96, and with the tags introduced below present only a small portion of the TEI Header tags available for resource documentation. For the full catalog of tags, see ibid.)

Naturally, the latter choice is best from the standpoint of data richness. The advantages of this second method to catalogers are clear: The structured system would certainly be more useful for mapping to a MARC record in an automated system. The trade-off is of course, as with every meta-information architecture, between a comprehensive data structure which is forbidding from a practical standpoint, and an easily completed one that is useless from a bibliographic control standpoint. The TEI Header is flexible in that creators can be very minimal with the information they choose to include, or they can include significant levels of detail, or any range in between. A very full header can at times be larger than the text it is documenting, as might be the case with a poem. The level of richness desired in the header depends on the purpose to which the creator wishes to put the text.

The four parts of the header are the file description <fileDesc>, the encoding description <encodingDesc>, the text profile <profile-Desc>, and the revision history <revisionDesc>. The file description is the first section, and it is required in any TEI Header. It is most closely correlated with the printed title page and with the MARC record. In this section, the creator includes traditional bibliographic information, such as title, author, publication information (such as publisher and date of publication) and source information (the source of the transcription), all of which are required. The creator can optionally include edition information, extent, series information, and notes. The file description was designed to be used as the basis for library catalog access records, but, as described above, was not required to be structured tightly, in order to encourage even those creators who are reluctant to document their texts.

The other three parts of the header include information not traditionally found in a MARC record (although see Hoogcarspel 1994, for recommendations for putting encoding information into a MARC record). The purpose of these sections was to give users of electronic texts information for determining whether a text was appropriate for the kind of analysis which they wished to do. The TEI Guidelines' design focused on the needs of humanities scholars, who might do advanced manipulation of an electronic text (as opposed to a simple search for a reference), such as examining a group of files to find certain themes or looking for trends in an author's style of writing. Knowledge of what was already encoded and the software required to process it would aid them in evaluating the text.

The optional sections are the encoding description, profile description, and revision description. The encoding description might describe which features of the text were tagged, such as proper nouns, common words, or homographs. Other encoding information might include the identity of the encoders, if it varied across the text, and other pertinent coding information. This kind of information is invaluable to humanities scholars, who often base their research on the identification and analysis of particular encoded elements.

The profile description is generally used for transcriptions of speech, which is important for electronic texts because many electronic texts which currently exist, especially some of the larger linguistic corpora, were created for linguistic research. The profile description also contains provisions for one of the most important parts of traditional cataloging practice, subject classification. These provisions include the <textClass> element, which contains the subelements <keywords> (containing classificatory terms, optionally from a controlled vocabulary such as LCSH) and <classCode> (which can be employed to give a shelflist number or other taxonomical identifier).

The revision description differs somewhat from a MARC edition statement because it does not document the "formal" stages through which an electronic text might go, but documents any changes which have been made to the text, addressing the "mutability" issue raised in section II above. The revision history, or change log, allows the listing of any changes which might be made to an electronic document, including who input it, who proofread it, who encoded it, and what changes were made at each point, including after it was published or distributed.

It is clear that the standard created by the TEI Header can be used not only as a title page for any electronic document, fulfilling the need for the cataloging chief source of information, but also, if used to its fullest, can be added to by the cataloging librarian to contain a wide range of useful meta-information, including subject analysis and shelflisting. The fact that only the file description section is required in the header would allow for any kind of electronic material to be documented with a TEI Header, regardless of the value of the other three sections for that type of material. The value of such a header is enormous to the cataloging librarian, who can use the information directly for AACR2 cataloging purposes. A standard format also aids in creating access to the text, and permits a prior evaluation of relevancy for the end user.

THE TEI HEADER AND THE MARC RECORD

The TEI Header, as a highly structured and rich meta-information record, allows for a wide range of applications for library catalog and network use. But having not been designed specifically for either, but rather for comprehensive electronic text documentation, some measure of incompatibility exists, and prompts the call for a generalized header structure in the subsequent section. It is important to understand the difference between the TEI Header and the MARC record as standards. The MARC record and the TEI Header are both intended to document materials, but there are a number of important differences, deriving from their goals. The TEI Header is intended to document a text to which it is attached (see discussion below regarding the Independent Header), and therefore contains internal pointers and explanations. At the same time, the text itself may point back to the header when clarification is needed. The Header is intended to assist users in determining the value of a particular text for their use, and in guiding them in its use. The MARC record was designed to give access. It is used to point to a physical object, but is not intended to aid a user in the use of the object. These clear functional differences mean that a number of other aspects of the two items differ as well.

The TEI Header was formulated to document an electronic text, but it was not intended to take the place of a library access record. The fact that a creator may choose to input the elements of the file description in prose is a significant difference between the header and the MARC record, and possibly a problem from the point of view of access. And even if the creator does use structured fields within the header, the authority work done by librarians is not required of the creator and is unlikely ever to be done by a scholar creating an electronic text, although it is possible that a commercial publisher may choose to help libraries by doing so. Thus the <author></author> field might contain "Edgar Allan Poe" instead of "Poe, Edgar Allan, 1809-1849." Additionally, the mapping from a structured TEI header to a MARC record does not necessarily correspond one-to-one. So although a structured TEI header can be mapped to a MARC record for some fields, the guidelines regarding its structure are much less rigorous than that for a MARC record, which is decidedly more granular. For example, the TEI header simply has an <author></author> field, while a MARC record distinguishes between personal, corporate and conference authors (Horowitz 1994, 30).

Certainly a structure such as the TEI Header allows the cataloger much greater room for description. The functional orientation of the TEI Header allows for far more information, which may not be necessary in a record intended to give access. Richard Giordano, a member of the TEI Committee on Text Documentation, emphasized that the information contained in three of the four Header elements are actually *non-bibliographic,* and thus should not be "shoe-horned" into a MARC record (Giordano, in Horowitz 1994, 13). The Independent Header is a TEI Header, but the fact that it is not attached to a text makes it seem more like a MARC record than an attached file descriptor. However, the differences remain. Although the Independent Header points to an electronic text which might exist at another location, much of the information in it still is not bibliographic. The information is not intended merely for access, but also to aid in human and machine analysis. The format of the Independent Header is identical to that of an attached TEI Header, so the issues of unstructured fields and the lack of one-to-one corre-spondence between fields remain the same. Should this extra-bib-liographic data then not be made available as meta-information to the patron? Two possible conclusions can be drawn—that the MARC record and systems built upon it are too constraining for the grow-ing variety and volume of useful meta-information available with electronic texts and network resources; and that with electronic texts and network resources the cataloging function can be enriched to include the recording of a greater amount of meta-information than current practice.

The TEI Header, URC, IAFA Template, and MARC record were designed for different purposes. They contain some duplicate in-formation, but the information is structured differently within each. It is desirable that some sort of standard meta-information scheme may some day be part of an overall system of bibliographic control, access, and search and retrieval system for network resources, and broad ideas for this are suggested below. However, the current prevalence of the MARC record in library environments means that a number of issues regarding the granularity and authority informa-tion which is currently lacking in a TEI header must be addressed to satisfy the access requirements developed for use in a MARC rec-ord in the library world. From the point of view of network applications, some of the same considerations apply. Schemes such as the URC owe much of their underlying design to existing network protocols, and they rely on systems and applications already in place for functionality. The TEI Header was not designed explicitly with network applications in mind, but most certainly could be used in the implementation of one of the meta-information architectures outlined above. It is important to emphasize, however, that although there is general agreement that some form of SGML/MARC inter-operation is a useful research direction, no discussions of systemic-level architecture for network resource meta-information involving the library community are occurring.

TOWARDS A GENERALIZED HEADER

Because of the highly structured nature of meta-information, the performance and acceptance of SGML as a text structuring standard, and SGML's growing acceptance and use in Internet applications, we conclude that an SGML structuring for meta-information is appropriate. Meta-information in SGML form will lend itself to a host of applications in libraries, such as the construction of finding aids and the interchange with MARC records in library catalogs explored above. It can also work with current network tools, and it can serve as the basis of future network protocols for document identification, organization, and automated retrieval. However, SGML is not a panacea, and does not in itself suffice as a meta-information structure for the "digital library." Some recent efforts to "SGML-ize" MARC, while useful and certainly fine for a library catalog that is SGML-aware, do not directly address network applications. A new meta-information structure needs to be part of a larger systemic architecture of meta-information on a network scale. Future meta-information efforts must be shaped by a vision of the new opportunities that the network environment and digital technology present.

At a descriptive level, the TEI Header is a useful example for a future network meta-information effort to consider, because of its highly structured nature and its richness in bibliographic description. Standardizing a method of coding electronic texts and creating a single model for a header (an electronic "title page") for electronic documents is a logical direction for organizers of information to take; after all, the title page itself was engineered as a meta-information structure for the printed volume. The fact that a single standard can speed processing of electronic materials as well as aid in access to and manipulation of these materials recommends the standardization process even further. In constructing a generalized header, some characteristics of the current configuration could be reconsidered. We recommend simplification, mandating structured not prose descriptions, moving the classificatory tags to their own area, and allowing room for the inclusion of inventive meta-information innovations currently in development. A problem which has not yet been addressed and in which the library community can make a substantial contribution is that of authority control in the network environment. A network authority-control server architecture could be established, from which authority records could be obtained, and these records themselves might contain all the known URLs network-wide in which the referent appears. The use of a generalized header together with a network-wide architecture for meta-information recording, control, organization, and sharing opens up a great number of possibilities for search, retrieval, access, and future agent-based or other automatic information-collection and processing applications whose mechanism depends on structured information. At the very least such a system would allow libraries and users to share network resources internationally, in a system-independent manner.

CONCLUDING REMARKS

Until the point in time in which some "intelligence" is embedded directly within information resources, the problem remains of recording and organizing meta-information and facilitating access through it. Our goal in this paper has been to propose the coordination of the networking community and the library community to address this problem. Our suggestion is a standard format for meta-information which has at least some minimum requirements for bibliographic control and access, and is usable in the existing, as well as future, network environment. This generalized header would combine the features required by both communities into a single standard. The suggested model addresses the limitations of the URC, the IAFA templates, the TEI Header, and the MARC record while taking the best they each have to offer. Moving toward a generalized header implies rethinking current cataloging, at least in the context of electronic materials, and we anticipate that this will be a long process of give and take between all parties involved. But what is needed is flexibility and communication between the library and networking communities in considering all the options for future standards. The proposal for a generalized header above is our effort to involve the library community in the establishment of meta-information architectures and structures for this broad new class of information resources. We hope this leads to more discussion and investigation into the best avenues for a single format for controlling and accessing as well as automatic processing and serving of networked resources.

WORKS CITED

Berners-Lee, Tim. 1993. *WWW Names and Addresses, URIs, URLs, URNs*. URL: http://www.w3.org/hypertext/WWW/Addressing/Addressing.html.

Bowman, C. M. et al. 1994. *Harvest: A Scalable, Customizable Discovery and Access System. Technical Report CU-CS-732-94*. Department of Computer Science, University of Colorado, Boulder, July 1994. URL: ftp://ftp.cs.colorado.edu/pub/cs/techreports/schwartz/Harvest.ps.Z.

Bunyip Information Systems. 1994. *About Archie 3.0*. URL: http://pubweb.nexor.co.uk/public/archie/readme.html.

Crocker, D. 1982. *Standard for the format of ARPA Internet text messages*, RFC 822. URL: http://ds.internic.net/rfc/rfc822.txt.

Daniel, R. 1995. *An SGML-Based URC Service*. June 16, 1995. URL: ftp://cnri.reston.va.us/internet-drafts/draft-ietf-uri-urc-sgml-00.txt.

Daniel, R. and M. Mealling. 1995. *URC Scenarios and Requirements*. March 24, 1995. URL: ftp://cnri.reston.va.us/internet-drafts/draft-ietf-uri-urc-req-01 .txt.

Deutsch P. et al. 1995. *Publishing Information on the Internet with Anonymous FTP,* 1/95. URL: ftp://cnri.reston.va.us/internet-drafts/draft-ietf-iiir-publishing-03.txt.

Goldfarb, Charles. 1990. *SGML Handbook*. Clarendon: Oxford University Press, 1990.

Gorman, M. and Paul W. Winkler, eds. 1988. *Anglo-American Cataloging Rules,* 2nd. ed., 1988 revision. Chicago: American Library Association.

Hoogcarspel, A. 1994. *Guidelines for Cataloging Monographic Electronic Texts at the Center for Electronic Texts in the Humanities*. New Brunswick, NJ: Center for Electronic Texts in the Humanities.

Horowitz, L. 1994. *CETH workshop on documenting electronic texts, May 16-18,*

1994, Radisson Hotel, Somerset, NJ. New Brunswick, NJ: Center for Electronic Texts in the Humanities.

IETF. 1994. *IETF Home Page.* Reston VA: IETF Secretariat, Network Working Group, *Corporation for National Research Initiative.* URL: http://www.ietf.cnri.reston.va.us/home.html.

Jul, Erik. 1994. *Building a Catalog of Internet-Accessible Materials.* Dublin Ohio: OCLC, Inc. URL: http://www.oclc.org/oclc/man/catproj/overview.htm.

Library of Congress. 1994a. *Proceedings of the Seminar on Cataloging Digital Documents October 12-14, 1994 University of Virginia, Charlottesville and the Library of Congress.* URL: http://lcweb.loc.gov/catdir/semdigdocs/seminar.html.

Library of Congress. 1994b. *USMARC Format for Bibliographic Data: Including Guidelines for Content Designation.* 1994 edition. Prepared by Network Development and MARC Standards Office. Washington DC: Library of Congress, 1994.

Malkin, G. 1994. *The Tao of IETF.* RFC 1718 Reston VA: IETF Secretariat, Network Working Group, *Corporation for National Research Initiative.* URL: http://www.ietf.cnri.reston.va.us/tao.html.

Monroe, H. 1994. *Alex: A Catalogue of Electronic Texts on the Internet.* URL: gopher://rsl.ox.ac.uk/00/lib-corn/hunter/About%20Alex.

NCSA. 1994. *Proposed Mosaic Common Client Interface* 11/4/94 URL: http://yahoo.ncsa.uiuc.edu/mosaic/cci.spec.

OCLC, Inc. 1992. *Assessing Information on the Internet: Toward Providing Library Services for Computer-Mediated Communication.* Dublin Ohio: OCLC, Inc. URL: http://www.oclc.org/oclc/menu/reschdoc.htm.

Postel, J. 1994. *Media Type Registration Procedure,* RFC 1590. URL: http://ds.internic.net/rfc/rfc1590.txt.

Raggett, D. 1995. *Document Type Definition for the HyperText Markup Language (HTML DTD).* Draft: Thu 19-Jan-95 12:02:46 URL: http://www.w3.org/hypertext/WWW/MarkUp/htm13-dtd.txt.

Roscheisen, M., C. Mogensen, and Terry Winograd. 1995. *Beyond Browsing: Shared Comments, SOAPs, Trails, and On-line Communities.* Stanford CA: Stanford University, 1995. URL: http://www-diglib.stanford.edu/diglib/pub/reports/WWW95/.

SoftQuad, Inc. 1994. *SoftQuad Panorama PRO–a New Era in Web Content Delivery.* URL: http://www.sq.com/products/panorama/panor-fe.htm.

Sperberg-McQueen, C. M., and Lou Burnard. 1991. Sidebar 5: The Text Encoding Initiative (TEI). *Library Hi Tech,* 9(3), 20.

Sperberg-McQueen, C. M., and Lou Burnard, eds. 1994. *Guidelines for Electronic Text Encoding and Interchange TEI P3.* Chicago: ACH-ACL-ALLC, Text Encoding Initiative.

Standards for Name
and Series Authority Records

Judith A. Kuhagen

SUMMARY. This article discusses the data content standards of authority work reflected in name and series authority records in the national authority file. It looks at how the standards have affected the content of the file and how the file's evolution from LC's local authority file to a national resource authority file has affected the standards. Difficult management issues are noted. *[Article copies available from The Haworth Document Delivery Service: 1-800-342-9678.]*

INTRODUCTION

The *USMARC Format for Authority Data* is the standard for the representation and exchange of authority data in machine-readable form in the United States. Name and series authority records are two categories of such authority data. What is the standard for the data content of records for names and uniform/series titles?

Judith A. Kuhagen, MA, is Senior Cataloging Policy Specialist in the Cataloging Policy and Support Office, Library of Congress, Washington, DC 20540-4305. She is one of the authors of the LC *Descriptive Cataloging Manual Z1* section. She was the chair of the CPSO/CCC Task Group on the 670 Field in Name and Series Authority Records and a member of both the LC Series Group and the CCC Series Authority Record Task Group.

The author thanks her division chief, Barbara B. Tillett, and her colleagues Robert Ewald, Kay Guiles, and Diane Humes for their advice and assistance in the writing of this paper.

[Haworth co-indexing entry note]: "Standards for Name and Series Authority Records." Kuhagen, Judith A. Co-published simultaneously in *Cataloging & Classification Quarterly* (The Haworth Press, Inc.) Vol. 21, No. 3/4, 1996, pp. 131-154; and: *Cataloging and Classification Standards and Rules* (ed: John J. Riemer) The Haworth Press, Inc., 1996, pp. 131-154. Single or multiple copies of this article are available from The Haworth Document Delivery Service [1-800-342-9678, 9:00 a.m. - 5:00 p.m. (EST)].

Reviewing the beginning and ongoing evolution of the national resource authority file (NAF), formerly known as the Library of Congress authority file, answers the question. The data content standard for names and titles has been composed of a mix of cataloging rules,[1] *Library of Congress Rule Interpretations* (LCRIs), and LC's *Descriptive Cataloging Manual Z* section (DCM Z1)[2] for NACO (the Name Authority Cooperative) and LC "local" practices and procedures.

The Name Authority Cooperative began in 1977 to encourage the shared creation and maintenance of name and uniform/series title authority records in a national resource authority file. LC catalogers doing descriptive cataloging plus an increasing number of NACO participants have joined in the development of both the authority file and the data content standard. As NACO involvement grew, the authority file and its data content standard became less "LC-centric" and more diverse. In addition to college and university libraries, NACO participants range from historical society libraries to public libraries and from museum libraries to other national libraries (National Agricultural Library and National Library of Medicine).

However, a certain amount of "LC-centric-ness" must remain since the NAF is in fact LC's authority file. The Library of Congress *does not* have its own separate local authority file. LC catalogers must work against all records in the file when creating new headings and are responsible for ensuring proper maintenance of all the records. LC catalogers contribute all LC name and series authority records to the file unlike NACO participants, who may choose what name and series authority records they will contribute. In addition, NCCP (National Coordinated Cataloging Program) participants contribute name and series authority records for the headings used in the bibliographic records they choose to contribute. NACO participants may download and modify any of the authority records for their local files, but LC does not have that flexibility.

The designation of the file as the "national" resource authority file has not been strictly accurate for some time. Since 1975 the Library of Congress has had an agreement with the National Library of Canada (NLC) to use NLC's headings when LC creates name authority records for Canadian corporate bodies; when creating new name authority records for Canadian persons, LC generally uses NLC's already-established personal name headings. Additionally, headings established by the British Library used in the Eighteenth Century Short Title Catalogue project have been added to the authority file since 1985. The British Library began submitting some personal name authority records in 1994. Discussions among the Library of Congress, the British Library, and the National Library of Canada related to the convergence of both cataloging policies and authority formats are taking place with the goal of an internationalized authority file. The immediate future will see the expansion of NACO to Australia when the University of Newcastle becomes a NACO participant in 1995.

NAME AUTHORITY RECORDS

The first automated name authority records (NARs) were created at LC on April 1, 1977; descriptive catalogers prepared paper worksheets and LC's MARC Editorial Division staff input the records. Instructions for filling out the worksheets were very specific since the records were being input by staff members who didn't see the items and might not know the languages. By 1990 nearly all LC staff in Washington, D.C. doing descriptive cataloging were creating their authority records online. LC staff members in overseas offices, who had been preparing worksheets and sending them to Washington for input, began creating MARC records in January 1995.

The U.S. Government Printing Office Library was the first NACO participant, beginning its contributions of NARs in October 1977. As of March 1995, there were 161 libraries participating in 72 NACO NAR projects. Some NACO projects are called "funnels" which enable many libraries to participate as a single project, e.g., art, music, Hebraic funnels. Initially, NACO participants also filled out paper worksheets and mailed them to LC where the MARC Editorial Division input the records. By 1987, the Linked Systems Project allowed online contribution of NACO records via a computer-to-computer link between LC and other systems. Yale University was the first RLIN library to transmit new NARs and additions/changes to LC in June 1987; the first OCLC library to do so was

Indiana University in March 1988. Now the exchange of data between LC and the utilities is handled via the Internet using file transfer protocols (FTP). The contributed records can be recognized by the alphabetic prefix to the Library of Congress Control Number, which indicates the system used for input (e.g., "no" for OCLC, "nr" for RLIN).

While LC catalogers were still using the manual Official Name/ Title Catalog for cataloging (through June 1983), LC had a policy to move as many headings with related information as possible from that manual file to the automated authority file. Catalogers reestablished name and uniform title headings by preparing "retrospective" name authority records based on the manual authority cards, usage in the card catalog, and usage in items in hand. In 1979, a contractor converted to automated form other manual authority records for headings used in MARC records; these records are in the "n50" series of control numbers. Some of the retrospective records may have some incomplete 670 fields (Source found) and may have 678 fields (Epitome note) containing summary information about persons or corporate bodies taken from separate, full citations on the manual authority cards.

At varying periods of time, name headings were coded to indicate the cataloging rules under which they were established. From late 1975-1980, LC serials cataloging staff were coding name headings according to cataloging rules to fulfill the requirement of supplying AACR 1 (*Anglo-American Cataloging Rules,* 1st edition) forms of names in CONSER (then meaning CONversion of SERials) records; when headings were not AACR 1 forms, references or notes were used to give the AACR 1 forms. During 1979-1980, in preparation for the implementation of the second edition of the *Anglo-American Cataloguing Rules* (AACR 2), LC coded as many headings as possible for the AACR 2 form through regular cataloging and a project identifying often-used headings. When headings were not AACR 2 forms, references or notes were used to give the AACR 2 forms. The heading considered to be the AACR 2 form could be either the "pure" AACR 2 form or a compatible form called "AACR 2-d"; the categories for compatible headings in use until September 1982 are given in LCRI 22.1 (personal names) and LCRI 24.1 (corporate body names). As of September 1982, all new headings, with only a few exceptions noted in the LCRIs just mentioned, had to be established as "pure" AACR 2; existing compatible headings continue to be used as established.

Scope of the Name Authority Component

One aspect of the data content standard of the national authority file is the policy on when a name authority record should be created. According to the DCM Z1 guidelines, an NAR is made

> . . . for a personal or corporate (including geographic) name heading that *may* be used as a main or added entry heading, whether it is actually first used as (or as part of) a main entry heading, a secondary entry (including a subject entry), or in certain cross references . . . NARs are not made for personal names when the only clue to the person's identity is a nonalphabetic or nonnumeric device . . .[3]

Pre-AACR 2 practice also excluded name authority records for personal authors when the person's identity was known only by an "Author of" statement or a characterizing word or phrase preceded by an indefinite article, e.g., "A Scholar;" such individuals were not considered capable of authorship prior to AACR 2. Entities eligible for use in bibliographic records only as subject entries (e.g., topical subject headings, fictional characters) are not represented by name authority records.

The conditions for making NARs for titles or name/titles other than those for series has changed over the years, too. Initial practice was to make these NARs only if it was necessary to trace cross references, to record documentation due to special problems, or to give the form for a related work added entry or subject entry when the bibliographic record for that work was not in the database. Today's guidelines (DCM Z1) add two more conditions for making these NARs: "special information needs to be recorded, e.g., citation title for a law; the authority record is needed as part of a project or program, e.g., creation of uniform title authority records for each of a composer's works."[4] (The last condition, the result of a request from the NACO music funnel project, is an example of NACO participation extending the boundaries of the authority file beyond the works being cataloged to all works that could be cataloged.)

NAR Level of Establishment

The authority format describes four levels of establishment (008/33): full, memo, provisional, and preliminary. The usual level is "full." The "memorandum" value is rarely used now since in a shared database it doesn't carry the original meaning of a heading not appearing in a bibliographic record. LC catalogers and NACO participants code NARs as "provisional" if usage is not available for establishing the heading in the language required by AACR 2, if further research should be done the next time the heading is used in case more information will be available to resolve a problematic situation, or if the title or body is being established subordinately to a name heading and that name heading's NAR is "provisional." A NACO participant may code an authority record as "provisional" if the library doesn't have the necessary language expertise or is unable to complete the related authority work/full reference structure; however, such an authority record can't be contributed if the heading conflicts with an existing heading. The Cooperative Cataloging team, the LC unit administering the NACO program, can arrange for assistance from another cataloging unit if the NACO participant makes such a request.

"Preliminary" authority records are based on headings in existing bibliographic records instead of being based on the forms of name as presented on items in hand. Preliminary authority records in the NAF represent specific past activities, e.g., records created by LC staff based on records contributed to the *National Union Catalog* when no LC usage was available; records created as part of special LC projects without items in hand (e.g., using other libraries' bibliographic records to upgrade existing CIP bibliographic records when publications hadn't been received in LC); and records created as part of retrospective projects, e.g., the University of Chicago retrospective cataloging project, the Cornell University retrospective conversion project for headings in non-current serial titles in the humanities. A "preliminary" record is upgraded to a "full" record, modified if necessary, when the heading is needed for a bibliographic record representing an item in hand.

The Cooperative Cataloging Council/Program for Cooperative Cataloging is proposing the addition of a code in 008/33 for machine-generated authority records.

Cataloging Rules/Options and Rule Interpretations

The Anglo-American Cataloguing Rules, 2nd edition, 1988 revision (with 1993 amendments) is the cataloging code for name authority records currently being added to the authority file. The *Library of Congress Rule Interpretations* record decisions on options presented in the rules, give instructions where there are lacunae in the rules, explain/elucidate context for particular rules, address specific needs of certain constituencies (e.g., music libraries) upon request, and record agreed-upon practices (including LC "local" practice if needed).

As noted above, the NAF includes records based on earlier cataloging rules. Headings not coded for AACR 2 are evaluated and modified as needed when the heading is used in an AACR 2 bibliographic record or needed as part of a new authority record. However, there have also been AACR 2 rule revisions and LCRI revisions affecting forms of headings and the making of references. Sometimes there is a project to change all the existing headings, e.g., headings both for and including British place names when the Chapter 23 rule changed. Otherwise, the change of rule/LCRI is applied to new headings and to existing headings when next used. Recently, specific instructions on the implementation of the change have been included in the appropriate rule interpretation. An example is the reference from local place for a church, cathedral, etc.; LCRI 24.10B says to remove that reference the next time the heading is used.

Some AACR 2 rules and LCRIs have direct impact on the number of name authority records made. For instance, LCRI 21.1B1 gives guidelines for deciding if a conference is named; if a conference is unnamed, a heading isn't established. Another example is when to make multiple headings/authority records for pseudonyms and different bibliographic identities (LCRI 22.2B).

One heading may be used for more than one person if possible additions (e.g., date, phrase) to persons' names are not available or suitable (AACR 2 rule 22.20 and LCRI 22.17-20). The resulting undifferentiated personal name authority records, formerly called non-unique name authority records, are coded with value "b" in fixed field 008/32. In 1988, in response to concerns about the length of these records, LC changed its policy to list no more than three persons in such a record; if the heading represented more than three persons, a 667 note, "Record covers additional persons," was added. In mid-1990, in response to concerns about the lack of information deemed important, the policy reverted to listing each person using the same name.

Other AACR 2 rules and LCRIs give instructions on inclusion, choice, order, and punctuation/spacing of data elements in the heading field (1XX) of an NAR. LCRI 23.2 includes a list of specific geographic names in English to be used instead of the forms provided by the U.S. Board of Geographic Names as well as special decisions about headings for China, Germany, Korea, etc. Lists of words in English, French, and Spanish meeting the criterion in 24.13, Type 2 and 24.18, Type 2 of " . . . a word that normally implies administrative subordination" are found in the LCRIs for those two rules; a common understanding of what names will be entered subordinately leads to consistency in a shared file.

LCRI 22.17 gives the instruction to apply the option in that rule to add dates in personal name headings even if the dates aren't needed to break a conflict. That LCRI also includes the policy *not* to add dates to existing headings already coded for AACR 2; questions are often raised about this policy when death dates or birth/death dates are available. The decision was made on the basis of economics for LC as well as for other libraries; if LC changes a heading to add date(s), other users need to change their headings. Bibliographic file maintenance is costly for LC and other libraries lacking global update capabilities. (The missing dates are recorded in 670 note fields.) The question of adding missing dates in headings raises the larger issue of whether a heading is just a standardized form of name or is also biographical information. LC has preferred to view headings as standardized forms of names.

NARs may have see references from forms not used as headings to the established forms used as headings and see also references leading to related headings. Decisions have to be made about the number and form of see references. AACR 2 Chapter 26 and LCRIs for some Chapter 26 rules address the need for see references in general categories. For example, LCRI 26.3 specifies inverted references from keywords for bodies entered under governments and for conferences, exhibitions, etc.; LCRI 26.3A7 indicates when to make references from jurisdictions. References for specific situations are included in AACR 2 Chapters 22-25 and corresponding LCRIs, e.g., references for joint committees, commissions, etc., in LCRI 24.15A.

The number of references was reduced in the mid-1980's in response to NACO participants' concern about time needed to record references. The current policy is to give only one reference for each variant form or approach, i.e., not to give variants of variants; there are some exceptions to that policy, e.g., the direction in LCRI 26.3 to give all English variants if the corporate body's heading is not in English.

The indexing capability of some libraries' local systems may mean that certain references aren't needed in those systems. For example, LC doesn't need the inverted references required by LCRI 26.3 (since its 1XX fields in NARs are indexed for keyword searching) but gives the references to benefit the libraries who need them. The policy for number of references may be changed in the future due to the possibility of using subfield $5 in reference fields to label local references; some NACO participants have expressed interest in this technique.

The general policy on form of see references is in LCRI 26: "All cross references on authority records in the automated name authority file must eventually be in accordance with LC/AACR 2 practice in matters of form, style, and choice of references." It was not possible to handle the references for AACR 2 when headings were being coded in preparation for AACR 2 implementation. The reference structure and the forms of the references are evaluated and adjusted as needed when the headings are used. Rule 26.1F1 says to give the reference in the same structure it would have as a heading; the associated LCRI says there will be some differences since the NAF contains headings based on earlier practices. So, the principle is to make the reference match the heading. For example, if the heading for a person has dates, a reference for a variant form of the name would also have dates. That same LCRI says to ignore the instruction in the rule to use combined references; the policy is to use such references only for situations needing special explanatory references, e.g., pseudonym references.

LCRI 26.1 has the further instruction not to include a reference in an authority record if its form normalizes to the same form as the heading in that record or a heading in another record. More information on normalization is given in the DCM Z1 introduction section.[5] Unfortunately, not all systems normalize headings the same way.

An NAR may also have another kind of reference called a "linking" reference. Although linking references are not addressed in AACR 2, LCRI 26 explains that they could be/were used as the " . . . connection between different pre-1981 and post-1980 forms" and " . . . as a mechanism for updating headings in pre-AACR 2 bibliographic records to the AACR 2 form." An NAR with a reference coded as the AACR 2 form in preparation for AACR 2 implementation had its heading and the reference flipped by program to put the AACR 2 form in the heading field; the former heading became the linking reference. LC catalogers and NACO participants included linking references in new NARs if the headings had been established prior to AACR 2 and the forms differed. Linking references are the exception to having all references in accordance with AACR 2 and the exception to making the reference match the heading. Linking references were required until February 1994 when their inclusion became optional at the suggestion of the NACO music funnel project members. If the linking reference normalizes to the same form as the heading in that record or in another record, the pre-AACR 2 form is given in a 667 note field: "Old catalog heading: _____."

Subject-to-name references were included in name authority records for corporate bodies in the 1970's and early 1980's. However, since these references weren't maintained and may not reflect current subject cataloging policy, they are removed when the authority records are being modified for other reasons.

Some references are supported by 670 field (Source found) citations showing when and where forms given as references were used. Other references do not need to be justified (i.e., supported) by citations; the types of these references are listed in the DCM Z1 guidelines:

1. References justified by rules or rule interpretations only, usually because the reference is derived from inverting, shortening, etc., the heading or giving a substitute form in the heading.
2. References made on the basis of the cataloger's awareness of different romanizations or orthographies.
3. Name/title cross references derived from the work being cataloged, from other works cataloged under the same heading, or from information in standard reference sources . . .
4. References made on the basis of information from the National Library of Canada . . .
5. References to earlier/later headings of corporate bodies reflecting changes due to national orthographic reform, changes in government headings due to an official language change, or changes involving only a parent body to which the body being established is subordinate.
6. References made on the basis of information from the British Library as part of the Eighteenth Century Short Title Catalogue project.
7. References from pre-AACR 2 forms on SARs and on retrospective NARs.[6]

Specific NAR Fields

Some fields included in name authority records when the NAF began are no longer included in new NARs. The 678 field (Epitome note), used in LC's retrospective records, was described above. Difficulties in LC's workflow for information references (references giving the entire history of the corporate body with indication of subject usage) and calls for simplification resulted in the decision to discontinue using field 665 (History reference). The substitute practice is to give see also references on each record only for the immediately preceding and succeeding headings with no explicit indication of subject usage (LCRI 26.3B-C).

The initial use and then abandonment of three LC local fixed fields also illustrate the development of the authority file. LC local fixed field 43 (Retrospective) was used to label those records created by LC staff and the contractor converting manual authority records to automated form; MARBI (Machine-Readable Bibliographic Information Committee, the American Library Association advisory group for the MARC format) considered and then decided against the distribution of this fixed field data. Local fixed field 11 (Heading used in LC), assigned by both LC staff and NACO participants, specified whether the heading was used in a record for a work in LC's collections; its use was abandoned in April 1988. Local fixed field 6 (GM MARC indicator) noted if the heading was created solely for a heading in a cartographic record or for a heading in a record for a work assigned to LC's Geography and Map Division; as of April 1990, this data was no longer recorded.

Information formerly recorded at LC only in the local cataloger's note field 952 (e.g., "Not same as: _____" or "Change heading if name _____ continues to be used") is found now in the 667 note field, because the local field 952 is not distributed. Since some groups of LC catalogers do their cataloging in OCLC and RLIN and since NACO participants generally view the NAF in a utility, this information must be available beyond LC's database.

However, the most "popular" field for discussions proposing change/abandonment is the 670 field (Source data found). As stated in the DCM Z1 guidelines,

> . . . the purpose of this field is to record information about the name or title represented in the 1XX field. It includes facts that contribute to the identification of the heading, that justify the choice of the name used as the 1XX heading and references to it, and that clarify relationships between it and other headings in the file.[7]

Because the abandonment of this field had been suggested as a time-saving factor by several libraries in their responses to the LC Series Group's report (see series authority record section below) and to several Cooperative Cataloging Council (CCC) task group surveys, the CCC appointed a task group to address the use and importance of the 670 field. The final report of the 670 group summarized the various uses of the 670 field by general and special interest groups:

Some are "merely" concerned about having enough information in the 670 to confirm that the person or body or series
represented by the record is the same as the person/body/series
in the item in hand. Others want that information plus enough
history for corporate bodies to identify earlier and later names.
Some, especially people working with manuscript or archival
material, include multiple 670 fields and give extensive biographical information about a person and her/his family and
extensive historical information about corporate bodies; thus,
the authority records themselves become resources for individuals seeking information on these persons or bodies. Individuals working with other kinds of special collections often
have very specific information to record.[8]

The report also described how information in the 670 field is just
beginning to be used to support automated authority control, such
as OCLC's attributes project.[9]

The CCC 670 task group's report included the recommendation
that "a 670 field for the work being cataloged *should be included* in
name and series authority records, especially if these records are
going to reside in a shared database."[10] Sometimes the bibliographic
record which generated the authority record contributed to the authority file is not itself contributed to a shared database. The second
recommendation addressed the minimal elements of a name authority 670 field: title and publication date of the work being cataloged,
recorded in subfield $a; the main entry could be given if the title was
generic or too short for identification. The task group included the
publication date as an element necessary for identifying a person or
corporate body's time period in a large/shared database. The location in
the item of the name or title in the heading, the usage (form of the
name/title) found in that source, and other data about person/body/title
would be given in subfield $b at the discretion of each library.[11]

The LC/NACO policy has been always to give the subfield $b
information (location, usage, and other data) in all 670 fields in a
name authority record. LC considered several simplification proposals from the CCC 670 task group and recently forwarded some
proposals to its own staff and to NACO participants for comment.
These latter proposals involved (1) requiring only the element of

information unique to that source for sources other than the work being cataloged, (2) generally not including subfield $b in a citation for National Library of Canada information in an LC rec-ord, and (3) not including the date of a database search or phone call if that 670 field was included as part of the original record. Also included was a modified proposal to condense information other than variant forms of name from other than the chief source of information into one set of parentheses. LC did not endorse and, therefore, did not forward for comment the proposal from the 670 task group stating a subfield $b was unnecessary in name authority records if the form on the chief source of information was the same as the form in the heading and if the authority record had no references or had references not needing justification. LC's years of database maintenance in a very large file have shown the importance of having location and usage in the 670 citation for resolving conflicts and for problem solving.

The presentation of information in the 670 field in LC/NACO records has become more flexible. As noted earlier, the guidelines for many years were very specific as to content and punctuation. Initially, the main entry was required; if the name authority record was made for a person or body connected to a series, both the main entry of the series and the main entry for the analytic record were required. In 1987, two 670 simplifications occurred: (1) not giving the reason for establishing the heading if it were other than the main entry in the bibliographic record; and (2) allowing catalogers to use any style and punctuation in the field as long as the information was clearly presented and the style/punctuation didn't need to be consistent from one record to the next. In March 1993, three other 670 simplifications were announced: (1) generally requiring only the title proper rather than the main entry in subfield $a; (2) not requiring the notation "[not analyzed in LC]" or "[not cataloged in LC]" at the end of 670 fields for issues of a series not analyzed/cataloged in LC; and (3) not giving the GMD in subfield $a. The original guideline to be selective in deciding how many 670 fields to record for reference sources consulted continues to be endorsed. The objective of clarity is still key.

SERIES AUTHORITY RECORDS

The first automated series authority records (SARs), in the "n83-"series of control numbers, were created at LC in August 1982. Manual series authority cards had been filed in the Official Name/Title Catalog for many years prior to 1981 and in the Add-On Official Catalog for 1981-August 1982. The manual authority cards in the Add-On Catalog were converted to automated records in the "n42-"series by a contractor. The U.S. Government Printing Office Library, the first NACO participant for NARs, was also the first NACO participant to contribute SARs to the authority file. As of March 1995, 31 NACO participants have contributed or are contributing SARs, some related only to their own cataloging and others for the series headings found in the bibliographic records they've chosen to contribute.

Since online series authority records didn't exist until after AACR 2 implementation, there were no existing MARC records to code for AACR 2 as there were for name authority records. However, because the bibliographic files were not "closed" when AACR 2 was implemented, any existing series had to be reestablished the first time an issue of that series was cataloged after AACR 2 implementation. The difference in choice/form of entry and title transcription for serials under earlier cataloging rules represented by monographic series analytic records in the "unclosed" bibliographic files made reestablishing series a challenge. The series added entries on those records were changed to the AACR 2 forms. The existing decisions on classification were maintained; little information about analysis practice for series classified as collections and for publishers before the AACR 2 time period is included in these SARs unless the LC cataloger needed to consult the manual authority records in the Official Name/Title Catalog for some other reason.

In August 1993 an LC Series Group was appointed to determine how LC's local processing instructions recorded in SAR treatment fields (see below) could be conveyed to LC staff if LC were to stop tracing series and stop creating SARs. That group's report[12] generated much discussion in the U.S. library community. The Cooperative Cataloging Council established a Series Authority Record Task

Group with the charge to " . . . define the content and functional uses of series authority records in the national authority file."[13] That task group, in its final report submitted in September 1994, concluded that "controlled access is needed to all types of series" and made the recommendation " . . . provide a series authority record for every series."[14] In early November 1994, LC announced its intention to continue tracing series in bibliographic records and creating SARs.[15]

Scope of the Series Authority Component

As noted above, one aspect of the data content standard of an authority file is the policy for when a record should be created. According to the DCM Z1 guidelines, series authority records (SARs) are made

> . . . for all monographic series, analyzable or partially analyz-able multipart items, occasionally analyzable serials other than monographic series, and series-like phrases that may be construed by some to constitute a series. A series-like phrase record also can be made to record information of general inter-est or application, e.g., the 1XX in the record is an imprint rather than a title.[16]

SARs are not made for a manifestation lacking the original series statement, an unanalyzable multipart item, an issue of a periodical even if it has a special title or consists of a single contribution, or a hardcover/softcover separate edition of a single issue of a periodical published in addition to the unbound issues received on subscrip-tion.

The propensity that serial publications in general have for varia-tion and change certainly is found in the subgroup monographic series; variations also occur among volumes of multipart items. So, another aspect of when series authority records should be made relates to how many SARs should exist to represent these varia-tions/changes. Such variations include a difference in title proper, a difference in responsible person/body, issues in different languages, change in presence/absence of volume numbers, and combination of main series and subseries. A listing of the various rules/LCRIs giving the policy for such situations is found in DCM Z1;[17] some are also summarized below.

Most titles of series and multipart items are clearly presented as titles on the works being cataloged. The words themselves, a publisher or editor statement, and sometimes the presence of numbering confirm that the words are titles. At the other extreme are words, letters, and combinations of letters and numbers that clearly are not titles of series or multipart items. In a shared database, usually it is easy to have agreement about these two extremes. It is the middle-ground situations that cause confusion. Are the words in these situations titles? For the sake of both consistency in the database and efficiency, decisions need to be made and recorded so the words will be handled the same way each time they appear without having to reconsider the situation each time. If the decision is that the words are not a title of a series or a multipart item, a series-like phrase SAR is created to record that decision; the phrase is recorded in the 1XX field (Heading) as if it were a title so it can be found in future searches of the authority file. Treatment fields for processing information (see below) are omitted since the phrase doesn't represent a bibliographic entity. A 667 note field is included in the phrase SAR to give instructions for handling the phrase, for example, to give the phrase as a quoted note in the bibliographic record.

The SAR counterpart of the "undifferentiated personal name" NAR is the "core record" for series-like phrases. Since the series-like phrase is not recorded in the bibliographic record as a series title, distinguishing identical series-like phrases from each other is not necessary. This combined series-like phrase SAR applies to any use of that phrase by any corporate body. (If one use of that "phrase" by a body is considered a series title, a separate SAR for that series is created.) Specific places of publication and publishers are not given. A standardized 667 note is included: "CORE RECORD. Covers all instances . . . "[18] After the concept of the phrase core record was implemented, some LC staff worked on a project to collapse individual SARs for the same phrases into one SAR. (This core record should not be confused with the Cooperative Cataloging Council's core bibliographic record. LC is considering a new name for this combined series-like phrase SAR to avoid such confusion.)

SAR Level of Establishment

The same four levels of establishment noted above for name authority records apply to series authority records. The usual level for SARs is "full." An SAR would be labelled as "provisional" in two situations: (1) if the main entry was under person or body and the NAR for that person or body itself was a "provisional" record; and (2) if an SAR is being made for a series having issues in different languages and the first issue is not available. The value "d" for "preliminary" has not been used for SARs since the policy for making an SAR requires having an item in hand. However, that policy was not followed for some short-duration projects in 1985 and 1988 that based the SAR heading on series statements in bibliographic records (for example, using other libraries' bibliographic records to upgrade existing CIP bibliographic records when publications hadn't been received in LC); these SARs were not coded as "preliminary" records.

Cataloging Rules and Rule Interpretations

The *Anglo-American Cataloguing Rules, 2nd edition,* 1988 revision (with 1993 amendments) is the cataloging code for SARs currently being added to the authority file. Rules in Chapter 12 (Serials) apply to transcription of series titles proper, including which form of title should be recorded when the title is present in both a full form and an acronym or initialism (12.1B2) and where the title starts (12.1B3).

As for name authority records, the code and the *Library of Congress Rule Interpretations* contain directions affecting how many series authority records should be made. For example, one part of LCRI 1.6 gives guidelines on number of records for series published in different languages; another part addresses when a new SAR is needed if numbering designations are added to or removed from series issues. Rule 21.2A was changed in the 1988 revision of AACR 2 to make the guidelines for when a title proper has changed be as close as possible to the guidelines of the International Serials Data System for a change in the key title; for example, a change from singular to plural form of a word doesn't require a new entry. The LCRI explains and expands on the other differences in form of title not defined as a "change in title proper." Some LC staff members worked on a project to condense separate series authority records that no longer represented title changes. Although this change has a positive impact for non-series serials since fewer new records need to be created, the impact of the change in relation to monographic series is mixed. Fewer SARs are needed since a difference in title proper covered by rule/LCRI 21.2A is added as a 430 field (See reference) to the existing SAR. However, the access point for the series title in that bibliographic record now becomes a form not found on the item in hand; the found form is transcribed in 490 1 field (Series traced differently) and the different (i.e., earlier) form from the SAR is given as the access point in the 830 field.

LCRI 21.2C1 lists other conditions when a separate entry isn't required. AACR 2 21.3B and the corresponding LCRI address the opposite condition: when a separate entry is required.

Prior to AACR 2, the choice of main entry for serials with generic titles and for serials with the body's name in the title was under the heading for the body. Under AACR 2, main entry for most serials is title. This change in main entry plus the use of same or similar non-generic titles by more than one serial meant it would not be possible to distinguish the titles used in linking fields of serial bibliographic records or distinguish the series added entries for one publication from those for another publication when the titles proper were the same. AACR 2 did not provide a solution for this problem. LC and the National Library of Canada (NLC in its role as a CONSER library) developed the concept originally called the "unique serial identifier." The guidelines for adding a qualifier to the title proper of a serial entered under title to distinguish it from another serial having the same title proper are in LCRI 25.5B. The guidelines have become more flexible, emphasizing cataloger's judgment in selecting the appropriate qualifier. Here, as in the area of dates in personal name headings, questions are raised whether the qualifier should just make the heading unique or whether the qualifier should identify the serial. The LCRI includes guidelines for adding qualifiers in other situations affecting series authority records (e.g., when the series title is identical to a corporate name, when a qualifier is added to a multipart item heading) as well as for adding qualifiers in non-SAR situations. LC and NLC presented the guidelines to the Joint Steering Committee for the Revision of AACR; the committee agreed with the guidelines but chose not to include them in rule 25.5B. The 1993 amendments to AACR 2 do include some series and non-series serial examples for that rule.

The guidelines for references in SARs were recorded in a predecessor document (DCM C11.9) to the current DCM Z1 document, rather than in an LCRI because AACR 2 Chapter 26 lacked a rule for series/serials. However, rule 26.5 (References to Added Entries for Series and Serials) was added in the 1988 revision of AACR 2. Now that LC has reconfirmed its intention to continue creating SARs, an LCRI for 26.5 will be developed. References in SARs fall into four categories: from the form not chosen as main entry (e.g., reference from name + title if the series is entered under title), from variant forms of title, to earlier and later headings, and from the pre-AACR 2 form (i.e., the linking reference). The principles applied to NARs of tracing only one form for each kind of reference and giving a reference for a variant in the form it would have if it were the heading apply also to SARs. Linking references became optional in SARs in February 1994 as they did for NARs.

All types of SARs, even series-like phrase SARs, may have references. Local processing decisions do not affect whether references are given in SARs. Prior to AACR 2, LC's practice was not to give references for a series classified as a collection in LC; any references connected to the series would duplicate added entries given in the collected set bibliographic record for the series. SARs in the NAF are for any library to use; the presence of references shouldn't be contingent on the classification practice of any specific library.

The technique of using qualifiers described in LCRI 25.5B for headings is applied to references if they conflict with other SAR headings/serial titles proper or normalize to forms that are the same as SAR headings. NACO participants are interested, for SARs as well as NARs, in adding local references using subfield $5 to identify the library. Some kinds of SAR references do not require justification by information recorded in a 670 field; they are included in the list given in the NAR section on references above.

Specific SAR Fields

When discussions were held in the mid- to late-1970's about online authority data for monographic series, two different possibilities, in either the Serials or the Authority format, were considered because of the basic difference between name and series authority data. A name authority heading is the authorized form of name to be used in any bibliographic record now and in the future where its use is appropriate; name authority data can be associated with many bibliographic entities. However, a series heading is always connected to one specific bibliographic entity; when that bibliographic entity changes in ways requiring a new entry, the "old" series authority data is no longer appropriate. New series authority data must be created. Due to the interrelationship of series authority data with the corresponding bibliographic entity, recording series authority data in the Serials bibliographic format was considered. However, problems were identified with that approach: the need to create serial collected set records for unnumbered series and series-like phrases, the need for new fields in the Serials format to record classification/analysis/tracing practice, the significant increase in serial catalogers' workloads. Changes to the Books format would also have been needed to record local processing information about multipart items. So, the decision was made to put series authority data in the Authorities format with other types of authority data.

Series authority records employ the following fields as found in NARs: 1XX (Heading), 4XX/5XX (REFERENCES), 670 (Source found), 675 (Source not found), and 667 (Note). The 675 fields were not included in SARs prior to the "n84-"series of control numbers. Until 1989, the first 670 field in a SAR did not have a subfield $b if the usage matched the heading; also, variant forms found in the item cited in the first 670 were not always included in subfield $b. These differences from NAR 670/675 practice were the result of an attempt to minimize the impact on descriptive catalogers' workload since the manual series authority cards had contained less information. However, having different practices for different kinds of authority records was in itself confusing; also, trying to resolve problems without location and usage in the SAR 670 was a difficult and time-consuming task.

The difference in the two kinds of authority data did result in the addition of certain fields unique to SARs in the Authorities format. Fixed field data includes type of SAR (008/12, with values for series, multipart item, phrase, and other serial) and whether the publication is numbered or unnumbered (008/13).

Unique variable fields fall into two categories, those giving bibliographic details and those recording local treatment practices. Fields 640 (Series dates of publication and/or volume designation), 641 (Series numbering peculiarities), and 643 (Series place and publisher/issuing body) contain information to help identify which specific bibliographic entity is represented by the SAR. Since place and publisher data change often for series, the DCM Z1 section for the 643 field gives guidelines for how much data to record and when summary data can be given in the 670 (Note) field.

Fields 642 (Series numbering example), 644 (Series analysis practice), 645 (Series tracing practice), and 646 (Series classification practice), collectively called the "series treatment fields," include a subfield $5 to indicate which library applies the treatment shown. LC catalogers must always include these treatment fields. When creating a new SAR, a NACO participant has the option of omitting one or all of these fields, predicting/recording only LC's treatment decisions, recording only its own treatment decisions, or recording both its and LC's decisions. NACO participants established the policy that no more than one NACO participant's decisions should be recorded in an SAR. NCCP participants must record LC's decisions. As noted earlier, SARs for series-like phrases lack treatment fields.

Since some groups of LC catalogers do their cataloging in OCLC and RLIN, some "local" information about publications at LC is given in the 667 note field because the more appropriate local 952 field is not distributed. Examples include location information for technical report series and changes in retention decisions for specific series.

Fixed field 008/32 (Undifferentiated personal name) was not being coded correctly for SARs until March 1991. Until then, only value "n" had been used in SARs. Incorrect "n" values can be changed when the record is used/modified.

CONCLUSION

The national authority file has developed from an LC-oriented file to a file trying to serve the sometimes disparate needs of a large and diverse group of contributors and consumers interacting with the file in contexts ranging from card catalogs to various online systems. Managing such a file becomes ever more complex as the size of the file itself and the number of contributors increase. How are the different needs of the consumers known and then met? How are decisions made about changes in cataloging rules, cataloging policies, use of data elements, etc., when the impact of any decision is not the same for all contributors/consumers? How does one know if consensus has been reached? Complicating all these issues is the reality that the national authority file is still LC's local authority file.

The final report from the Cooperative Cataloging Council's Task Group on Authorities contains six recommendations/assumptions[19] addressing both the management issues noted above as well as other steps in the development of the file, for example, merger of the name authority file and LC's subject authority file. Decisions on the future of the file will shape and be shaped by the standards exemplified by the authority records.

NOTES

1. *Anglo-American Cataloging Rules,* 1st edition; *Anglo-American Cataloguing Rules,* 2nd edition, and 2nd edition, 1988 revision with updates and amendments; also the *A.L.A. Cataloging Rules for Author and Title Entries* and earlier rules to some degree due to LC's superimposition policy. Rules cited/quoted in this article are from the 2nd edition, 1988 revision of *Anglo-American Cataloguing Rules* as updated by the 1993 amendments.

2. The Z1 section of LC's *Descriptive Cataloging Manual* (DCM) is printed on pages to be interfiled in the *USMARC Format for Authority Data*; it gives specific NACO and LC practices and procedures. Distribution of this documentation for name and series authority records is to NACO participants and LC cataloging staff. The current version, first published in 1993 and updated as needed, is not a stand-alone document. Earlier versions of LC's name and series authority records guidelines were summarized in *Cataloging Service Bulletin,* 42 (fall 1988): 37-64 [NARs only] and 24 (spring 1984): 22-55 [NARs and SARs].

3. Library of Congress. Cataloging Policy and Support Office. *Descriptive Cataloging Manual,* Z1, Introduction, p. 2.

4. Ibid.

5. Ibid., p. 4-6.

6. Ibid., 670, p. 3-4.

7. Ibid., p. 1.

8. CPSO/CCC Task Group on the 670 Field in Name and Series Authority Records. Final report (1994), p. 2. (Available via the LC MARVEL gopher via the path Libraries and Publishers (Technical Services), Cataloging at the Library of Congress: Programs & Services, Cooperative Cataloging Programs at the Library of Congress, Cooperative Cataloging Council, 670 Field (Sources Found) Task Group.)

9. Ibid., p. 2-3.

10. Ibid., p. 4.

11. Ibid.

12. Library of Congress. Collections Services. Series Group. Report (1993). (Also issued in AUTOCAT [electronic bulletin board], s.l. ca. 1990-; [cited 15 December 1993], available from listserv @UBVM.BITNET.)

13. Cooperative Cataloging Council. Series Authority Record Task Group. Final report (1994). (Available via the LC MARVEL gopher via the path Libraries and Publishers (Technical Services), Cataloging at the Library of Congress: Programs & Services, Cooperative Cataloging Programs at the Library of Congress, Cooperative Cataloging Council, Series Authority Record Task Group (Final Report/Appendix).)

14. Ibid.

15. Sarah E. Thomas. Memorandum of Nov. 4, 1994: "Series Authorities;" also "Series Description and Access," *Cataloging Service Bulletin,* 67 (winter 1995): 22. (For a fuller version, see in COOPCAT [electronic bulletin board], s.l., July 1992-; [cited 7 November 1994]; available from listserv@iubvm.ucs.indiana.edu; INTERNET.)

16. Library of Congress. Cataloging Policy and Support Office. *Descriptive Cataloging Manual,* Z1, Introduction, p. 2-3.

17. Ibid., p. 7-10.

18. Ibid., p. 10.

19. Cooperative Cataloging Council. Task Group on Authorities. Final report (1993), p. 2-6. (Available via the LC MARVEL gopher via the path Libraries and Publishers (Technical Services), Cataloging at the Library of Congress: Programs & Services, Cooperative Cataloging Programs at the Library of Congress, Cooperative Cataloging Council, Task Group 3 Final Report (Cooperative Cataloging Council).)

Standards and Rules for Subject Access

Nancy J. Williamson

SUMMARY. Standardization of subject access to bibliographic information systems is an important factor in national and international networking, cooperation, and exchange of bibliographic data. Standards, guidelines, and rules are needed to ensure consistency and quality in the design, development and application of indexing languages to documents and their citations. This paper defines the terms "standards" and "guidelines" as they apply to subject analysis used in library catalogs and bibliographic databases. It identifies and discusses the most important national and international "standards" that influence subject access to bibliographic data. Included are the tools of subject cataloging which have become standards in their own right, as well as formally prepared and approved guidelines. Each "standard" or "guideline" is described in terms of its origins, characteristics, and control and its importance in the design of bibliographic retrieval systems. Emphasis is given to the importance of the relationship between alphabetic and systematic access. *[Article copies available from The Haworth Document Delivery Service: 1-800-342-9678.]*

INTRODUCTION

Providing subject access to documents involves a two-step process—the conceptual analysis of the intellectual content and the

---

Nancy J. Williamson, BA, BLS, MLS, PHD, is Professor Emeritus, Faculty of Information Studies, University of Toronto, 140 Saint George Street, Toronto, M5S 1A1, Canada.

[Haworth co-indexing entry note]: "Standards and Rules for Subject Access." Williamson, Nancy J. Co-published simultaneously in *Cataloging & Classification Quarterly* (The Haworth Press, Inc.) Vol. 21, No. 3/4, 1996, pp. 155-176; and: *Cataloging and Classification Standards and Rules* (ed: John J. Riemer) The Haworth Press, Inc., 1996, pp. 155-176. Single or multiple copies of this article are available from The Haworth Document Delivery Service [1-800-342-9678, 9:00 a.m. - 5:00 p.m. (EST)].

translation of that analysis into the terminology of the system. In the best of all worlds, standards, codes, and rules for subject analysis should be provided for both steps. However, there are few, if any, formal rules for the conceptual analysis of documents. Derek Langridge[1] has produced a useful discussion of the process of "summarization" in both theoretical and practical terms, F. W. Lancaster[2] refers to the two-step process and several theoreticians have written on the characteristics of "aboutness."[3,4] Standards, guidelines, and rules that do exist are all related to the tools and systems that make the translation process possible.

The tools of translation are of two basic types–alphabetical descriptor systems (e.g., subject heading lists, and thesauri) and systems for the systematic ordering of documents and files by topics and subtopics (e.g., classification schemes). In the ideal retrieval system, both alphabetical and systematic methods for organization and/or display are used to provide alternative methods of retrieval that complement and supplement each other. For example, the alphabetical descriptors used in most library catalogs function as index terms leading to the location of documents and permitting the browsing of related items on shelves. In contrast, a classified display of bibliographic records in a classified catalog or bibliographic database permits systematic browsing but also must be accompanied by alphabetical indexes. While retrieval using both methods usually produces overlapping results, research has shown that each method results in the location of some documents and/or surrogates not retrieved by the other. That which is scattered by the alphabet is grouped by classification and vice-versa. Moreover, most alphabetical systems have some classificatory elements in them.[5] The degree to which classification is applied depends of the nature of the system.

Standards, guidelines, and rules are needed for the design, construction, application, maintenance and control of these systems. This paper defines the terms "standards" and "guidelines" as they apply to subject analysis systems in general. It identifies and discusses some of the most important national and international "standards" that influence subject access to bibliographic files and databases. Each "standard" or "guideline" is described in terms of its origins, characteristics and control, and its importance in the design of bibliographic retrieval systems. Emphasis is given to the importance of the relationship between alphabetic and systematic access.

STANDARDIZATION DEFINED

As defined in *The Oxford Dictionary of Current English* a standard is an "object, or quality, or measure serving as a basis or example, or principle, to which others should conform or by which others are judged; [or a] required or specified level of excellence." In this context, the process of standardization is described as "cause to conform to a standard." As these definitions suggest, "standardization" can have different meanings in different contexts. As described in the author's paper on "Standards and Standardization in Subject Analysis Systems: Current Status and Future Directions"[6] "standards" exist on a continuum which ranges from formal, obligatory rules and regulations, through less regulatory "guidelines and principles" to the common use of tools and instruments. Their origins vary, as do their spheres of influence and degree of application. Some standards are mandated by government or by collective agreement among organizations, while others are applied (or not applied) according to the policies of institutions. Most of the "standards" and rules which pertain to subject analysis, and described here, have either been developed as guidelines, or they are the tools themselves. Some of these guidelines and rules are now mandated, and made obligatory in part, by the requirements of networking, cooperative exchange of bibliographic records and economic constraints. The terms which stand out in the definitions are "quality," "measure," "level of excellence," and "conform[ity]." However, not all accepted standards meet these criteria. In conforming to standards a certain level of quality is accepted. However, this does not necessarily result in excellence.

Are standards, guidelines, and rules for subject analysis systems necessary? The brief answer to this question is "yes," but there are a number of reasons for this. Subject analysis is one of the most complex and least understood aspects of bibliographical control. In the current environment of global bibliographic information systems, it is essential to provide guidance in the design and development of the tools used in order to achieve, insofar as possible, inter-system and intra-system consistency and compatibility. Users of systems must be permitted to move with ease from one system to another and it is important to make bibliographic data available as quickly and efficiently as possible at reasonable cost. The major dilemma in the application and use of a common standard is that it may not be the best solution for all needs of all users, in all situations. While standards and rules may be modified, adapted, and supplemented by individual institutions, this may result in adverse effects on networking, cooperation, national, and international exchange of bibliographic data and maintenance. Unfortunately, while it is possible to determine time, effort and money expended in developing and maintaining a system, it is much more difficult to measure accurately the time, effort, and effectiveness of the retrieval process.

ALPHABETICAL DESCRIPTOR SYSTEMS

Alphabetical descriptor systems are of two kinds. Those which by nature are precoordinated string systems (e.g., subject headings, PRECIS strings) and those which are primarily single concept systems designed for use in post-coordinate retrieval (e.g., thesauri). While these systems have some common roots, there are also basic distinctions. String systems have their origins in card catalogues and printed indexes, whereas concept based systems, such as thesauri, had their beginnings in the design of automated systems. The information systems for which they were designed are different. For example, subject heading lists are designed on the assumption that access to documents will be supplemented by the use of a classification scheme, whereas thesauri were originally developed to be used in systems where a classification scheme has not been applied to the citations. Hence many thesauri have supplementary codes, hierarchical displays, facet categories and, in some cases, classification schemes attached. These displays are designed to provide users with alternate search aids which, in varying degrees, compensate for the lack of a classified arrangement of documents and/or citations.

While in terms of use, the two types of systems have developed along divergent paths, they are not mutually exclusive. In online systems the distinction has become somewhat superfluous, since subject headings hardly ever "head" anything any more, and there is no reason why thesaurus descriptors as opposed to subject headings can't be used in online catalogs. Indeed, in some cases they are. Also, keyword searching of subject headings is, in part, analogous to the searching of concepts. Nevertheless, in practice, in most cases subject headings continue to be used in catalogs, while thesauri are identified with online bibliographic databases. The primary reason for this is historical. Library catalogs have a long history and subject headings are a long established "standard." Subject headings have continued to be used because of the existence of large catalogs and in spite of the introduction of online catalogs. The result is that not only the systems but the standards, guidelines and rules that apply to the two types of systems have developed separately and a distinction continues to be made.

STRING SYSTEMS: LCSH

While there are some experimental string systems,[7] those in common use tend to be products of national libraries and the distribution of cataloging data. Through their wide application in networks and exchange of catalog records these systems themselves have become the "standards." They are not codes of rules, but they are the embodiment of such rules insofar as they are correctly applied. While beginning with Cutter[8] in 1876, rules and broad principles have existed under which subject heading lists have been developed, there has never been a formal code or "standard" for use in the development of subject heading lists. This does not mean that there have not been efforts to produce such a code. There were at least two early attempts to develop codes of rules for subject access.[9,10] While recently, there has been a revival of interest and considerable debate on the need for a formal code,[11,12] it doesn't appear that a "subject heading code" as such will emerge. Past history suggests that producing a theoretically-based code would not be an easy task and perhaps the time has passed when it would have been regarded as essential. However, there is need for a common set of broad principles which can be applied internationally and which will accommodate language differences. As described later in this paper, some progress is being made in this direction.

Best known of the national systems is the *Library of Congress Subject Headings* (LCSH). This subject heading list serves as a national and, to some extent, an international "standard." It is not a formal code or standard in the legalistic sense; it does not result from formal agreement by a representative group of users; nor is its wide acceptance based on any exceptional quality which it possesses. Rather it is the product of practice and the day-to-day operations of a working library. It is through extensive use that LCSH has become the model or "standard" on which other libraries determine the quality and level of their subject cataloging. The application of LCSH may not result in the quality of subject cataloging which libraries most desire, but it is the quality that they can afford. Its status is further enhanced by the fact that it is used to provide controlled vocabulary for catalog records in several large cataloging databases that are widely available. As well, the list itself is conveniently available in a variety of physical formats—print, microform, MARC tapes, and CD-ROM. The Library of Congress controls the policy and development of LCSH. However, LC welcomes professional input from individuals through direct contact and through the work of the Subject Analysis Committee (SAC) of the American Library Association. Over the past twenty-five or thirty years, SAC has carried out a number of projects which have influenced the development of LCSH considerably.

LCSH traces its origins back to Cutter and is the product of his very broad set of rules. Over many years, these rules have been extended and developed by the Library of Congress and other national libraries, while the nature and characteristics of LCSH have been described and interpreted in the works of David Haykin[13] and Lois Mai Chan[14] who have provided subject catalogers with valuable aids to understanding its development and application.

LCSH does not stand alone. It is actually only one item in the "family" of tools which together make up the "standard." Essential support is provided through four additional publications. The most important of these support tools is the *Subject Cataloging Manual: Subject Headings* (SCM)[15] now in its fourth edition. By default it is regarded by many as a "code of rules," although it is not a formally organized document. Consisting of two looseleaf volumes it is updated with periodic additions and changes and sets out LC subject heading policy in a series of memoranda primarily intended for LC staff. Many of these contain interpretations and instructions that are also absolutely essential for non-LC subject catalogers. The Manual provides general directions on cataloging policy and practice at LC, describes the nature of subject authority work and explains the current rules for establishing syndetic structure. Essential to the application of LCSH are the extensive lists of free-floating subdivisions, subdivisions for special topics and pattern headings. Since much of this material is not contained in LCSH itself, the SCM is an essential companion to it. Because of its peculiar origins, it is somewhat cumbersome to use, but it has an index and, along with the second member of the "family" of tools, the *Cataloging Service Bulletin*,[16] it is the definitive statement on LC cataloging policy and on the development and application of LCSH. The Bulletin, published quarterly, announces new policy decisions, explanations, and interpretations on all aspects of LC's cataloging operations including it's subject heading work. Two other important members of the LCSH "family" are the *Free-Floating Subdivisions: An Alphabetical Index*[17] which brings together alphabetically in one place all of the free-floating subdivisions and locates them in their respective memoranda, and *LC Period Subdivisions Under Names of Places.*[18]

While global networking and extensive international use of the OCLC database have resulted in world-wide use of LCSH and its relatives, its development in one country, in one language presents problems as a standard for international use. In countries where there are language and cultural differences, adaptation and modification of the terminology is needed for its most effective use. Because of the ethnocentric nature of the list, subject areas such as history, politics and government, literature, native peoples and general culture are not adequately covered for non-American collections. Some indication of the magnitude of the problem can be seen in the findings[19] of a random sample of two hundred terms taken from the 1988 annual index to the *British National Bibliography* (BNB) and the 11th edition of LCSH also published in 1988. "LEAD" terms from PRECIS strings were compared with main subject headings from LCSH. Geographic, personal, and corporate names were excluded. Exact matches were found in 36% of the cases. Partial matches were found in 48% of the cases. Of the latter, 41%, or 20% of the total sample, was represented by see references, an indication that the two tools sometimes used different terms for the same subject. For example, "Bibliographic control" was the preferred term in BNB, whereas in LCSH there was a reference from "Bibliographical control" to USE "Bibliography-Methodology." In 16% of the cases, for terms in BNB no equivalent was found in LCSH. In some instances there were no equivalents, in others terms were different, while in still other cases the same term had completely different meanings in different national contexts. For example, when lecturing on PRECIS, Derek Austin would use "Underground Railway" to refer to the "London Underground." In a North American context, this same term describes the escape route by which the slaves were shepherded into Canada during the American Civil War. Also, in Canada the preferred term for Eskimos is "Inuit" whereas the 11th edition of LCSH, still preferred "Eskimos," with references from "Inuit" and "Innuit." However, some things do change. In its 17th edition, LCSH includes "Inuit" as a Narrower Term to "Eskimos" to be used to describe these people in particular parts of the world.

Depending on the situation, this kind of problem might be handled on a descriptor-by-descriptor basis. However, in many cases a more effective method is the production of supplementary and complementary tools. Examples of such tools are *Canadian Subject Headings*[20] and *A List of Australian Subject Headings*,[21] both of which are designed to be companions to LCSH. Language problems are sometimes more difficult to solve. Translation is one solution, but differences in semantics and syntax from one language to another create their own problems. Nevertheless, LCSH has been translated into other languages. One example of this is the *Répertoire de vedettes-matière*,[22] a French translation of LCSH, which is published by l'Université Laval and applied by the National Library of Canada in its MARC records and the national bibliography *Canadiana*. Another project is a multi-lingual system produced in Belgium. The NEWWAVE database of the Koninklijke Bibliotheek in Brussels incorporates LCSH in English, French, and Dutch. Other methods of attacking the problem are the development of completely new subject heading lists based on the "standard model," or the use of a switching language which would act as an intermediary between systems. However, up until now there has been little success in developing switching languages for practical use.

OTHER STRING SYSTEMS

A number of other string systems have been developed, for example PRECIS, NEPHIS, and POPSI.[23] All are based on semantics and syntactic relationships and have a logic and elegance not present in LCSH. Developed by Derek Austin at the British Library for use in the indexes of BNB, the Preserved Context Indexing System (PRECIS) is based on a set of procedures (not a list) that, when applied, result in subject strings in which the terms are ordered logically in a one-to-one relationship and are context dependent within a string. Drawn from natural language, the concepts are controlled in a thesaurus of terms which includes a fully developed syndetic structure.

At one time, PRECIS had the potential to become an international standard for subject access to library catalogs. Regrettably this goal is now unlikely ever to be realized. Until recently, maintained by a national library and used to provide subject access in catalog records available in MARC format, PRECIS has also been successfully applied to bibliographic files in some other languages, including French and German. Early in its development it appeared that PRECIS might be in a position to challenge the supremacy of LCSH as the "standard." However, time and effort involved in abandoning one system and implementing another was found to be too expensive. Even the British Library has recently abandoned PRECIS for LCSH. In response to a recommendation from the Subject Analysis Committee of ALA, in late 1977, the Library of Congress conducted a pilot project to assess PRECIS as a replacement for LCSH. It was concluded that the LC subject catalogers could learn the PRECIS system and apply it, but it was felt that the "differences in terminology were great,"[24] that the PRECIS thesaurus developed at the British Library could not be used, and LC would need to create its own thesaurus using American terminology. This situation is analogous to the difficulties of using LCSH outside of the U.S. To implement PRECIS, LC would not only have had to train its staff to apply the system, it would have had to build a new subject authority system from the ground up. While it is not impossible to start a new system, the time and effort required comes at considerable cost.

Standards can be a good thing and they have many advantages, but they can also stifle innovation and hinder progress. Nevertheless, while PRECIS is not likely to come into general use, it may still have a future in special types of retrieval systems, particularly media databases. One very successful example of its continuing application is the index to the National Film Board of Canada *Film Catalogue* where PRECIS strings serve admirably as a kind of "precis" of each film title. Frequently, film titles are not very expressive of the subject content of the film, whereas the presence of the PRECIS strings in the index, permits catalog users to make preliminary selections of films by subject from the index.

INTERNATIONAL GUIDELINES FOR STRING SYSTEMS

For historical reasons and peculiarities of language, there are still many countries which have their own subject analysis systems and rules. However, in a climate of international exchange of bibliographic data, there is a need for common principles, guidelines, and rules upon which national systems can be based. Experience has shown that this is not easy to achieve. Many variations exist across national and local systems world-wide and technical terms used by subject catalogers across nations and across languages are often defined differently. However, recently, the Section on Classification and Indexing of the International Federation of Library Associations and Institutions (IFLA) has been working on two projects that will create guidelines and principles for international use in compiling subject heading lists and carrying out subject authority work.

The recently published *Guidelines for Subject Authority and Reference Entries*[25] prepared by a Working Group of the Section is a major step in the direction of an international standard. The purpose of these guidelines is to provide libraries and information centers with a broad set of rules that may be applied to a wide variety of subject descriptor systems and that would permit ease in the international exchange of subject cataloging data. They attempt to be international in scope and contain a spectrum of examples from a number of countries and languages. Their application is not obligatory, but they were drawn up by a representative international committee and scrutinized for suggested changes in a world-wide review prior to their approval. Because of extensive variations in subject heading practices and language requirements across the world, the approach taken in these guidelines is necessarily very broad. However there are many explicit examples gathered from a range of sources in various countries and languages. Only time will determine whether these *Guidelines* are accepted as a "standard," but they represent a giant step in the right direction.

Another document which will be forthcoming in the near future and which is international in scope, is "Principles Underlying Subject Heading Languages." It will also be the product of a Working Group of IFLA's Section on Classification and Indexing. This document will contain the background, definitions, and principles themselves and will have illustrations from rules for subject heading systems in Germany (*Regeln für den Schlagwortkatalog*), Iran (*Rules and Regulations Concerning Subject Headings*), Portugal (*SIPORbase-Sistema de Indexação em Português: Manual*), and the US (*Subject Cataloging Manual*) plus examples from *Canadian Subject Headings*. The Working Group hopes that the final version will also include excerpts from rules used in Brazil, Croatia, France, the Netherlands, Norway, Poland, Russia, Spain, and the UK. A revised and expanded draft of these "Principles" was discussed at the IFLA Conference in Istanbul, Turkey, in August 1995. Soon after, the draft is expected to be sent out for world-wide review. This document should serve as a companion volume to the previously published *Guidelines.* Together they should provide a truly international basis for improved compatibility for the international exchange of subject analysis data.

CONCEPT SYSTEMS: THESAURUS STANDARDS

In the standards and guidelines, thesaurus descriptors are described as "concepts." However, the word "concept" has never been satisfactorily defined in terms of controlled vocabularies. Some years ago Loll Rolling[26] illustrated the notion of "concept" as the second stage of a continuum of descriptor types, moving from simple to complex—from uniterms (or keywords) through uniconcepts to subject headings. The end result was some descriptors that could be differentiated in this manner, while other descriptors that were uniterms also qualified as uniconcepts as well as subject headings. For example, the descriptor "petroleum" met the criteria for all three categories. In her paper on "Indexical Contexts,"[27] Elaine Svenonius describes concepts as basic "units of meaning," that is units of thought, or mental constructs. Lancaster[28] discusses the problem and uses the term "concept headings" in referring to thesaurus terms, and the ISO 2788 *Guidelines for the Establishment and Development of Monolingual Thesauri*[29] defines an indexing term as "the representation of a concept" but does not define "concept" itself.

In spite of this confusion, thesauri are the most obvious examples of what might be called "concept systems," as opposed to "string systems." An examination of such tools suggests that the "true" concept is an elusive thing, correctly or incorrectly defined by individual thesaurus compilers in their own terms. It is difficult to generalize on the nature of "concepts," since the need for compound versus factored terms seems to vary greatly from one discipline or one subject to another. While thesaurus guidelines endeavor to explain "concepts" through examples, the most visible criteria for determining whether a controlled vocabulary is a thesaurus or not are the non-use of precoordinated subdivisions, the use of the symbols BT, NT and RT, and the inclusion of hierarchical, rotated, and other types of supplementary displays. Today the term "thesaurus" is used very loosely. Thus the presence of these criteria does not necessarily mean that a particular tool is a thesaurus. In the strict sense of the guidelines, some descriptor lists are not thesauri even though they describe themselves as such. The nature and structure of controlled vocabularies is changing over time. Because of the effects of changing technologies, by the 21st century the term "thesaurus" may be legitimately applied to vocabularies and terminologies that are very different from those currently being developed, or new terminology may emerge to describe such vocabularies.

In contrast with the rules for subject headings, the historical development of thesaurus standards, guidelines and rules has been much more orderly and precise. From a very early stage the compilation of thesauri was accompanied by the parallel development of guidelines for their construction. While these guidelines are not obligatory, they are set out as formal rules and development has been gradual and cumulative. As illustrated by F. W. Lancaster in his arrowgraph of the "evolution of thesaurus standards"[30] guidelines for thesaurus construction have their origins in both alphabetical subject indexing (Cutter's Rules) and bibliographic classification (Ranganathan's alphabetico-synthetic classification).

From the alphabetical indexing perspective, four early thesauri were constructed using simple terms or concepts and syndetic structure analogous to the structure used in subject heading lists. The construction of these thesauri led to the development of the COSA-TI[31] guidelines, from which emerged ANSI Z39.19 (1974)[32] and the *Unesco Guidelines for the Establishment and Development of Monolingual Scientific and Technical Thesauri* (1970).[33] As new thesauri were developed and the need for guidelines increased, the Unesco guidelines spawned French[34] and German[35] guidelines as well as the first edition of ISO 2788.[36] All were the products of standards organizations as opposed to library associations and institutions.

From the perspective of classification, Ranganathan's influence manifested itself through two lines of development—on the one hand through the work of the Classification Research Group (CRG) in the United Kingdom leading to the development of PRECIS, and on the other hand through the application of faceted classification (by a member of the CRG) in the construction of *Thesaurofacet*.[37] The latter was one of the first thesauri to integrate an alphabetical thesaurus with a fully developed faceted classification system. Since the COSATI guidelines were also used in the compilation of *Thesaurofacet*, this work represents a completed link between the guidelines for alphabetical thesauri and the application of the principles of faceted classification. Ultimately, all of these developments, PRECIS, *Thesaurofacet*, and ISO 2788 (1974) converged in the British standard BS 5723[38] which in turn spawned a new edition of the Unesco guidelines and the second edition of ISO 2788. The

ANSI Z39.19 guidelines were not part of this merger, but the compilers of ANSI Z39.19 (1993)[39] have stated clearly that they drew heavily on the previous ANSI guidelines and on ISO 2788. While initially, much effort went into the development of guidelines, recent activity has focused on the consolidation of the status quo. Little new ground has been broken, although there is still room for clarification and perhaps for revisiting the guidelines in the light of recent technological developments. The existing ISO 2788 guidelines, now approximately 10 years old, were developed at a time when most thesauri were in printed form. More and more thesauri are being created and used online. ANSI Z39.19 (1993) addresses this change in part but more intensive consideration of this factor may be needed. Certainly more attention needs to be given to role of faceted classification in the structuring of thesauri and ISO 2788 should be re-examined in the light of recent technological changes and future requirements.

In spite of the well controlled historical development of thesaurus guidelines, there is some doubt as to how much direct impact they have on actual thesaurus construction. In 1990 in his paper on "The Standards Jungle," Alan Gilchrist stated that "virtually the only recommendation in ISO 2788 which has become "standard" is the use of the symbols BT, NT, RT, etc., to denote Broader Term, Narrower Term and Related Term."[40] A brief examination of a sample of published thesauri suggests that this may very well be the case. There is a wide variation in the nature and quality of thesauri in both printed and electronic form. Why should this be so? A major factor is the lack of standardization of features across databases. Moreover, these databases are not exchanging data with each other, so for the vendors the need to standardize is not a compelling concern. However, there is a high level of frustration among information professionals, who are users of bibliographic databases and who are concerned about compatibility and convertibility of indexing languages, particularly in disciplines such as the social sciences and subject areas such as medicine. Another reason for the lack of rigor in the application of thesaurus guidelines could be the focus of most thesauri on specific disciplines and subject fields, where the issue of standards is sometimes local, rather than national or international. Unfortunately, work with databases and controlled vocabularies is not confined to those who have education and training in the information professions. Inevitably, that there are database vendors and systems designers who are unaware of even the existence of guidelines. As the information highway extends itself and the demand for global access to databases increases, information professionals have a responsibility to take the initiative in standardization issues in order to bring order out of what could otherwise become chaos.

CLASSIFICATION SYSTEMS AS STANDARDS

The facility for systematic browsing of documents and surrogates is an essential component of most information systems. Among the various methods for providing this facility, are the application of standard classification schemes and the use of various other kinds classificatory structure, such as faceting, clustering, and categorization, in the organization of documents or their surrogates on the basis of subject content or other appropriate characteristics. There are no formally written standards or guidelines for classification systems, although there are definitely stated principles. For practical purposes, the major general classification systems are themselves standards. Other types of classificatory grouping in information systems are more apt to be individual in nature. Three general classification systems warrant consideration as international "standards" in their own right. These are the Dewey Decimal Classification (DDC), the Library of Congress Classification (LCC), and the Universal Decimal Classification (UDC).

Of these, DDC best fits the requirements of an international standard. While it had its origins in the work of one individual, Melvil Dewey, it has developed into a truly international tool. During much of its history it has been controlled and developed under the guidance of an internationally representative Editorial Policy Committee. It is well supported financially and is revised and updated on a continuing basis. It has been translated into many languages and uses a notational system which is language independent. Also DDC is centrally applied to catalog records which are internationally accessible. The schedules have been published in both abridged and full form. A "Manual" of instruction is integrated into both editions and the full edition is available in both printed and electronic form. However, as an international "standard" DDC does have weaknesses. In spite of intensive efforts to revise and improve it, it still exhibits some cultural biases and some 19th century approaches to the organization of knowledge. While DDC may be a less than perfect standard, it is an important tool which can be expected to remain an international standard well into the future.

In contrast to DDC, LCC is the product of one library and is controlled and updated by that library. It is, at present, available only in English. Its notation is also language dependent and its content and development reflects the needs of one library, albeit a large library with a broad coverage of topics. Thus it has a built in bias not only to one language, but also to one culture and one collection. Like DDC, it is assured of having strong financial support and there is a policy of continuous revision. It has achieved status as a standard in North America and English speaking countries elsewhere in the world, mainly because of its application to catalog records which are widely available in both printed and machine-readable form. However, like its companion LCSH, it has its limitations for countries other than the United States, particularly in areas of history, politics, and literature. In some cases solutions to this problem have been found. National schedules have been developed to handle these deficiencies. For non-English speaking countries LCC presents even greater problems, not only because of the non-existence of schedules in other languages, but also because of the notation. The mixed notation is a problem where non-Roman alphabets are the norm and the extensive use of Cutter numbers as an integral part of the schedules is a limiting factor in all countries where the predominant language is not English. Yet it has an international future as a result of its availability on records contained in the OCLC database and on USMARC tapes which include many rec-ords for documents in languages other than English. While, the schedules are not yet available to users in machine-readable form, the Library of Congress staff is working to eliminate this limitation.

UDC is somewhat more problematic as a "standard." While its origin is the 5th edition of DDC, the two systems have developed over their long history along very different paths. While UDC is published by some standards organizations and is used by a number of national bibliographies, mostly in non-English speaking countries, in a paper on the "Present Role and Future Policy for UDC as a Standard for Subject Control," I. C. McIlwaine states that "it cannot truly be described as a standard."[41]

Nevertheless, UDC does have some of the qualities important to a classification system which is a "standard." It has some 40,000 users across the world, a notation which is language independent and it has been translated into many languages. It is also available in both printed and machine-readable form (in CDS-ISIS). Historically, there were optimistic signs that UDC might have an important role to play in computerized information retrieval. It was the first of the general classification systems to be investigated in experimental information retrieval using classification systems, and serious thought was given to the possible use of UDC as a switching language between one classification system and another. Neither of these ideas bore fruit for a number of reasons. For much of its existence, UDC's financial support has been uncertain. UDC does not have the advantage of wide application to readily available catalog records which LCC and DDC have. Also, in the past it has not had the advantage of consistent continuous revision under the guidance of a strong representative editorial board. The original mode of revision was through revision committees of users and an editor who responded to committees' suggestions. While democratic, this process of revision is sporadic at best and results in ad hoc development of the schedules.

Recent changes in the management of UDC show promise for the future. A Consortium of FID and 5 major publishers is now managing UDC. Some progress has been made toward a more stable financial situation, but there is still much to be done. A new Editor-in-Chief has been appointed with a mandate to carry out an organized program of revision with the support and advice of an Advisory Board. A new *Guide to the Use of UDC*[42] has been prepared. Also publication is being streamlined. Efforts to try to produce and maintain three levels of schedules–full, medium and abridged–have been abandoned and plans for the future are to publish one "standard" edition of approximately 60,000 terms, roughly equivalent in size to the recently published English Medium Edition. This "standard" edition is to be published in English and it is assumed that it will be the basis for all other editions in all languages. These decisions could do much to expedite revision and updating of the system and attract more users, particularly in non-English speaking countries.

However, this may not be enough to raise the status of UDC as a "standard." An important question which must be addressed is: "What kind of bibliographic classification is most likely to be needed in the future?" There is no easy answer to this question, but it warrants serious thought. Could UDC be converted or restructured into a system which would be more effective in online systems? Currently an experiment[43] is underway which will convert one UDC class (61 Medicine) into a faceted classification with a thesaurus to serve as the index. While this project will not provide a definitive answer to the question about a more effective classification for online systems, it is one small step in that direction. There is an assumption here that a faceted classification linked with a thesaurus might be more useful as a search aid in online bibliographic systems than the traditional systems. Only time and testing will determine whether this is so.

RELATED STANDARDS

The standards and rules discussed here are those most directly related to the subject analysis of textual content, its analysis and representation. However, the provision of subject access, specifically in online catalogs is also controlled by the MARC formats for bibliographic records, subject authority records, classification data, and shelflisting. While they are part of the MARC "family" and discussed elsewhere, these formats control the kind of subject analysis data which may be included in catalog records and the ways in which the data can be manipulated. As the production of full-text systems progresses, another aspect of standardization with implications for subject access is text-encoding standards.

CONCLUSION

Standards, guidelines, and rules for subject access have developed along two distinct paths. On the one hand indexing languages for use as subject analysis tools have been accepted by default as "standards," while on the other hand formal "guidelines" have been drawn up. Clearly, it is the application of the tools which has resulted in standardization of subject access, while the carefully stated guidelines are applied (or not applied) on an individual basis. It is apparent that the existence of standards or guidelines does not necessarily lead to standardization. There must be some compelling reason to apply standards if that goal is to be achieved. In terms of subject access, this translates into networking, cooperation and exchange of bibliographic data nationally and internationally. It also follows from economic constraints and ease of availability. The result is "conformity." Although it is difficult to believe that this kind of standardization leads to either "quality" or "excellence," these remain desirable goals for which to strive. As access to information becomes more global, standards and their application will become increasingly important and need to be rethought. Among concerns which should be addressed are compatibility and convertibility of indexing languages.

NOTES

1. Derek Langridge, *Subject Analysis: Principles and Procedures* (London: Bowker-Saur, 1989), 56-97.

2. F. W. Lancaster, *Indexing and Abstracting in Theory and Practice* (Champaign, IL: University of Illinois, Graduate School of Library and Information Science, 1991), 5-18.

3. Clare Beghtol, "Bibliographic Classification Theory and Text Linguistics: Aboutness Analysis, Intertextuality and the Cognitive Act of Classifying Documents" *Journal of Documentation* 42 (1986): 84-113.

4. M.E. Maron, "On Indexing, Retrieval and the Meaning of About." *Journal of the American Society for Information Science* 28 (1977): 38-43.

5. B.C. Vickery, "Classificatory Principles in Natural Language Indexing Systems," in *Classification in the 1970's: A Second Look,* edited by Arthur Maltby (London: Clive Bingley, 1976), 119-41.

6. Nancy J. Williamson, "Standards and Standardization in Subject Analysis Systems: Current Status and Future Prospects," in *Subject Indexing: Principles and Practices in the 90's: Proceedings of the IFLA Satellite Meeting, Lisbon, Portugal, 17-18 August, 1993,* edited by Robert P. Holley, Dorothy McGarry, Donna Duncan, Elaine Svenonius. (Munchen: K.G. Saur, 1995), 278-91.

7. Timothy C. Craven, *String Indexing* (New York: Academic Press, 1986).

8. Charles A. Cutter, *Rules for a Dictionary Catalog,* 4th ed. rewritten (Washington, D.C.: Government Printing Office, 1904).

9. John W. Metcalfe, "Tentative Code of Rules for Alphabetico-Specific Entry," in *Subject Classifying and Indexing,* by John Wallace Metcalfe (New York: Scarecrow, 1959), pp. 263-92.

10. R.K. Olding, "The Form of Alphabetico-Specific Subject Headings and a Brief Code," *Australian Library Journal* 10 (July 1961): 127-37.

11. Sally Jo Reynolds, "In Theory There is No solution: the Impediments to a Subject Cataloging Code," *Library Quarterly* 59 (July 1989): 223-38.

12. Lois Mai Chan, "A Subject Cataloging Code? *Cataloging & Classification Quarterly* 10 (No. 1/2): 199-202.

13. David Haykin, *Subject Headings: A Practical Guide* (Washington: Library of Congress, 1951).

14. Lois Mai Chan, *Library of Congress Subject Headings: Principles and Application,* 3rd ed. (Littleton, Colo.: Libraries Unlimited, 1995).

15. Library of Congress, Office of Subject Cataloging Policy, *Subject Cataloging Manual: Subject Headings,* 4th ed. (Washington: Library of Congress, Cataloging Distribution Service, 1991-).

16. *Cataloging Service Bulletin* (Washington, D.C.: Library of Congress, Cataloging Distribution Service, 1978-).

17. Library of Congress, Office of Subject Cataloging Policy, *Free-Floating Subdivisions: An Alphabetical Index,* 7th ed. (Washington, D.C.: Library of Congress, Cataloging Distribution Service, 1995).

18. Library of Congress, Office of Subject Cataloging Policy, *LC Period Subdivisions Under Names of Places,* 5th ed. (Washington DC: Library of Congress, Cataloging Distribution Service, 1994).

19. These "findings" have been excerpted from the author's paper on "Subject Cataloguing and LCSH" published in *Standards for the International Exchange of Bibliographic Information: Papers Presented at a Course Held at the School of Library, Archive and Information Studies, University College London, 3-18 August 1990.* Edited by I.C. McIlwaine (London: Library Association, 1991), pp. 143-44. While the study was not replicated on later data for this present paper, there is no reason to believe that the percentages would have altered significantly in the interim.

20. National Library of Canada, *Canadian Subject Headings,* edited by Alina Schweitzer, 3rd ed. (Ottawa: The Library, 1992).

21. J.A. McKinlay, *A List of Australian Subject Headings: Compiled for the Cataloguers' Section of the Library Association of Australia* (Sydney: Library Association of Australia, 1981).

22. *Repértoire de vedettes-matière,* 10e ed. (Quebec: Bibliothèque de l'Université Laval, 1989).

23. Craven, *Ibid.*

24. "Precis Project," an unpublished report prepared by the Library of Congress, Subject Cataloging Division, January 1978, 3.

25. International Federation of Library Associations and Institutions. Division of Bibliographic Control. Section on Classification and Indexing. Working Group

on "Guidelines for Subject Authority Files," *Guidelines for Subject Authority and Reference Entries* (München: K.G. Saur, 1993).

26. Loll N. Rolling, "Compilation of Thesauri for Use in Computer Systems," *Information Storage and Retrieval* 6 (1968): 341-50.

27. Elaine Svenonius, "Indexical Contexts" in *Subject Analysis Ordering Systems: Proceedings 4th International Study Conference on Classification Research, Augsburg, Aug. 28-July 2, 1982* (Frankfurt: Indeks Verlag, 1982), v. 1, 125-38.

28. F.W. Lancaster, *Indexing and Abstracting in Theory and Practice, Ibid.*, 10.

29. International Organization for Standardization. *Guidelines for the Establishment and Development of Monolingual Thesauri*, 2nd ed. (Geneva, ISO, 1986). (ISO 2788 1986).

30. F.W. Lancaster, *Vocabulary Control for Information Retrieval*, 2nd ed. (Arlington, VA: Information Resources Press, 1986), 30.

31. U.S., Federal Council for Science and Technology, Committee on Scientific and Technical Information, *Guidelines for the Development of Information Retrieval Thesauri* (Washington, D.C.: Government Printing Office, 1967).

32. American National Standards Institute, *Guidelines for Thesaurus Structure, Construction and Use* (New York: ANSI, 1974). (ANSI Z39.19 1974).

33. Unesco, *Guidelines for the Establishment and Development of Monolingual Thesauri* (Paris: Unesco, 1970).

34. Association Francaise de Normalization, *Règles d' Establishment des Thesaurus en Language Française* (Paris: AFNOR, 1974). (NFZ 47-100).

35. Deutsches Institut für Normung, Richtlinen für die Herstellung und Weiterentwicklung *von Thesauri* (Berlin: DIN, 1976). (DIN 1463-1976).

36. International Organization for Standardization, *Guidelines for the Establishment and Development of Monolingual Thesauri* (Geneva: ISO, 1974). (ISO 2788 1974).

37. Jean Aitchison et al., *Thesaurofacet: A Thesaurus and Faceted Classification For Engineering and Related Subjects* (Leicester: English Electric Company, 1969).

38. British Standards Institution, *Guidelines for the Establishment and Development of Monolingual Thesauri* (London: BSI, 1979). (BS 5723).

39. National Information Standards Organization (U.S.), *Guidelines for the Construction, Format, and Management of Monolingual Thesauri* (Bethesda, Md.: NISO Press, 1994). (ANSI/NISO Z39.19 1993).

40. Alan Gilchrist, "The Standards Jungle," in *Standards for the International Exchange of Bibliographic Information: Papers Presented at a Course Held at the School of Library, Archive and Information Studies, University College London, 3-18 August 3-18 August 1990,* edited by I.C. McIlwaine (London: Library Association, 1991), 12.

41. I.C. McIlwaine, "UDC as a Standard for Subject Control," in *Standards for the International Exchange of Bibliographic Information: Papers Presented at a Course Held at the School of Library, Archive and Information Studies, Univer-*

sity College London, 3-18 August 1990, edited by I.C. McIlwaine (London: Library Association, 1991), 151.

42. I.C. McIlwaine and Andrew Buxtion, *Guide to the Use of UDC,* (The Hague: International Federation for Information and Documentation (FID), 1993). (FID Occasional Paper 5).

43. Nancy J. Williamson, "Future Revision of UDC: Second Progress Report on a Feasibility Study for Restructuring," in *Extensions and Corrections to the UDC, 1994* (The Hague: UDC Consortium, 1994), 19-27.

Automating the Library of Congress Classification Scheme: Implementation of the USMARC Format for Classification Data

Rebecca S. Guenther

SUMMARY. Potential uses for classification data in machine readable form and reasons for the development of a standard, the US-MARC Format for Classification Data, which allows for classification data to interact with other USMARC bibliographic and authority data are discussed. The development, structure, content, and use of the standard is reviewed with implementation decisions for the *Library of Congress Classification* scheme noted. The author examines the implementation of USMARC classification at LC, the conversion of the schedules, and the functionality of the software being used. Problems in the effort are explored, and enhancements desired for the online classification system are considered. *[Article copies available from The Haworth Document Delivery Service: 1-800-342-9678.]*

INTRODUCTION

The standard format for machine-readable cataloging in the United States is USMARC, which allows for the communication of

Rebecca S. Guenther, MS, BA, is Senior MARC Standards Specialist, Network Development and MARC Standards Office, Library of Congress, Washington, DC 20540-4102. rgue@loc.gov.

[Haworth co-indexing entry note]: "Automating the Library of Congress Classification Scheme: Implementation of the USMARC Format for Classification Data." Guenther, Rebecca S. Co-published simultaneously in *Cataloging & Classification Quarterly* (The Haworth Press, Inc.) Vol. 21, No. 3/4, 1996, pp. 177-203; and: *Cataloging and Classification Standards and Rules* (ed: John J. Riemer) The Haworth Press, Inc., 1996, pp. 177-203. Single or multiple copies of this article are available from The Haworth Document Delivery Service [1-800-342-9678, 9:00 a.m. - 5:00 p.m. (EST)].

bibliographic and related information between computer systems. Institutions can thus exchange records in a standardized format, so that systems can predict record content and know how to process the records. The family of MARC formats include: bibliographic, authority, holdings, classification, and community information.

The *USMARC Format for Classification Data* was completed and approved by the American Library Association's Machine-Readable Bibliographic Information Committee (MARBI) in June 1990. The Network Development and MARC Standard Office of the Library of Congress (LC) developed the format, and in 1991 initiated an experiment to use the format in the conversion of classification data. Several schedules were later included, and the Cataloging Directorate at LC made a commitment in 1993 to complete the conversion of all *Library of Congress Classification (LCC)* schedules. The implementation of the USMARC Classification Format for *LCC* will result in many benefits both for the Library of Congress and for other users of *LCC*.

POTENTIAL USES FOR ONLINE CLASSIFICATION

Online classification data has many potential uses for information access. It provides the authority for classification numbers, terms, and shelflist information; can be used for printing and maintaining a classification scheme; enhance subject retrieval; assist the classifier; facilitate maintenance tasks for classification numbers in bibliographic records; and provide the basis for an online shelflist.

Authority Control for Classification Data

Online classification data may provide authority control for the classification number and caption (a heading that corresponds to a classification number(s) and describes the subject covered). An authoritative file of classification records may be used by the classifier to assign classification numbers to bibliographic records. It may also provide a system with the mechanism to validate the correct assignment of classification numbers.

In addition, online classification data can support authority control for synthesized classification numbers, i.e., numbers that have been made more specific by adding other numbers from a table or other parts of the schedule to a base number. A synthesized classification number need not appear in the classification scheme itself, since it is built by following add instructions, which instruct the classifier to add or append other numbers from the schedule or a table to a base number.

Printing and Maintenance of Classification Schedules

Online classification data is an efficient method for printing a classification schedule. A print program that uses the USMARC records for publishing the schedules may have different system requirements than the program for online user display.

The *Library of Congress Classification* is an enumerative scheme, with new classification numbers inserted where appropriate based on bibliographic material when the need arises. The Library of Congress publishes *LC Classification–Additions and Changes,* which communicates new, changed, and deleted numbers and captions. Classification numbers are updated weekly.

Prior to the conversion effort, *LCC* consisted of some forty-six separate schedules, developed over a period of time by different people. It was designed as a shelf location and browsing device and has been maintained as such.[1] Over the years, the Library of Congress revised some schedules using word processing software, although many were not in machine-readable form. Most of the schedules, including many that are machine-readable (but not in MARC), have required editing to make the references and notes more consistent with one another and to allow for the classification number records to be input into the USMARC format.

Producing the *LCC* from an online file will facilitate the cumbersome process that the Library of Congress has used to publish revised editions. Generally the publication of revised editions of specific subject areas have been sporadic, and some are badly out-of-date. Online classification data will allow for additions and changes to the classification schedules on a timely basis and for the ability to include back-of-the-book indexing on a routine basis.

Providing Subject Access

In previous research, scholars and researchers have recognized the possibilities of classification data providing subject access to library material. The DDC Online Project demonstrated the usefulness of classification data for subject access, browsing, and display, opening up potentially powerful new search strategies.[2] Explorations on the use of the *LCC* for online subject access have also been conducted.[3] Online classification data enhances retrieval of bibliographic records by providing a different type of subject access, through a classed catalog approach, rather than through controlled subject headings. It enables the library user to see the interrelationships between topics and classification numbers, and facilitates browsing from more general to more specific topics and numbers. Shelflist access, usually unavailable to the library user prior to the online era, collocates material regardless of its circulation status, oversize dimensions, or institutional sublocation. It thus has value even in open-stacks libraries. In addition, more precise searching of bibliographic records is possible through classification numbers for certain types of searches. For example, a well-known individual author or work may have its own classification number in the *LCC*, and a search by class number may retrieve a listing of bibliographic records on that author or work more efficiently than a traditional author or title search. Having the classification data accessible online will facilitate this process.

Assistance for the Classifier

Online access to classification numbers may save time for the classifier. The classifier may perform a keyword search to quickly locate the possible classification numbers through captions, notes, or index terms. The classifier may be able to trace the formation of synthesized numbers to assist him in classifying. In addition, online classification may assist the classifier in obtaining consistency in the assignment of classification numbers to library materials. The Library of Congress is exploring the integration of schedule and table numbers in its implementation so that the system provides the calculation function formerly done by the classifier. Applying add instructions or tables to classification numbers and validating the accuracy of synthesized classification numbers can both save time for the classifier and increase accuracy. In addition, the system can provide online links between classification records and subject authority records both to facilitate the subject cataloging and classification function and to provide greater subject access to library material.

Maintenance of Classification Numbers in Bibliographic Records

An online system could use an automated classification database to facilitate a library's conversion to a different classification scheme. By maintaining the classification schedule online, an institution may be able to perform global updates of the bibliographic file when a classification number is added or changed. The classification format allows for tracing the history of a number and to provide specific links to the new or old number.

Providing a Basis for an Online Shelflist

The online classification system provides a basis for an online shelflist, it is a building block for the assignment of item numbers. An automated shelflist would be a valuable resource for bibliographic material, especially if classification records can be linked to bibliographic records.

WHY USMARC FOR CLASSIFICATION?

It has often been argued that classification schemes are basically text files that, if automated, would best be encoded in Standardized Generalized Markup Language (SGML) which is intended to handle large amounts of text. However, there are several advantages to using a MARC format.

Model of Library of Congress Subject Headings

Library of Congress Subject Headings (LCSH) are input into separate USMARC authority records with tracings provided from unused to used forms and links to broader, narrower, and other related terms. Tracings are an efficient method for assuring database integrity, as references for changing headings do not need to be found and changed in many places. LCSH are updated on a daily or weekly basis at the Library of Congress and historically have been controlled by LC. Essentially a database of USMARC classification records can provide the same type of control as name and subject authority records do; references can be supplied as tracings from unused to used numbers and terms.

Changes are made to classification numbers and captions on a daily or weekly basis as well. Thus, the ability to communicate changes on a record-by-record basis, rather than an entire database, is essential.

Interaction with Other USMARC Files

As mentioned above, online classification data can be linked to other USMARC data. The consistency in structure and data elements between the USMARC formats for bibliographic, authority, especially subject authority, and classification data facilitates the linking between files. Most large library systems know how to process and interpret MARC data. Integrating classification records into this structure can provide advantages for future use of the records. In addition, for any interactive links to occur, such as validation of classification numbers in bibliographic records, global changes, or subject term and number comparisons, using the data in the same format will facilitate the process. MARC has proven to be flexible, efficient, and easy to maintain for library automation systems.[4] It is used worldwide for storing, sharing, and manipulating bibliographic information by computer. The *USMARC Format for Classification Data* joins the other established formats with a similar structure and goals.

Using USMARC Classification Locally

The Library of Congress envisions a new MARC record distribution of classification records, based on the model of MARC bibliographic and authority record distribution. *LCC* schedules will be distributed in USMARC records, and, eventually, once conversion is complete, the entire scheme can be so distributed. Local institutions that choose to acquire the records can use them in local systems (assuming local implementation of the classification format). Those institutions will then be able to create local classification records, since many may wish to expand certain areas of the classification, or provide local notes. Using the MARC format, institutions could create individual records or notes in existing records as needed locally, rather than be limited to using only the records as distributed by LC. They would then be able to communicate in a standard format these local records to other institutions if desired.

DEVELOPMENT OF THE USMARC CLASSIFICATION FORMAT

The Library of Congress recognized the need for a USMARC format for communicating and storing classification data and began the development of the USMARC classification format in 1987/1988. It was developed in close consultation with the two major classification schemes in use in the United States, the *Library of Congress Classification,* and the *Dewey Decimal Classification,* although its data elements are intended to be generic enough to accommodate other classification schemes. The Network Development and MARC Standards Office began work on a proposal to include classification data as an extension of the *USMARC Format for Authority Data.* The Library of Congress followed several assumptions in developing the format: certain types of data that need to be displayed or searched must be identified separately; all types of notes and classification numbers need to be accommodated by the format; the schedules themselves should drive the format rather than vice versa. For the *Library of Congress Classification*, it might be necessary to make editorial changes, but in general the format should allow for printing the schedules as they are now.

After the USMARC Advisory Group and the Machine-Readable Bibliographic Information (MARBI) Committee of the American Library Association partially reviewed a draft of proposed changes to the Authority format to accommodate classification data, the Network Development and MARC Standards Office decided to rewrite the proposal as a separate format. The Office made the decision because it found that there was less overlap with the Authority format than originally anticipated, and because the codes and conventions in that format were too constraining. After several revisions, and in further consultation with representatives from the publications of the *Library of Congress Classification,* the *Dewey Decimal Classification,* the *National Library of Medicine Classification,* and the *Universal Decimal Classification,* the MARBI Committee approved the USMARC Classification Format in June 1990.[5]

STRUCTURE AND CONTENT OF USMARC CLASSIFICATION FORMAT

Content designation in the *USMARC Format for Classification Data,*[6] as in the other USMARC formats, are codes and conventions used to explicitly identify data elements in a record. The goal is to characterize the data elements with sufficient precision to support manipulation of the data for various functions.[7] Functions supported include display, both formatting in an online display and in producing a printed or other type of product, and online information retrieval. How an institution displays the data is not specifically covered in the USMARC formats, although they do provide for display constants, which are terms, punctuation, or spacing that are system generated for display. For instance, the hyphen separating the beginning and ending numbers of a classification number span is not carried in the record but may be generated as a display constant by the display system based on the structure of the classification number field of the record. The system itself, that is, the implementation of the format, will largely determine how well those intended functions are met. It is difficult to predict the limitations a system might encounter in using the data; however, the format itself has allowed for great specificity in coding to maintain optimal flexibility and to satisfy likely uses.

The Library of Congress has implemented USMARC Classification using a PC-based cataloging program called Minaret, which allows for a user-defined format, indexes, and displays. How the program uses the content designation for manipulation is described in this section; more information on the software environment is detailed below under Implementation.

Similarities to Other USMARC Formats

The USMARC Classification Format retains much of the structure familiar from the USMARC bibliographic and authority formats. The Leader is a required element which defines the parameters for the processing of the record, and the Directory gives information on the fields, field length, and starting and ending character positions in the record so that a system can process a file of multiple records (Figure 1). The format has a 1XX block of fields, functioning like heading fields in the authority format. Most records include a field 153 (Classification Number) that contains the authorized classification number and caption representing a topic, as well as the full caption hierarchy. In rare cases a field 154 (General Explanatory Index Term) can be used instead. The structure of reference notes (2XX and 3XX) and tracings (4XX and 5XX) mirrors the USMARC authority format and is used in a similar fashion. The 6XX block of fields contains notes, and tag names

FIGURE 1. USMARC Classification Tags
USMARC CLASSIFICATION FORMAT FIELDS

LEADER

DIRECTORY

0XX	Control information, numbers, codes (010-084)
1XX	Classification numbers and terms (153, 154)
2XX	Complex see references (253)
3XX	Complex see also references (353)
4XX	Invalid number tracings (453)
5XX	Valid number tracings (553)
6XX	Note fields (680-685)
70X-75X	Index term fields (700-754)
76X	Number building fields (761-768)

from the USMARC authority format that apply to classification have been retained. The 7XX block retains the structure of the USMARC bibliographic format added entries, allowing for including in the classification record controlled authority headings when there is a relationship with the classification number. These fields are intended to supplement terms contained in other parts of the USMARC record, such as the caption data in 153, for additional subject access to the classification number.

Kinds and Types of Records

The *USMARC Format for Classification Data* identifies three kinds of classification records: schedule record (an authority for a classification number from the schedule itself); table record (an authority for a classification number from a table, intended to be added to a base number from the schedule); and an index term record (a record for a general explanatory term from a classification index that represents a concept and cannot be associated with one classification number or span). The processing of the record will be largely dependent on the kind of record being coded; for instance, all numbers from the same table will need to be processed and displayed together for comprehensibility. In addition, the type of number, identified as either single number, defined number span (a range of numbers defined by a separate table or subarrangement), or summary number span (a range of numbers that summarize a topic and is not defined by a separate table or subarrangement) determines how the number will be displayed. These data elements, along with others that provide coded information about the record as a whole or about the data in the Classification Number field, are defined in field 008 (Fixed-Length Data Elements) of the record.

In the LC implementation of the format, the system can use the code in the Kind of record (008/06 in Fixed-Length Data Elements) to separate schedule and table records; the code in Type of number (008/07) is used to suppress the numbers in a summary number span for display purposes; the code in Classification validity (008/08) may allow for suppression of invalid numbers or generation of parentheses around obsolete numbers.

Classification Number and Caption

Generally, each line in the classification schedule that includes a caption is a separate USMARC classification record. The classification number and caption for which the record is created is contained in a 153 field. The field may include a single number in a single subfield ≠ a or a span of numbers in two subfields (separated into beginning and ending number of the span). The caption is included in a subfield ≠ j, which contains the term that the number represents. In many cases in the printed *LCC* schedules there are captions that do not have explicit corresponding numbers, although a span of numbers is implicit. These are given summary number spans, indicating the first and last classification number to which this caption applies, and the numbers can then be suppressed in printing or online display if desired (based on the code in the Fixed-Length Data Elements).

The Library of Congress classification system implementation contains separate searchable indexes for the classification number span and the captions. Classification number sorting rules have been defined so that the records display in the correct order; this also will allow for a classed catalog approach to the collection. The caption index supplies the user with rich terminology to search the schedules.

Caption Hierarchies

Field 153 also communicates the hierarchical relationship between captions by including repeatable subfields (≠ h) that contain the superordinate caption hierarchy, i.e., all captions to which the caption describing the number(s) is subordinate. This structure not only gives a context for the classification caption, which in some cases may be meaningless (e.g., General works, Study and teaching), but also provides for a hierarchical display either in an online system or a printed product. By counting the number of subfield ≠ h's (caption hierarchy subfield) a classification system could then calculate the indention level of the caption; the caption itself is in a different coded subfield ≠ j.

In the LC classification system, the caption hierarchies are used to create indentions on the browse display, showing how topics are related to each other. When a caption is highlighted, the entire caption hierarchy is displayed on the top of the screen in a box. They also are used by the program for properly sorting the classification number spans so that a span encompassing a larger group of numbers will sort before a span beginning with the same number but encompassing fewer numbers. It is expected that in a later release this information could be exploded to create outlines (as are currently provided in the printed schedules) based on hierarchy level.

In addition, the format provides for tracings to superordinate or subordinate captions in the hierarchy to facilitate online browsing; this is accomplished in field 553 (Valid Number Tracing) subfield ≠ w, which may be coded to show that the number and caption refers to a broader or narrower topic (similar to coding for broader or narrower heading in the USMARC authority format). The potential for providing links up and down the hierarchy using this special type of tracing is dependent on the capabilities of the systems used for implementation; at this stage LC has not used this feature.

Tracings

The classification format includes tracing fields similar to those in the USMARC authority format. These fields are used to direct the user to another number in cases where the given number is not valid for use or where a different number needs to be considered for classifying the topic. A simple cross reference display is generated from a tracing field. The tracing field itself is tagged as a field 453 (Invalid Number Tracing) or 553 (Valid Number Tracing) in the record for the number to which it refers. Tracings in the USMARC authority format work essentially the same way for name and subject authority records and have proven to be very powerful retrieval tools. The format also allows for Complex See References (field 253) and Complex See Also References (field 353), when more detailed instruction is required to convey the information or they cannot be accommodated in a tracing field for some reason; in these cases the reference leads the user *away* from the number in the classification number field (field 153) to that in field 253 or 353, in contrast to a tracing in fields 453 or 553, which leads *to* the number in field 153.

In the LC implementation, the content designation in the tracing structure has allowed for direct links between tracings and the numbers to which they refer. The user can jump from one place in the schedule to where the reference is leading him. Because the number in the tracing is in a classification number index, it can be used for maintenance purposes, where previously there was no way to find all the places where a certain classification number was referenced.

In addition, the coding in the tracing field is used to generate specific displays. A code in subfield $\neq$ w of the tracing field (453 or 553) determines the text of the reference note. If coded as an invalid tracing (field 453) with code "j," the display text is: "[data in 453 $\neq$ t Topic subfield] see [data in 153 $\neq$ a];" if coded as a valid tracing (field 553) with code "j," display text is: "For [data in 553 $\neq$ t] see [data in 153 $\neq$ a];" if coded as a valid tracing with code "l," display text is: "Cf. [data in 553 $\neq$ a] [data in $\neq$ t]." A classification number is assigned to each tracing field to allow for the proper sorting of the data in the browse display.

Notes

Several note fields may be used to instruct the classifier about the use and application of classification numbers. The Scope Note (field 680) explains topics classed in the number. The Classification Example Tracing Note (field 681) documents the use of a number in another record to facilitate updating of fields when a change is made to the classification number. (Note that there is a similar field in the USMARC authority format, but in LC's classification implementation this field has not been used.) The Application Instruction Note (field 683) instructs the classifier on the application of tables, subarrangements, etc., sometimes for a particular institution. The History Note (field 685) may be used both for the guidance of classifiers and for computer processing of records to link between old and new numbers. It allows for indicating the type of change recorded, new or previous classification numbers, implementation dates, and institution to which the information applies. Potentially this field can be used to perform global updates for reclassification projects if there is interaction between the system's classification and bibliographic records, although LC has not yet used it.

Index Terms

The USMARC classification format includes a group of fields for recording index terms. These fields (700-754) are intended to supplement terms contained in data within the USMARC record itself for additional subject access to the classification number. Fields 700-751 and 754 contain subject access terms controlled by a subject heading system or thesaurus such as the *Library of Congress Subject Headings* (LCSH) or *Medical Subject Headings* (MeSH). These fields allow for linking to a subject authority file or to subject headings in bibliographic records. Field 753 (Index Term—Uncontrolled) contains textual index terms that are not controlled by an established thesaurus, particularly terms in a back-of-book index to a classification schedule. Separately identified subfields are used in the field to establish hierarchical relationships between terms or for reference to other index terms. Because the terminology in the classification captions, indexes, and subject headings may all be different within one classification record, subject access is enhanced by providing both controlled and uncontrolled index terms. Field tags in the classification format and a comparison to subject added entry fields in the bibliographic format is given in Figure 2, showing the similarity in structure.

In the conversion of *LCC* so far, only field 753 has been used for index terms, although the use of controlled index term fields will be considered in the future. Additional terms can be added to the classification record to supply enhanced subject access.

Number Building Fields

Fields 761-768, the Number Building Fields, provide instructions for the classifier in building classification numbers from sources within the schedule and tables. The fields are heavily coded, and it is intended that they may be used for computer processing, particularly computer-assisted classification. These fields are intended to make it possible for the computer to perform the necessary computations to create synthesized numbers, rather than the classifier.

Field 761 (Add or Divide Like Instructions) contains instructions for adding numbers from other parts of the schedule or tables,

FIGURE 2. Classification Index Fields in Comparison with Bibliographic Subject Access Fields

70X-75X INDEX TERM FIELDS

CLASSIFICATION FORMAT

700   Index Term—Personal Name

710   Index Term—Corporate Name

711   Index Term—Meeting Name

730   Index Term—Uniform Title

750   Index Term—Topical

751   Index Term—Geographic Name

753   Index Term—Uncontrolled

754   Index Term—Faceted Topical Terms

6XX SUBJECT ACCESS FIELDS

BIBLIOGRAPHIC FORMAT

600   Subject Added Entry—Personal Name

610   Subject Added Entry—Corporate Name

611   Subject Added Entry—Meeting Name

630   Subject Added Entry—Uniform Title

650   Subject Added Entry—Topical Term

651   Subject Added Entry—Geographic Name

653   Index Term—Uncontrolled

654   Subject Added Entry—Faceted Topical Terms

resulting in a synthesized number. Field 762 provides a reference to a table to be applied to the classification number. Field 763 (Internal Subarrangement or Add Table Entry) is used to specify an internal classification subarrangement (i.e., one that applies to a span of numbers and that has appeared within the schedule).

LC has implemented fields 761-763, but not used the other number building fields, field 765 (Synthesized Number Components) and field 768 (Citation and Precedence Order Instructions), which were created essentially to accommodate the *Dewey Decimal Classification*. The use of the number building fields in the initial experimentation with the format has led LC to request changes to content designation and coding practices.

ONLINE CLASSIFICATION EXPERIMENT AND FURTHER IMPLEMENTATION AT LC

Background

In 1992 the Network Development and MARC Standards Office initiated an experiment to test the new classification format, which resulted in the conversion of the H schedule (Social Sciences) to the USMARC format. The project used PC-based software called Minaret, which can create MARC records. Minaret allows for the user to define data elements, indexes, and display forms, and its flexibility proved essential for experimenting with a new format. Because the individual record approach does not adequately represent classification information which must be viewed in its hierarchical context of subject terms, the developer of the software prepared an enhancement for LC to enable the user to access a classification browse display. This display brings the classification records together according to defined specifications to display the data on the screen in a format similar to the page of a classification schedule, showing relationships between numbers and captions.

Use of the Software

The program provides links to other records to facilitate use of the classification schedule. The user can jump to another number referred to through the tracing in the record by pressing the enter key. In addition, the user can bring up a table window when the record refers the user to a table or subarrangement, allowing him/her to create a more specific classification number.

Several indexes are available to search the schedule: classification number, record control number, classification caption, index term (primarily those that would appear in a printed index), and a combined caption/term index. Other terminology may be added in the 753 (Index Term–Uncontrolled) field or in controlled subject heading fields in the individual classification records when desired and then be accessible by the term indexes. The indexes provide quick access to numbers and topics as well as the potential for effective maintenance of the schedules on a frequent basis.

USMARC records created in Minaret can be exported as MARC or ASCII for use by other systems or programs.

Conversion of Schedules

When the classification format experiment began, LC selected a portion of the H-HG (Social Sciences: Economics) schedule for conversion. Records were initially created for two subclasses, and later the entire H schedule (including HM-HX, which had previously been published as a second volume) was included.

In order to determine potential use of the *Library of Congress Classification* in machine-readable form, a Technical Committee on LC Classification conducted a survey on several Internet discussion lists. As a result of the responses to the query and the enthusiastic comments expressed by those who attended demonstrations of the Minaret classification database, the Technical Committee decided that the USMARC format should be used for the conversion of the *LCC* schedules into machine-readable form and that all the schedules should be converted.[8]

Conversion efforts continued, with outside contractors delivering converted USMARC classification records for several schedules in 1992 and 1993. Network Development and MARC Standards Office staff trained internal LC staff responsible for *LCC* schedule maintenance, and additional schedules were converted, as well as online maintenance functions incorporated into the workflow. By the end of 1994, about two-thirds of the *LCC* schedules had been converted; what seemed like an impossible task several years earlier had rapidly become a reality. The conversion is the first step in the effort to develop an online classification system, which will have a large impact on the assignment of classification numbers, subject access to the classification and ultimately to a library's collection, and future automation and use of an online shelflist. It also could facilitate cooperative programs for LCC development. At the end of 1995 the Library of Congress had all of the schedules converted except for small portions of a few, using LC staff and outside contractors.

Cataloger Use

As part of the initial online classification experiment one cataloger on the Business and Economics Team of the Social Sciences Cataloging Division has used the classification database daily for classification of new material since 1992. The cataloger experimented with enhancing the database with additional index terms related to classification numbers. Later several other catalogers in other subject areas began to participate in the use of the system. Responses were generally positive to the use of online classification data.

Online Environment

The Minaret program for classification at LC is a UNIX-based multiuser system running on a minicomputer that is accessible using remote login (telnet). It fits into the LC environment of client/ server applications and can be accessed through LC's Bibliographic Workstations within the context of the catalogers' other work. Thus, catalogers can access the database in one session while working in other LC internal files. Potentially they could search across databases or copy data from one to another.

In-house staff converting schedules are working in the master classification database, and records prepared by outside contractors are being incorporated into it. Because of licensing issues and the need for the records to be reviewed, the classification database is not currently available for users outside of the Library of Congress.

RESULTS OF THE ONLINE CLASSIFICATION EXPERIENCE

As a result of its experience of converting and using an increasing number of USMARC classification records, the Library of Congress has modified the format and will institute changes in the appearance of the printed schedules. The Network Development and MARC Standards Office initiated several changes to the US-MARC classification format since its original acceptance in 1990 based on the online experience. In addition, coding decisions have had to be made to accommodate the often inconsistent nature of the *LCC* schedules, which in some cases will result in editorial changes in the printed product.

Use of the Format

After experimentation with the format, the following modifications were made: (1) conventions for parsing LC classification numbers into subelements were changed; (2) a separate field was defined to contain the table reference, for linking a number in the schedule to the appropriate table. Previously the data was included in a field with other add or divide like instructions; (3) table names were concatenated into one subfield instead of parsing the schedule name and table number; and (4) a subfield was defined to facilitate the coding and use of internal tables. The USMARC Advisory Group and Machine-Readable Bibliographic Information Committee (MARBI) approved proposals for these changes based on LC's experience. As of the writing of this article, no other institution had yet implemented the USMARC classification format, although plans were underway for the conversion of the *Dewey Decimal Classification's* Editorial Support System records into USMARC. In addition, a UNIMARC classification format is under development, particularly for use by the *Universal Decimal Classification.*

Coding Decisions

As new situations have been encountered in the conversion of the schedules, the Library of Congress has had to make many decisions on specific MARC coding. Because much of the data in the schedules was based on the appearance on the printed page, modifications have been necessary. In many of the printed schedules, instructions have been redesigned. All page dependent data, such as the frequent use of footnotes referring the user to another page, have been made explicit in individual records.

Some specific coding decisions are indicated below. Each will have an effect on the way the information appears in the printed product, since it is produced from the MARC records.

Invalid Numbers

Invalid numbers are assigned to anchor a caption that refers the user to another part of the schedule. These numbers will generally be suppressed in the printed product and the online display by a code in the Fixed-Length Data Elements field. A classification number span can have an invalid beginning or ending number of the span. Users may thus find references to invalid numbers within the new schedules.

Internal Tables

The classification format includes a field for inputting a list of subarrangements from a table within the schedule. As a result of the online experience and to allow for flexibility in the future, the Library of Congress decided to avoid using this technique where possible. In some cases separate records have been created, making the subarrangement explicit. Other subarrangements are coded in separate table records, rather than embedded in repeating fields of one record. A mechanism was devised to allow for their display within the schedule (as they previously have) instead of as a table external to the schedule. In these cases there are explicit references within the record for each number/caption that applies the subarrangement to the appropriate table. In the revised schedules, many numbers will now instruct the user to apply a table that is located at a given classification number, while previously a footnote was used to refer the user to a particular page. In the online system, a direct match is made through the table reference, and the applicable table can be accessed in a window. There are also cases where subarrangements which previously appeared internally have been coded as external tables. For instance, the H schedule as it was last published contained ten tables plus several lists of regions to be applied throughout the schedules; the edition generated from the USMARC records now contains thirty tables, some of which were previously internal tables. This allows for a direct link in the online system from a classification number to its subarrangement, rather than a footnote to another number in the schedule.

Tracings

As with the USMARC authority format, the tracing structure in the classification format provides a direct link to the number to which the reference refers, thus facilitating maintenance. Although other fields are provided for complex reference notes, LC prefers to use tracings wherever possible. Initially it was felt that few if any complex reference notes would be used for *LCC*. However, the conversion process has shown that the use of the complex reference notes has been necessary in some situations. These instances are: (1) if a reference refers to a span of numbers that does not exist in a separate classification record (i.e., it cannot be established because it does not have a corresponding caption); (2) if the reference refers to more than three numbers (e.g., for different aspects of a topic); (3) if the number in the reference is a synthesized one (formed from applying a subarrangement to a base number) and it is not desirable to create a record for it; (4) if it refers to a whole class for which a record does not exist; and (5) if it is a general textual reference. Generally the distinction between the use of the complex reference versus tracing note is not apparent to the user in the display or print product.

Since tracings are included in the record for the number to which they refer, LC has had to make many explicit where previously they were not (e.g., use of the + sign after the first number of a span) or correct blind references. Some references may appear with an invalid number as part of the span. In addition, in cases where a reference directed the user to three or fewer numbers in the schedule, these have been broken into separate tracings, each located in the record for the number to which they refer. In display or print they will appear as separate references, not attached as one statement by semicolons, as in previous editions. The user can thus jump from one classification number to another by highlighting the reference desired.

Divide Likes

In cases where the schedules used the divide like technique to save space (divide one area of the schedule like another one), the subarrangements have either been explicitly input wherever they apply, or a table created and a reference to it input into each record. Thus, there will be few instances where the user will have to apply a subarrangement from another number span. This coding decision should save time for the classifier; in cases where a table has been created, a future machine calculation function could further expedite the classification function.

Index Terms

Terms from the back-of-book classification index are input into individual USMARC classification records for the numbers to which they refer. Currently the Library of Congress is exploring how terminology can be enhanced and how references to other terms should be accommodated. In the early phases of the conversion, contractors primarily input terms from the latest edition of the printed schedule. Recently LC has established rules for applying index terms in an attempt to provide more consistency.

PROBLEMS TO BE RESOLVED

The Library of Congress has undergone the conversion of the *LCC* schedules very quickly. Both internal LC staff and outside contractors have contributed to the effort of automating over forty volumes of classification data with more than 16,000 total pages in a relatively short period of time. The conversion began as an experiment to test the format, and gradually grew into the reality of USMARC records that would be used for printing, online display, and distribution.

LC made the assumption early in the project that it would be easier to modify the data in the schedules once it had been keyed. Thus, inputting staff has generally revised schedules only where needed to make the information explicit or to correct obvious errors. One exception has been the J schedule (Political science), which was so outdated that LC performed a thorough revision before input into the online classification database. Staff is reviewing the data as the USMARC records are used by the CDS print program for new editions of separate schedules. It is expected that even after conversion there will be a lag time before the data is ready for distribution after a review process.

A study of *LCC* prepared by Nancy Williamson has assisted the Library of Congress in identifying problem areas. The conversion experience confirmed the need for many of the recommendations given in the study.[9] In many cases LC will need to investigate further to consider how much revision is needed to make the machine-readable data more useable. Daily use of the growing classification database is providing valuable experience for determining even better ways to access and utilize the data.

Consistency of Table Application

As different schedules were converted, it became obvious that the application of tables was highly inconsistent throughout the scheme. In some cases tables appeared at the end of the schedule, in others within the text, in others by footnotes referencing other locations. Even more disturbing was the fact that how those tables are applied to a number was inconsistent. In some cases the number from the table is appended to the base number; in other cases it is necessary to perform addition to calculate a number resulting from adding from a table to a base number.

Because it is highly desirable for a classification system to perform the function of synthesizing numbers (since all the information to do so is in the records), it will be necessary to make the data consistent so that only one rule is followed. In addition, most of the subarrangements that were coded as internal tables (encoded in repeatable 763 fields in one record) during the early stages of the conversion will be changed to separate table records to facilitate a calculator function.

Consistency in Indexes

The indexes to the schedules provide rich terminology, but they vary greatly because schedules were developed individually and revised at different times. The depth of indexing from one schedule to the next is dependent upon the subject matter and the perspective of the indexer.[10] As the different schedules are being brought together into one master classification database these inconsistencies have become obvious. A thorough review is needed both within and between separate schedules. LC has formed a task force to consider indexing issues.

CLASSIFICATION SYSTEM ENHANCEMENTS

The system being used at the Library of Congress for the online classification schedules has proven to be generally effective in its display and search capabilities. Numbers and captions can be viewed in the context of their hierarchies, links are made between records, and several indexes are available as entries into the data. There are several improvements that LC hopes to make to allow for utilizing the potential of the data in the online classification system.

Integrated Display

In the current system, the user can bring up a table in a window through a link in the record which is applied to the particular classification number. It is desirable to have the table information integrated into the schedule display such that the user does not need to view a separate table window. Instead, the information from the table could be integrated on the screen with the schedule records so that the computer calculates the number for each possible caption that could be created by synthesizing the schedule and table numbers. Thus, the system would show all the possible numbers with their captions that could exist within a classification number span by proper application of tables. In essence, this would result in the retrieval of classification numbers similar to what might be in a shelflist, without the item numbers. In this type of implementation, it would appear as if separate USMARC records had been created for each number within the span, while actually the system would be utilizing information in the database that had not been integrated. This function could prove extremely useful in saving cataloger time, assuring accuracy in assignment of classification numbers, linking to bibliographic records, and performing machine validation of synthesized numbers.

Isolating Portions of Schedules

LC is exploring the possibility of isolating separate classes or subclasses as desired by the user. Because of the many references between schedules and the tracing structure inherent in the classification format, a master database contains records from all schedules. In some cases users wish only to view their particular subject areas, defined by classes or subclasses. It is desirable to add a feature which runs a query to isolate the records brought into the browse display for any given user.

Expanding Hierarchies

Many users have expressed an interest in navigating through the schedules by hierarchy level. This could allow for expanding from a general to a narrower approach to a topic. In addition, a hierarchical approach would be useful for searching a nondistinctive caption (such as Other countries, General works, etc.).

Links Between Numbers

Currently it is possible to jump to a table or from a tracing to the number referred to. Machine linking between additional fields is also desirable, since classification numbers are also contained in notes in the records.

Cataloger Notes and Bookmarks

Catalogers have expressed the need to maintain private notes in their own "copy" of the schedule. Local notes could be stored for a particular classification number in a private database for each cataloger. In addition, bookmarks containing the classification numbers of records that a user wants to mark for future reference is desirable. The user could then browse their private list of book marks and jump to the desired place in the schedule. In this way catalogers could use a shared database, but still be able to customize it for their individual needs.

Linking Between USMARC Files

LC is exploring a mechanism to link the data in the online classification database with the bibliographic and authority files in the

LC systems. This type of integration of data between systems could enhance retrieval of bibliographic material by opening up potentially powerful new search strategies, as well as integrate cataloging functions.

DISTRIBUTION ISSUES

The Cataloging Distribution Service (CDS) has developed a print product using the USMARC records. In late 1994, it published the H (Social Sciences) schedule using the new system, and it intends to publish several others in 1995. By the end of 1994, the printed E-F (American history), L (Education), and R (Medicine) schedules were undergoing review for upcoming publication.

Once a schedule is published it will be maintained both online and manually for a period of time, until the conversion is fully completed. Since additions and changes are made to the *LCC* classification schedules on a weekly basis, the USMARC records in the classification database are changed accordingly. The new publishing process will enable CDS to publish revised editions of schedules on regular basis compared to the previous manual effort.

CDS is also exploring using CD-ROM as a storage device for the classification with links to *Library of Congress Subject Headings*. In addition a MARC record distribution is planned. It is expected that other institutions, system vendors and/or utilities will develop classification systems, using the MARC record distribution for most of the data.

CONCLUSIONS

Standards are critical to the usefulness of large databases, such as that developed for the *Library of Congress Classification* in its machine-readable form. When the USMARC classification format was completed, it was questionable whether the major undertaking of converting the massive amounts of data in schedules could be possible in a reasonable amount of time. Now that the endeavor is approaching completion, the challenge has become using the data effectively. There is great potential in utilizing the wealth of information in the online schedules effectively and efficiently. Designers of future retrieval systems for classification records need to utilize online classification as a powerful tool for subject access, the maintenance of classification schedules, and machine-assisted classification. In our age of increasing use of networked information resources, classification data can provide an alternative approach for retrieval of information.

NOTES

1. Lois Mai Chan. "The Library of Congress Classification System in an Online Environment," *Cataloging & Classification Quarterly* 11: no. 1 (1990), p. 9.

2. Karen Markey and Ann Demeyer. *Dewey Decimal Classification Online Project: Evaluation of a Library Schedule and Index Integrated into the Subject Searching Capabilities of an Online Catalog: Final Report to the Council on Library Resources.* (Dublin, OH: OCLC Online Computer Library Center, 1986).

3. Lois Mai Chan. "Library of Congress Classification as an Online Retrieval Tool: Potentials and Limitations," *Information Technology and Libraries* 5: no. 3 (September 1986).

4. Walt Crawford. *MARC for Library Use.* 2nd ed. (Boston: G.K. Hall, 1989), p. 7.

5. "Proposal No. 89-1: Proposed Classification Format" (Washington, D.C.: Network Development and MARC Standards Office, Library of Congress, 1991).

6. *USMARC Format for Classification Data: Including Guidelines for Content Designation.* (Washington: Cataloging Distribution Service, Library of Congress, 1991).

7. *The USMARC Formats: Background and Principles.* (Washington: Network Development & MARC Standards Office, 1989), p. 4.

8. "Final Report: Technical Committee on LC Classification in Machine-Readable Form" (Washington, D.C., Library of Congress, September 1992).

9. Nancy J. Williamson, "The Library of Congress Classification: a Content Analysis of the Schedules in Preparation for their Conversion into Machine-Readable Form" (Washington, D.C.: Library of Congress, Cataloging Distribution Service, 1994).

10. Williamson, p. 10.

Recent Research on the Sequential Bibliographic Relationship and Its Implications for Standards and the Library Catalog: An Examination of Serials

Gregory H. Leazer

SUMMARY. Recent work on bibliographic relationships is evaluated. Tillett's taxonomy of bibliographic relationships and Smiraglia's taxonomy of the derivative bibliographic relationship provide the context for a discussion of recent research and standards work. Research on the sequential relationship drawn from work conducted on serials is evaluated, and the implications of that research is applied to catalog system design. Leazer's and Gorman's conceptual designs are evaluated, and are used in a critique of the USMARC format for bibliographic description. *[Article copies available from The Haworth Document Delivery Service: 1-800-342-9678.]*

Lubetzky succinctly stated the principles of descriptive cataloging in 1946. He wrote that the catalog must present "an integrated and intelligible description of the book and indicate clearly its *relation* to other editions and issues of the book, and to other books recorded in the catalog" (1986, p. 106; emphasis mine). The cata-

Gregory H. Leazer is Assistant Professor, Department of Library & Information Science, University of California, Los Angeles.

[Haworth co-indexing entry note]: "Recent Research on the Sequential Bibliographic Relationship and Its Implications for Standards and the Library Catalog: An Examination of Serials." Leazer, Gregory H. Co-published simultaneously in *Cataloging & Classification Quarterly* (The Haworth Press, Inc.) Vol. 21, No. 3/4, 1996, pp. 205-220; and: *Cataloging and Classification Standards and Rules* (ed: John J. Riemer) The Haworth Press, Inc., 1996, pp. 205-220. Single or multiple copies of this article are available from The Haworth Document Delivery Service [1-800-342-9678, 9:00 a.m. - 5:00 p.m. (EST)].

log functions by expressing all of the manifestations of a work as a bibliographic relationship—that is, two bibliographic entities (books and other artifacts of recorded knowledge such as sound recordings and maps) are related by virtue of the fact that they contain the same intellectual work. Additionally two different works can be related by virtue of the fact that they share some other common feature, for example, two works that are issued as part of the same series, or one cites the other.

Tillett has sparked an investigation into the general nature of bibliographic relationships and has developed a taxonomy of relationships (1991b, p. 156). She defines seven in total:

1. Equivalence relationships that "hold between exact copies of the same manifestation of a work, or between an original item and its reproductions . . ."
2. Derivative relationships hold between a work and a modification based on that same work. "These include: (a) variations or versions of another work, such as editions, revisions, translations, summaries, abstracts, digests; (b) adaptations or modifications that become new works but are based on earlier works; (c) changes of genre, as with dramatizations and novelizations; and (d) new works based on the style or thematic content of another work, as with free translations paraphrases imitations, and parodies."
3. Descriptive relationships "hold between a bibliographic work or item and a criticism, evaluation, or review of that work."
4. Whole–part relationships "hold between a component part of a bibliographic item or work and its whole, as with an individual selection from [the work] and the whole anthology, collection or series."
5. Accompanying relationships "hold between a bibliographic item and the bibliographic item it accompanies."
6. Sequential relationships "hold between bibliographic items that continue or precede one another, as between successive titles of a serial."
7. Shared characteristics relationships "hold between a bibliographic item and other bibliographic items that are not otherwise related but coincidentally have a common author, title, subject, or other characteristic used as an access point in a cat-

alog, such as a shared language date of publication, or country of publication."

Relationships between bibliographic entities are often expressed through two general techniques in the contemporary catalog: through the use of coordinated access points and through narrative (often transcribed) information. The multiple manifestations of a common work are usually entered under the same access point (the "main entry") which might include a standardized form of the title ("uniform title") if there is variation among titles of the work, as is often the case with translations. This is a form of implicit linkage that expresses a relationship among bibliographic entities by bringing descriptive surrogates together into physical or display proximity, a process called collocation.

The second general technique for relating bibliographic entities is through narrative information in the body of the description. An example of narrative information is a statement such as "Contains excerpts of "Badge of evil" from the earliest printed edition . . . ." Current descriptions of serials generally use this technique to express the sequential relationship.

Knowledge of these bibliographic relationships is used to assemble all of the manifestations of a bibliographic work, including its derivative manifestations: translations, amplifications, descriptions, successive editions, etc. Another way of stating this is that the control of the relationships aims to reconstitute all of the members of a bibliographic family–all of the offspring that are somehow derived from a progenitor work. Unfortunately, bibliographic relationships have not been rigorously controlled throughout the history of cataloging. Tillett states (1991a, 393):

> history has shown no rationale and little consistency in how we relate bibliographic entities. A review of cataloging rules since 1841 reveals differing methods and devices used over the years to show bibliographic relationships, but also reveals a lack of any theoretical rationale for the devices prescribed.

A general problem with diffuse and varied techniques for controlling bibliographic relationships is the lack of a clear mandate to the cataloger that this information should be controlled. Smiraglia (1992) focuses on Tillett's definition of the derivative relationship, and further refines it, providing a taxonomy of his own (p. 28). He differentiates among:

1. Simultaneous derivations. Works that are published in two editions simultaneously, or nearly simultaneously . . .
2. Successive derivations. Works that are revised one or more times, and issued with statements such as "second . . . edition," [and] works that are issued successively with new authors . . .
3. Translations . . .
4. Amplifications including illustrated texts, musical settings, and criticisms, concordances and commentaries . . .
5. Extractions, including abridgments, condensations and excerpts.
6. Adaptations, including simplifications, screenplays, librettos, arrangements of musical works, and other modifications.
7. Performances, including sound or visual . . . recordings.

Examining derivative relationships, Smiraglia confirms Tillett's finding about the control of bibliographic relationships in general: the contemporary catalog contains varying and inconsistent mechanisms for handling relationships. Smiraglia measured the extent of derivative relationships in an examination of bibliographic entities. He then examined catalogs to see if they contained information about those derivative relationships. He found that less than half of all derivative relationships in the bibliographic universe were explicitly stated in the catalog (1992, 60; and restated again in briefer form in Smiraglia 1994). These relationships could be overlooked, for example, because of the lack of common main entry access point, or because the same main entry access points were formulated differently.

THE SEQUENTIAL RELATIONSHIP

Of special interest to serials catalogers (and catalog users) is the sequential bibliographic relationship. The evolution of a serial over time–all of the title changes, absorptions, splits, and mergers–can be modeled as a sequential relationship between the earlier title(s) and the later title(s). Henderson (1992, p. 10) has compared serials with human genealogical development: serials are born and die, often have children and parents, and relationships are formed between two serial titles, like a marriage, and often divorce at a later date. The sequential relationship is generally controlled through notes information in the *Anglo-American Cataloging Rules*, 2nd ed. (AACR2). The *USMARC Format for Bibliographic Data (UFBD)* has special provisions for this type of relationship in the 780 (Preceding Entry) and 785 fields (Succeeding Entry).

There has been little theoretical work done on the sequential relationship along the lines of Tillett's work on all types of bibliographic relationships and Smiraglia's work on the derivative relationship. *UFBD* distinguishes among types of sequential relationships by use of the second indicator of the 780 and 785 fields. The second indicator of the 780 field can be used to generate suggested display constants as follows: Continues; Continues in part; Formed by the union of _____ and _____; Absorbed; Absorbed in part; or Separated from. Each code is followed by the title from the related record. The 785 field reciprocates these relationships, by coding in the opposite direction, e.g., "continued by" rather than "continues." Such values demonstrate the existence of subtypes of the sequential relationship, and appear to be an exhaustive breakdown of this relationship.

While there has been little published theoretical work on the sequential relationship, there has been a more practical approach to its control than the derivative relationship. In fact, serials relationships have been the subject of several papers that propose a mechanism for mapping out sequential relationships. Gorman and Burger (1980) apply a general bibliographic retrieval system design (described in Gorman 1982) to the problems of serials relationships. They state (p. 14) that two descriptive records in a catalog could be related by a linking field in one record that contains:

a. a code expressing the nature of the link, and
b. the control number of the related record.

The second record would also contain a reciprocal relationship back to the first record. These criteria for a machine design that is already in place: the bi-directional references customarily included in descriptive records for serials could be used to relate records explicitly and automatically. The second indicator of the 780 and 785 fields expresses the nature of the relationship, and these fields also contain subfields for control numbers such as the International Standard Serial Number (ISSN), Library of Congress Control Number (LCCN) or a system record number.

Bernhardt (1988) contains a proposal to display to the user the matrix of records related to a single serial title. Bernhardt's vision is to display to the user a list of related records so that the user can understand the entire context of the serial family. Such a system has the potential to display the serial cataloger's comprehensive understanding of the evolution of a serial title over time. The underpinnings for her proposed system are the same USMARC data Gorman and Burger would use.

Leazer (1993, and rephrased in shorter form in 1994) also describes a conceptual model for the control of all types of relationships, of which the sequential relationship is just one kind. This model contains a structure that is similar to the structure proposed by Gorman (1982) for modeling bibliographic relationships. Leazer moves beyond Gorman by taking advantage of the recent work done by Tillett and Smiraglia; Leazer's model specifies the types of relationships modeled in a catalog that contains a linking structure. Leazer also emphasizes that the linkages among descriptive records should be used to control entire bibliographic families. Gorman and Leazer share the characteristic that sequential relationships are but one type of relationship, and their models call for the control of relationships of all types.

Alan (1993) contains the most concrete advances to date in the area of controlling and expressing sequential relationships. Alan found that 71% of the time all of the records of a serial family could be linked up using OCLC record numbers, ISSNs, or LCCNs (p. 410). Thus, a simple linkage-creation algorithm can create explicit linkages among records. Users of a catalog could then follow a computer-generated trail to the appropriate record for a serial, and use the whole set of related records to understand the evolution of a serial title over time. Plans should be made to prepare the remaining 29% of serial families whose members are only partially linked together. Clues already in the bibliographic record could be used by the computer to recognize a sequential relationship and automatically create linking fields without substantial human effort.

The effort then is to move from controlling individual serial titles (and incidentally expressing their relationships to other serial titles) to controlling clusters of sequentially-related serial titles. For serial titles without sequential relationships no change is needed. But for complex serial titles, a matrix of computer linkages among records could model these relationships.

Implicit in Gorman and Burger's (1980) and Leazer's (1993) conceptual models is the potential of finding new ways to present bibliographic data to the user. The display of serial families can be presented graphically by providing details of the entire family in a snapshot, rather than displaying serial records sequentially one at a time. Visual forms, as Langer (1963) has pointed out, has at least one advantage over textual language (p. 93):

> Visual forms—lines, colors, proportions, etc.—are just as capable of *articulation*, i.e., of complex combination, as words. But the laws that govern this sort of articulation are altogether different from the laws of syntax that govern language. The most radical difference is that *visual forms* are not *discursive*. They do not present their constituents successively, but simultaneously, so the relations determining a visual structure are grasped in one act of vision. Their complexity, consequently, is not limited, as the complexity of discourse is limited, by what the mind can retain from the beginning of an appercetive act to the end of it.

Gorman and Leazer do not specifically address how to display families of related records to catalog users. However, both proposals include schematic designs to model the relationships included in the catalog, and these schematics serve as preliminary sketches on how a multitude of related bibliographic records might be displayed. Gorman and Burger's schematic (Figure 1) provides the simultaneous display of four bibliographic records, with the relationships among them. Each record, displayed as a node, includes a brief description. Obviously, the extent of each description is limited by factors such as screen size and the number of nodes displayed, but at least brief identifying information can be provided. The online catalog, based on hypertext linkages, could provide a fuller bibliographic description if the user clicked on the node.

FIGURE 1. Schematic of sequentially related serial records, excerpted from Gorman and Burger (1980, p. 17).

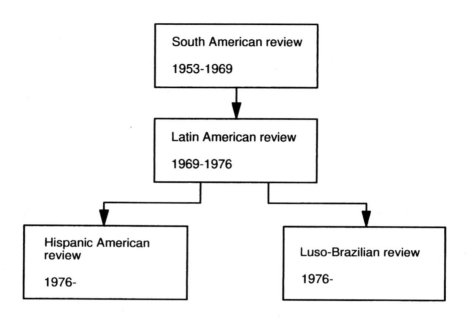

Separate windows could provide separated graphical representations and textual bibliographic descriptions.

Leazer provides a simple graphical display as well (1993, p. 103). For the control of serials and their relationships, his model is very similar to Gorman and Burger's model. As with Gorman and Burger, entire bibliographic families can be displayed to the user to convey quickly the family's relative complexity or simplicity. Furthermore, the graphic display can serve as a map to help position the user within the bibliographic family and guide the user to the most appropriate bibliographic record.

Bernhardt, in contrast to the other models, explicitly addresses display issues for catalog users. Unlike Gorman or Leazer's model, she concentrates on the arrangement of textual matter, rather than a more purely graphical display (see Figure 2). An ordered display of a number of related serial records appears to be the motivation for her model. The textual display has simplicity for its virtue, though it is not as adequate for sequential relationships other than the simple *continues/continued by* relationship because the linear up-down listing functions only in one dimension. Mergers and splits, for example, would be more difficult to display with this technique.

A display, whether graphical or textual, could be generated on the fly using the information about links in each bibliographic record. An additional bibliographic record for the description of the entire family, manually created and updated, would not be required as the online catalog could create such a record at the time of retrieval that synthesizes information for all linked records. Thus, a set of related serial records would form a "cluster of successive-entry records in [a] bibliographic database" (Alan, p. 413), without having to create a meta-level cluster record. A simple title change would necessitate only the update of the ceased publication, and the creation of a new serial record—no other records would need to be revised and no cluster record would ever have to be manually created or modified.

FIGURE 2. Textual display of sequentially related serial records, excerpted from Bernhardt (1988, p. 38).

The serial <u>Lois Lane's Daily gazette</u> has been published under various titles.

It is located at UCLA under the following entries:

Titles:		Volumes held by UCLA:
1	Clark Kent's Daily planet	1-4 (1932-1935)
2	Daily planet	5-8 (1936-1939)
3	Lois Lane's Daily gazette	No holdings

Enter 1, 2, etc., to see complete holdings and call number information:

THE PROMISE OF LINKS IN THE LIBRARY CATALOG

The linking structure described for sequential relationships among serial records can easily be extended to linkages of any type. Sequential relationships are but one type of bibliographic relationship. A generic linking structure could accommodate all the bibliographic relationships described by Tillett and Smiraglia. Both Gorman 1982 and Leazer 1993, in fact, are models for general bibliographic relationships, and Leazer's model makes distinctions among the various types of bibliographic relationship. Any type of association between descriptive records could be included with this structure, including citation relationships.

A linking structure could also be used to express the relationships between descriptive bibliographic records and the authority records that generally describe people or corporate bodies. Gorman 1982 most specifically describes a multidimensional database whereby an authority record is linked in turn to every bibliographic description associated with that authority record. Moreover, the associations between an authority record and a bibliographic record could distinguish between types of relationships between these two records, such as:

book <is authored by> name
book <is illustrated by> name
sound recording <is published by> name
book <is biography of> name

This structure of linkages could be used to express relationships between subject authority records and descriptive records, and also to express the associations between subject terms within the authority file. Generic relational terms such as "broader term," "narrower term," and "related term" could easily be converted into linkages so that the user could follow a computer-generated trail to the most appropriate term—the linkages could help the user build or modify a subject query. These relationships could be combined in a textual and hierarchical display like Bernhardt's proposed display for serial records, and could allow the user to move up, down, and across hierarchies. The same model could be used in classifications as well.

IMPLEMENTING LINKS IN THE LIBRARY CATALOG

Linked records are difficult to accommodate in today's US-MARC record communication environment. USMARC's strength is its granular or modular structure: each individual record can stand alone. Records can be uploaded from a local system to a national utility and downloaded into the local systems of thousands of libraries with very little difficulty. Each record is a kingdom to itself, with access points that allow it to stand on its own if needed, or it can synchronize with other records that share the same access points–if everyone does their authority work consistently.

A system that contains a network of linkages does not readily lend itself to rapid communication in support of many local databases of bibliographic records. A library might purchase a single member of a very large bibliographic family, e.g., an issue of a periodical that underwent a title change, or a copy of *Gone With the Wind*. Downloading a record could mean that one also has to download all the records that are linked to that record–each record is best understood in the context of related records. The strength of the designs proposed by Gorman and Burger, Leazer, Bernhardt, and Alan is that they attempt to model the entire bibliographic universe rather than a single library collection. A liability of these models is that they do not easily transmit individual records between systems. Downloading a single record might be similar to weeding crabgrass: one plant has a massive root structure that connects it to many other shoots. The library that owns only one title of a periodical family faces a dilemma: either include a bibliographic record for a title that the library does not own, or ignore the title change and therefore mislead the catalog user about the constitution of this serial family.

USMARC records function so well in the current cataloging paradigm because they are so granular–*UFBD* is a communication format, after all. This characteristic is a benefit in a distributed record environment, but a liability in an explicitly-linked record environment. USMARC's granularity might make it difficult to implement a linked-record structure. Explicit serials relationships are theoretically possible to control but difficult to achieve in practice.

The USMARC record formats now stand in the way of substantial progress in bibliographic control. Linking records is simply not amenable to the USMARC formats. Attempts to make it more so are now currently underway, such as the amendments described in the American Library Association Machine-Readable Bibliographic Information Committee's (MARBI) "Proposal No. 95-6: Linking Code for Reproduction Information." Such adaptations of the US-MARC format offer minor improvements, and represent complicated and obtuse methods for expressing bibliographic relationships. Furthermore, such improvements are piecemeal and promise only partial solutions for the control of all bibliographic relationships. Clearly, a more general record-linking structure is needed—one that probably cannot be achieved by tweaking USMARC.

USMARC is ideally suited to a national bibliographic control enterprise that consists of thousands of parallel catalogs, functioning in comparative isolation. A local catalog based upon USMARC controls a single library collection and that collection is contained in a building or on a campus. The local catalog does not necessarily control the bibliographic universe, per se, but only a portion of it. These local catalogs are generally drawn from national repositories of bibliographic records—the bibliographic utilities—that act as large union catalogs and can help with resource sharing, but generally do not offer the same depth of control as local catalogs, and are not as frequently utilized by end users. These national utilities (such as RLIN or OCLC) are an appropriate model for a data communications mechanism that existed from the time of the first application in bibliographic control until now—expensive telecommunications links between computers for the transmission of bibliographic records could be justified because they offered cost advantages. Data transmission is now much more pervasive than it was during the last three decades, many households and almost all libraries can now get access to centralized databases. Libraries could all pool their resources into a single centralized bibliographic control tool, or a small number of such tools.

Such a centralized control tool would be a catalog for the nation, or for an international community, and would be the foundation for a single virtual library. All libraries could pool their resources much more effectively. A user could consult the catalog to find all the members of a bibliographic family without regard to whether all members of that family are contained in a single library. The model of a single national catalog for all libraries helps answer how local libraries should catalog electronic resources (such as those on the Internet) that don't belong to a particular institution or library collection but are yet accessible to an institution's users.

How do we get there from here? Obviously current bibliographic databases are too big and the result of too much work to simply abandon them. Moreover, much of the data content for a catalog with a national or global scope that controls items without regard to their location—whether that item is in a small town, at a large research university, or on a hard drive on a distant continent—already exists in current bibliographic databases, especially those massive union catalogs such as those owned by the major bibliographic utilities. A coherent unified catalog of such a scope, would exist in lieu of the many parallel local catalogs replicated at each individual library. Such a unified catalog would provide the platform for a bibliographic database that includes linkages between records.

Such linkages could be automatically generated from information contained in current bibliographic records. Alan has already demonstrated that most sequential relationships can be controlled this way. Further research could certainly recognize these relationships and increase the extent of control over them. Links could be forged for additional types of bibliographic relationships using this same basic technique. Tillett (1987) contains an appendix of the various ways bibliographic relationships are encoded in USMARC records. All the various methods for the current control of relationships could be converted into a single mechanism that could provide better assistance to the user.

Proponents of the current MARC formats ought to test them for adequacy in accommodating systematically the full range of relationships. The serial sequential relationship could be first priority, to be used as a demonstration of the effectiveness of a catalog that incorporates hypertextual linkages and controls entire bibliographic families. If not up to the task, perhaps these unit-record-based formats need to give way to some type of database structure that allows linking mechanisms to express relationships.

This examination should assess whether it is more efficient to build the desired displays of bibliographic families on an as-needed basis in response to user queries, or to preformulate them for ready reference. If the former, what requirements are needed, either in the database system or in the bibliographic data? If the latter, what investment of human and machine resources would be required? In either case, would the display of bibliographic families entail the revision or replacement of the USMARC format?

How could the "added dimensions" of other serial bibliographic relationships be integrated effectively into these displays and still permit intelligible, holistic overviews for the user?

What changes in systems, standards, and cataloger values would need to occur before we could move to a model of a single centralized bibliographic control tool? As the bibliographic universe expands and budgets stagnate, or even contract, is there any other way to hang onto our current standards for high-level, quality cataloging?

CONCLUSION

Recent work in the area of relationships between serial titles has recently underscored the lack of a consistent and simple mechanism for relating bibliographic records. This activity has taken place against a background of theoretical research on the nature and extent of bibliographic relationships. It is unclear that the USMARC formats will ever be able to effectively accommodate information regarding sequential bibliographic relationships, or any other type of relationship.

Research has shown an effective way to control serial relationships, but thus far it has done so in isolation from other types of bibliographic relationships. Gorman and Leazer have both proposed models that could apply to all bibliographic relationships, including the sequential relationship. Adopting a system like the one Gorman promotes will result in better bibliographic control of serials. As Gorman and Burger state (1980, p. 25):

> the exhaustive analysis of the relationships between serials [that] has characterized serial cataloging for many years will, at last, be put to productive use. The complexities which the

cataloger unravels will no longer be obscured by the limitations of the card catalog or its derivative—the MARC system. Serial cataloging, always an exact and demanding art, will become an effective process.

The discipline of sociology serves as an instructive metaphor to understand bibliographic control. In order to understand the fabric of human society, the sociologist studies the pattern of social relations formed by groups of individuals—human society is revealed by the network of social relationships that bind individuals together into families and communities. Bibliographic control, as a theory and an activity that results in tools like the library catalog, must also account for textual interactions and bibliographic relationships in order to achieve a complete understanding of the bibliographic universe. Just as a description of a human individual would be incomplete without acknowledging this person's relationships to others, the description on the bibliographic entity is incomplete without an account of its bibliographic relationships to other entities. The incorporation of relationship information into library catalogs will allow users to explore the bibliographic universe via a simple and effective mechanism. The unit of control for the library catalog must grow beyond the simple publication to a more complex notion of the bibliographic family and the relationships among its members.

WORK CITED

Alan, Robert. 1993. "Linking Successive Entries Based upon the OCLC Control Number, ISSN, or LCCN." *Library Resources & Technical Services* 37: 403-13.

American Library Association. Machine-Readable Bibliographic Information Committee (MARBI). 1994. "Proposal No. 95-6: Linking Code for Reproduction Information."

Anglo-American Cataloguing Rules, 2nd edition, 1988 revision. 1988. Prepared under the direction of the Joint Steering Committee for the Revision of AACR, a committee of the American Library Association, the Australian Committee on Cataloguing, the Library Association, the Library of Congress. Ed. by Michael Gorman and Paul Winkler. Chicago: American Library Association.

Bernhardt, Melissa M. 1988. "Dealing with Serial Title Changes: Some Theoretical and Practical Considerations." *Cataloging & Classification Quarterly* 9, no. 2: 25-39.

Gorman, Michael. 1982. "Authority Control in the Prospective Catalog." In *Authority Control: The Key to Tomorrow's Catalog: Proceedings of the 1979 Library and Information Technology Association Institutes*, ed. by Mary W. Ghikas. Phoenix, Ariz.: Oryx Press, p. 166-80.

Gorman, Michael and Robert H. Burger. 1980. "Serial Control in a Developed Machine System." *Serials Librarian* 5, no. 1 (Fall): 13-26.

Henderson, Kathryn Luther (1992). "Personalities of Their Own: Some Informal Thoughts on Serials and Teaching About' How to Catalog Them. In *Serials Librarian* 22, no. 1/2: 3-16.

Langer, Susanne. 1963. *Philosophy in a New Key: A Study in the Symbolism of Reason, Rite, and Art*, 3rd ed. Cambridge, Harvard University Press.

Leazer, Gregory H. 1993. *A Conceptual Plan for the Description and Control of Bibliographic Works*. D.L.S. diss., School of Library Service, Columbia University.

Leazer, Gregory H. 1994. "A conceptual schema for the control of bibliographic works." In *Navigating the Networks: Proceedings of the ASIS Mid-Year Meeting*, ed. by D. L. Andersen, T. J. Galvin, and M. D. Giguere. Medford, N.J.: American Society for Information Science, p. 115-35.

Lubetzky, Seymour. 1986. "Principles of descriptive cataloging," in *Foundations of Cataloging: A Sourcebook*, ed. by Michael Carpenter and Elaine Svenonius. Littleton, Colo.: Libraries Unlimited, p. 104-12.

Smiraglia, Richard P. 1992. *Authority Control and the Extent of Derivative Bibliographic Relationships*. Ph.D. diss., Graduate Library School, University of Chicago.

Smiraglia, Richard P. 1994. "Derivative Bibliographic Relationships: Linkages in the Bibliographic Universe." In *Navigating the Networks: Proceedings of the ASIS Mid-Year Meeting*, ed. by D. L. Andersen, T. J. Galvin, and M. D. Giguere. Medford, N.J.: American Society for Information Science, p. 167-83.

Tillett, Barbara Ann Barnett. 1987. *Bibliographic Relationships: Toward a Conceptual Structure of Bibliographic Information Used in Cataloging*. Ph.D. diss., Graduate School of Library and Information Science, University of California, Los Angeles.

Tillett, Barbara B. 1991a. "A Summary of the Treatment of Bibliographic Relationships in Cataloging Rules," *Library Resources & Technical Services* 35: 393-405.

Tillett, Barbara B. 1991b. "A Taxonomy of Bibliographic Relationships," *Library Resources & Technical Services* 35: 150-58.

USMARC Format for Bibliographic Data: Including Guidelines for Content Designation. 1988. Washington, D.C.: Network Development and MARC Standards Office, Library of Congress.

Index

AACR1. *See Anglo-American Cataloguing Rules,* 1st ed.

AACR2. *See Anglo-American Cataloguing Rules,* 2nd ed.

AAP markup (ISO 12083), 12

Access. *See* Subject access

Accompanying bibliographic relationships, 206

ACRL, 18

ALA (American Library Association), 62,63,142, 160,178,183-184,195

A.L.A. Catalog Rules, Author and Title Entries, 63

Alan, Robert, 210,217

A.L.A. Rules-Advance Edition, 62

Alphabetical descriptor systems vs. classification schemes, 156

concept systems: thesauri, 165-169

string systems

international guidelines, 164-165

Library of Congress Subject Headings, 159-163

PRECIS, 163-164

thesauri and, 158-159,167

American Library Association (ALA), 62,63,142,160,178, 183-184,195

American National Standard for Bibliographic Information Interchange on Magnetic Tape, 86

American National Standards Institute (ANSI), 15

ANSI/NISO Z39 (ISO 2709), 6, 7,11-12,15,167-168

development, 6-7

EDIFACT applications, 11-13,14

Internet Engineering Task Force influence on, 10

MARC development, 86

MARC Pilot Project, 83

sale of standards, 10

Anderson, Dorothy, 18-19, 41

Anglo-American Authority File (AAAF), 72,102

Anglo-American Cataloguing Rules, 1st ed. (AACR1), 64

national authority file name records, 134

Anglo-American Cataloguing Rules, 1st ed., British edition, 47

Anglo-American Cataloguing Rules, 2nd ed. (AACR2), 2

development, 7

internationalizing, 37-57

China, 43-44

French-speaking Canada, 54-56

Kenya, 44-47

Nordic countries, 47-53

reasons for wide-spread adoption, 38-42

Singapore and Malaysia, 42-43

Library of Congress Rule Interpretations, 61-73

national authority file

name records, 137-141

series records, 145,148-150

sequential bibliographic relationships, 209

user-centered approach, 104-105

Anonymous Classics, 27-28

ANSI. *See* American National

Standards Institute
ASCII, 6
Asia, 42-44
Austin, Derek, 162,163
Australia, 133
Authority records, 3
    international standards, 27-28
    language in, 24
    linking structures, 214
    name
        AACR implementation,
            134-135
        automation, 133-135
        cataloging rules and rule
            interpretations, 137-141
        level of establishment,
            136-137
        Name Authorities Cooperative
            Program, 133-134
        scope of, 135-136
        specific fields, 141-144
    National Coordinated Cataloging
        Program, 67
    in network environment, 128
    for online classification, 178-179
    Program for Centralized
        Cataloging, 102
    series
        AACR2 implementation, 145
        automation, 145
        cataloging rules and rule
            interpretations, 148-150
        level of establishment, 148
        scope of, 146-147
        Series Authority Record Task
            Group, 145-146
        specific fields, 151-152
    USMARC, 183-184,185-186
Authors. *See also* Name authority
        records; Names in AACR2
    international issues, 21
        corporate authors, 47,48,49,
            50,55
        Kenya, 45-47
        Sweden, 53

national authority file, 135
Automated catagloging. *See* MARC;
        Networked information
        resources;
        Online classification; UNIMARC;
        USMARC
Automated vs. manual bibliographic
        control, 70-71
Avram, Henriette, 81,83,84,86

Belgium, 162
Bernhardt, Melissa M., 210,212,
        213,214
Bibliographic commons, 98
Bibliographic control, 3
    International Federation of
        Library Associations and
        Institutions, 17-34
    bibliographic record sharing,
        22-23
    international standards, 25-28
    language and culture in, 23-25
    limitations, 28-33,36
    principles, 20-21
    responsibilities, 18-19,28-29
    Third World countries, 32
Bibliographic records
    format standards, 11,12-15
    national libraries as source, 20-21
    Program for Centralized
        Cataloging, 99-104
    sharing, 21-23
    USMARC, 185-186,191
Bibliographic relationships, 205-219
    linking structure for catalog,
        214-219
    sequential, 208-213
    techniques for controlling,
        207-208
    Tillett's taxonomy, 206-207
Bibliographic utilities
    *Library of Congress Rule
        Interpretations* use, 66-67
    OCLC, 134,142,152,216
    in bibliographic control, 33

CONSER support, 93
electronic text cataloging
guidelines, 111
LC bibliographic records, 98
RLIN, 133-134,142,152,216
Birth dates, 138
Bishoff, Liz, 94
Boissonnas, Christian, 102
Book Industry Study Advisory
Committee (BISAC), 13
Bregzis, Ritvars, 82
British Library, 14,72,133,141,163
British National Bibliography, 85,
161-162
Buckland, Lawrence, 79,80,82
Burger, Robert H., 209,210,211,
212,218-219
Byrum, John, 95

CALS markup, 12
Canada
French-speaking, *Anglo-American
Cataloguing Rules, 2nd
Edition* (AACR2), 54-56
machine-readable cataloging, 77,
82
National Film Board of Canada,
164
Canada, National Library of, 14,72,
132-133, 162
Canadian Subject Headings
(National Library of
Canada), 162
Captions, USMARC, 187-188
Cartographic materials, 48
Catalogers
online classification, 180-181,
194,201
role in Program for Centralized
Cataloging, 104-106
Cataloging
copy vs. original, 66,92
decentralized, 97-98
electronic texts and network

resources, 111-113
Library of Congress, 96-97
outsourcing, 97-98
sequential bibliographic
relationships, 205-219
linking structures, 214-219
techniques for controlling,
207-213
Tillett's taxonomy, 206-207
simplification and modification,
67-68
"Cataloging Decisions," 64
Cataloging Distribution Service
(CDS), 202
Cataloging In Publication (CIP), 67
"Cataloging Memoranda," 63
"Cataloging Must Change" (Gregor
and Mandel), 93
Cataloging Service Bulletin (Library
of Congress), 65,161
Cataloging Service (Library of
Congress), 64,65
CCC (Cooperative Cataloging
Council), 68-72,94-96,
142-144,145-146
Chan, Lois Mai, 160
Chicago, University of, 67
China, 43-44
CIP (Cataloging In Publication), 67
Classification. *See also* Library of
Congress Classification;
Online classification
international standards, 24-25
as subject access standards, 156,
158,167,169-172
USMARC
advantages, 181-183
development, 183-184
distribution issues, 202
enhancements, 200-202
modification, 194-198
pilot study and Library of
Congress implementation,
192-194
problems to be resolved,

198-200
structure and content, 184-192
Columbia-Harvard-Yale Medical
Libraries, 78
Columbia University, 92
Committee on Scientific and
Technical Information
(COSATI) guidelines,
167
Commons, bibliographic, 98
Company standards, development,
8-9
Computers, decentralized cataloging,
70-71,97-98
Concept systems of subject access,
158-159,165-169
Conference on Machine-Readable
Catalog Copy, 1965,83
CONSER (Cooperative Online
Serials), 68,93-94
Cooperative cataloging
*Library of Congress Rule
Interpretations* needs,
67-68
National Coordinated Cataloging
Program (NCCP), 67-68
Program for Cooperative
Cataloging (PCC), 91-108
benefits to be provided,
106-108
core bibliographic record,
96-104
documentation and training,
104-106
need for, 93-94
reconstructing National
Coordinated Cataloging
Program, 94-96
Cooperative Cataloging Council
(CCC), 68-72,94-96,
142-144,145-146.
See also National Coordinated
Cataloging Program;
Program for Cooperative
Cataloging

Copy cataloging, 66
vs. original cataloging, 92
Core bibliographic record in
Program for Centralized
Cataloging, 99-104
Core record in series authority file,
147
Cornell University, 102-103
Corporate authorship in AACR2, 47,
48,49,50,55
Corporate bodies, name authority
records, 140,141
COSATI (Committee on Scientific
and Technical Information)
guidelines, 167
Council on Library Resources, 78,
79,83,93
Crawford, Walt, 1
Cromwell, Willy, 104
Cross-references
national authority file, 138-141
USMARC, 182,188-189,197
Culture
Dewey Decimal Classification,
170
Library of Congress Subject
Headings, 161-163
in universal bibliographic control,
23-25
Cutter, Charles A., 159,160

Databases, thesauri, 168-169
Datatrol Corporation, 81
DCM Z (*Descriptive Cataloging
ManualZ*),132,135,141,142,
146,150,153
Death dates, 138
De facto standards, 9
De jure standards, 9
Denmark, 47-49
Derivative bibliographic
relationships, 206
Descriptive bibliographic
relationships, 206
Descriptive Cataloging Manual Z

(DCM Z), 132,135,141,
142,146,150,153
*Descriptive Cataloguing Rules for
Western Language
Materials* (DCR- WLM)
(China), 44
Dewey Decimal Classification
(DDC), 169-172,183,192,
195
development, 7
as international standard, 24-25
Dewey Decimal Classification
Online Project, 180
Dewey, Melvil, 169
Directory model in meta-information
architecture, 113-114
Documentation
MARC, 79
Program for Centralized
Cataloging, 106
Document Type Definition (DTD),
119

EDIFACT (*Electronic Data
Interchange for
Administration, Commerce
and Transport*, ISO 9735),
11-13, 14
*Electronic Data Interchange for
Administration, Commerce
and Transport* (EDIFACT,
ISO 9735), 11-13,14
Electronic documents
cataloging, 111-113
format standards, 11,12
Electronic document transfer
international standards, 22-23
ISO 9735,11-13,14
Equivalence bibliographic
relationships, 206
"Eskimos," 162
Ewald, Robert, 2, 61

Fields in automated records
MARC, 76-77,82-83,84,85
national authority records
name, 141-144
series, 151-152
USMARC, 190-192
File transfer protocol (FTP), 93
Film Catalogue (National Film
Board of Canada), 164
Financial issues
automating bibliographic data,
78-79
cooperative cataloging, 96,98-99
ISO and ANSI sale of standards,
10
Library of Congress cataloging,
97
Finland, 47,49-50
Florida Atlantic University, 77
Formal standards, development, 6-7,
9,10
Format standards, ISO, 11,12-13
*Free-Floating Subdivisions: An
Alphabetical Index* (Library
of Congress), 161
Freitag, Ruth, 81
French-speaking Canada, 54-56
FTP (file transfer protocol), 93

General Bibliographic Description
(China), 43-44
Geographic names in AACR2, 55,
138
Germany, 165
Gilchrist, Alan, 168
Giordano, Richard, 126
Gorman, Michael, 209,210,211,
212,214,218-219
Government bodies, in AACR2
entries, 51,55
Government Printing Office,
67,79,133,145
Gredley, Ellen J., 39,40-41
Gregor, Dorothy, 93
Guenther Rebecca, 3,177

*Guidelines for Authorities and
    Reference Entries*
    (International
    Federation of Library
        Associations and
        Institutions), 57
*Guidelines for Authority and
    Reference Entries (GARE)*,
    28
Guidelines, for subject access,
    156-158
*Guidelines for Subject Authority and
    Reference Entries*
    (International Federation of
        Library Associations and
        Institutions), 164-165
*Guidelines for Subject Authority and
    Reference Entries
    (SGARE)*, 28
*Guidelines for the Application of the
    ISBDs to the Description of
    Component Parts, 27*
*Guidelines for the Establishment and
    Development of
    Monolingual
    Thesauri* (ISO), 166
Guiles, Kay, 2,61,81

Harvard University, 67
Haykin, David, 160
Header model in meta-information
        architecture
    advantages, 113-114
    standardizing, 127-129
    Text Encoding Initiative, 121-128
Henderson, Kathryn Luther, 208
Holley, Robert, 2,17
Horowitz, Lisa, 3,109
HTML (Hypertext Markup
        Language), 12,119
Humanities scholars, 123
Hypertext Markup Language
        (HTML), 12,119

Iban names, 43
IFLA. *See* International Federation
        of Library Associations and
        Institutions
Illinois, University of, 67,76
"Indexical Contexts" (Svenonius),
        166
Index terms, USMARC, 190,198,
        199-200
Industry group standards, 7,13
Informal standards, development, 8-9
Inforonics, Inc., 79
International bibliographic control
    International Federation of
            Library Associations and
            Institutions (IFLA),
            2, 17-34
    *Library of Congress Rule
            Interpretations*s, 72-73
    Library of Congress Subject
            Headings, 161-162
    sharing of MARC II records, 85
International Conference on
            Cataloguing Principles,
            1961,19
International Federation of Library
            Associations and
            Institutions (IFLA),
            2, 17-34
    *Guidelines for Authorities and
            Reference Entries,* 57
    implementation, 30-31
    international standards and,
            25-28,30
    language and culture in standards,
            23-25
    limitations, 31-32,36
    networks in standard setting, 32-33
    principles in universal
            bibliographic control, 20-21
    responsibilities, 18-19
    role of, 28-29
    sharing of bibliographic records,
            22-23
    subject headings, 164-165

Third World countries, 32
  voluntary nature, 29-30
International Meeting of Cataloging
    Experts, Copenhagen,
    1969,38-39
International Organization for
    Standardization (ISO)
  development, 6-7
  electronic communication use,
    10-11
  International Federation of
    Library Associations and
    Institution
    relationship, 32
  Internet Engineering Task Force
    influence on, 10
  ISO 2709 (ANSI/NISO Z39), 6,
    7,11-12,15,167-168
  ISO 2788,166-168
  ISO 8879 (SGML), 11-13,14,
    110,115,119-121,181
  ISO 9735 (EDIFACT), 11-13,14
  ISO 12083 (AAP markup), 12
  sale of standards, 10
International Standard for
    Bibliographic Description:
    Monographs (ISBD(M))
  vs. AACR2, 38,39,41
  in China, 43-44
International standards
  AACR2, 37-57
    China, 43-44
    French-speaking Canada,
      54-56
    Kenya, 44-47
    Nordic countries, 47-53
    reasons for wide-spread
      adoption, 38-42
    Singapore and Malaysia, 42-43
  International Federation of
    Library Associations and
    Institutions (IFLA), 17-34
  International Standards for
    Bibliographic Description
    (ISBD), 23-24,26-27,36,47,
      48,49
Internet, 112
  standard development, 911
  TCP/IP, 9
Internet Anonymous FTP Archives
    (IAFA), 117-119
Internet Engineering Task Force
    (IETF), 9-11,112
"Inuit," 162
Iran, 165
ISBD. *See* International Standards
    for Bibliographic
    Description
Islam, 46
ISO. *See* International Organization
    for Standardization

Japan, 39

Kenya, 44-47
Kiswahili language, 44-45
Koninklijke Bibliotheek, 162
Kuhagen, Judith, 3,131

Lancaster, F. W., 156,166,167
Langer, Susanne, 211
Langridge, Derek, 156
Language
  in AACR2 internationalization,
    44-45,49-50,51,54-56
  Dewey Decimal Classification,
    170
  Library of Congress Rule
    Interpretations, 71
  Library of Congress Subject
    Headings, 161-163
  "Principles Underlying Subject
    Heading Languages"
    (International
    Federation of Library
    Associations and

Institutions), 165
in universal bibliographic control,
23-25,29
Universal Decimal Classification,
171-172
Laval, Université, 162
LC. *See* Library of Congress
LCC. *See* Library of Congress
Classification
LCRIs. *See Library of Congress Rule
Interpretations*
LCSH. *See* Library of Congress
Subject Headings
Leazer, Gregory,
3,205,210,211,212,214
Legal deposit, 20-21
Legal publications, AACR2, 52, 55
Library of Congress authority file.
See National resource
authority file
Library of Congress Classification
(LCC)
as international standard, 24-25
printing and maintenance of
schedules, 179
subject access, 169-172
USMARC implementation,
177-203
development of format,
183-184
distribution issues, 202
enhancements, 200-202
modifications, 194-198
pilot study, 192-194
potential uses and advantages,
178-183
problems to be resolved,
198-200
structure and content of
format, 184-192
Library of Congress (LC), 3
AACR2 involvement, 104-105
backlog in cataloging, 96-97
cooperative cataloging, 68,93-94
copy vs. original cataloging, 92

machine-readable cataloging
history of, 78-81
MARC II format, 84-86
MARC pilot project, 81-84
name authority records, 133-134
national resource authority file,
influence on, 132
Network Development and
MARC Standards Office,
15,178,183-184,193,195
original cataloging, 96
Serial Industry Systems Advisory
Committee standards, 13
standards implementation, 31
Technical Committee on LC
Classification, 193
vendor use of records, 98
*Library of Congress Period
Subdivisions Under Names
of Places,* 161
*Library of Congress Rule
Interpretations* (LCRI), 2,
61-73,134-135
automated vs. manual
bibliographic control, 70-71
availability, 73
bibliographic utility use, 66-67
categories, 69-70
content, 71
Cooperative Cataloging
Council/CPSO Task Group
report, 68-72
cooperative cataloging efforts,
67-68
criticisms of, 105
development, 8-9,61-66
function, 61-62
institution-specific, 73
international efforts, 72-73
language, 71
limitations, 72
national authority file
name records, 137-141
series records, 148-150
presentation, 71-72

Library of Congress Subject
      Headings (LCSH), 159-164
   development, 8
   USMARC, 181-182,190
LIBRIS automated system, 53
Linguistic research, 124
Linked Systems Project, 133
Linked Systems Protocol (LSP), 93
Linking reference, 140-141
*A List of Australian Subject
      Headings* (McKinlay), 162
Local index model in
      meta-information
      architecture, 113-114
Local systems
   references, 139
   USMARC classification, 182-183
Lubetzky, Seymour, 205

McCallum, Sally, 2,5,15
Machine-Readable Bibliographic
      Information Committee
      (MARBI),142,178,183-184,
      195
Machine-readable catagloging. *See*
      MARC; Networked
      information resources;
      Online classification;
      UNIMARC; USMARC
McIlwaine, I. C., 171
Main entries. *See* Subject access
MAJOUR, 12
Malaysia, 42-43
Mandel, Carol, 92, 93, 95
Manual bibliographic control, 70-71
MARBI (Machine-Readable
      Bibliographic Information
      Committee),142,178,
      183-184,195
MARC, 2,3,6,162. *See also*
      UNIMARC; USMARC
   advantages, 13-14
   development of format, 75-86
      Library of Congress in, 78-81

MARC II, 84-86
      pilot project, 81-84
      university libraries in, 75-78
   distribution, 202
   harmonizing USMARC and
      UKMARC, 57,85
   integration with USMARC, 182
   International Federation of
      Library Associations and
      Institutions, 19
   international use, 14
   Library of Congress Network
      Development and MARC
      Standards Office, 15,178,
      183-184,193,195
   in network resource cataloging,
      limitations, 112-113
   Serial Industry Systems Advisory
      Committee version, 13
   in subject access, 172
   Text Encoding Initiative and,
      122-127
MARC Editorial Division, 133
MARC II, 84-86
Markuson, Barbara, 78
Medical Subject Headings, 190
Meta-information structures, 3,
      109-129
   cataloging of electronic text and
      network resources, 111-113
   characteristics, 113-114
   defined, 110
   Internet Anonymous FTP
      Archives, 117-119
   pilot studies, 110
   standardizing, 127-128
   Text Encoding Initiative
      independent header and,
      121-124
      MARC record and, 124-127
      Standard Generalized Markup
      Language and, 119-121,
      127
   Uniform Resource
      Characteristics, 115-117

Michigan State University, 98
Microforms, 48
Minaret software, 184-185,
     192-193,194
Minimum-level-cataloging (MLC),
     99,101-104
Monographs, 92
     Cooperative Cataloging Council,
          107
     MARC II, 84-86
Mosaic Common Client Interface,
     119
Multi-media, 48-49
Mumford, L. Quincy, 79
Music, Cooperative Cataloging
     Council core record for,
     107
Music uniform titles, 53
Muslim names, 46

NACO. *See* Name Authorities
     Cooperative Program
Name Authorities Cooperative
     Program (NACO), 67,
     93-94,136,140,142,
     143-144,145,152
     purpose and participants, 132-134
Name authority records, 3
Name authority records in national
     authority file, 133-144
     AACR implementation, 134-135
     automation, 133-135
     cataloging rules and rule
          interpretations, 137-141
     level of establishment, 136-137
     Name Authorities Cooperative
          Program, 133-134
     scope of, 135-136
     specific fields, 141-144
Names in AACR2. *See also* Authors;
     Name authority records
     Kenya, 45-47
     language in, 24
     Malay, 42-43

Norwegian, 51-52
National Coordinated Cataloging
     Program (NCCP), 67-68,
     93-94,152
     See also Cooperative
          Cataloging Program;
          Program for Cooperative
          Cataloging
     limitations, 93-94
     national resource authority file
          contributions, 132
     reconstructing, 94-96
National Film Board of Canada, 164
National Information Standards
     Organization (NISO), 6-7,
     13,15
National libraries, as bibliographic
     record source, 20-21
National Library of Canada, 72,
     132-133,162
National Library of Medicine, 67
National Library of Medicine
     Classification, 184
National resource authority file,
     131-153
     history, 132-133
     name authority records
          AACR implementation,
               134-135
          automation, 133-135
          cataloging rules and rule
               interpretations, 137-141
          level of establishment,
               136-137
          Name Authorities Cooperative
               Program, 133-134
          scope of, 135-136
          specific fields, 141-144
     series authority records
          AACR2 implementation, 145
          automation, 145
          cataloging rules and rule
               interpretations, 148-150
          level of establishment, 148
          scope of, 146-147

Series Authority Record Task Group, 145-146
specific fields, 151-152
National Union Catalog, 136
NCCP. *See* National Coordinated Cataloging Program
NEPHIS, 163
Network Development and MARC Standards Office, LC, 15, 178,183-184,193,195
Networked information resources cataloging, 111-113
characteristics, 112
defined, 110
distributed components, 112,114
meta-information structures, 109-129
characteristics, 113-114
Internet Anonymous FTP Archives, 117-119
pilot studies, 110
standardizing, 127-128
Text Encoding Initiative independent header and, 121-124
MARC record and, 124-127
Standard Generalized Markup Language and, 119-121, 127
Uniform Resource Characteristics, 115-117
mobility, 112,113-114
mutability, 112,114
Networks, in bibliographic control, 32-33
Newcastle, University of, 133
NEWWAVE database, 162
NISO (National Information Standards Organization), 6-7,11-13,14
Norway, 47,50-52
Numeric tagging in automated records, 82,84
Nwapa, Flora, 45

OCLC (Online Computer Library Center), 134,142,152,216
in bibliographic control, 33
CONSER support, 93
electronic text cataloging guidelines, 111
LC bibliographic records, 98
Office of the Information Systems Specialist, 81
Online classification
authority control, 178-179
bibliographic record maintenance, 181
classifier assistance, 180-181
as online shelflist basis, 181
printing and maintenance of schedules, 179
subject access, 180
USMARC
advantages, 181-183
development, 183-184
distribution issues, 202
enhancements, 200-202
modification, 194-198
pilot study and Library of Congress implementation, 192-194
potential and advantages, 178-183
problems to be resolved, 198-200
structure and content, 184-192
Online Computer Library Center. *See* OCLC
Ontario New Universities Library Project (ONULP), 77
Open Systems Interconnection (OSI), 9
Original cataloging, vs. copy cataloging, 92
Outsourcing of cataloging, 97-98

Pakistani names, 52
Palowitch, Casey, 3,109
Panorama[TM], 119
Paris Principles, 19,22,38-40
Phillips, Sue, 94

POPSI, 163
Portugal, 165
PRECIS (Preserved Context
     Indexing System), 161-162,
     163-164,167
"Present Role and Guture Policy for
     UDC as a Standard for
     Subject Control"
     (McIlwaine), 171
Preserved Context Indexing System
     (PRECIS), 161-162,
     163-164,167
"Principles Underlying Subject
     Heading Languages"
     (International
     Federation of Library
     Associations and
     Institutions), 165
Program for Cooperative Cataloging.
     See also Cooperative
     Cataloging Program;
     National Coordinated
     Cataloging Program
Program for Cooperative Cataloging
     (PCC), 72-73, 91-208
  benefits to be provided, 106-108
  core bibliographic record, 96-104
  documentation and training,
     104-106
  need for, 93-94
  reconstructing National
     Coordinated Cataloging
     Program, 94-96
Pseudonyms, 53
Publication process
  Internet standards vs. ISO and
     ANSI, 10
  Kenya, 44-45
Public libraries, 39,52

Ranganathan's alphabetico-synthetic
     classification, 167
References
  national authority file, 138-141

USMARC, 182,188-189,197
"Reflections on Bibliographic
     Standards and the Processes
     of Standardization"
     (Anderson), 19
Reimer, John J., 1
Repértoire de vedettes-matière
     (l'Université Laval), 162
RLIN, 133-134,142,152,216
Roberts, Winston, 28,29
Rolland-Thomas, Paule, 54,55,56
Rolling, Loll, 166
Rules for Descriptive Cataloging, 63

Schottlaender, Brian, 103
Schultheiss, Louis, 77
Seals of Approval (SOAPS), 116
"See" references
  national authority file, 138-141
  USMARC, 182,188-189
Sequential bibliographic
     relationships, 205-219
  linking structure for catalog,
     214-219
  techniques for controlling,
     207-213
  Tillett's taxonomy, 206-207
Serial Industry Systems Advisory
     Committee (SISAC), 13
Series cataloging
  AACR2, 48
  bibliographic relationships,
     205-219
     linking structure for catalog,
        214-219
     sequential, 208-213
     techniques for controlling,
        207-208
     Tillett's taxonomy, 206-207
  national authority records, 3
     AACR2 implementation, 145
     automation, 145
     cataloging rules and rule
        interpretations, 148-150
     level of establishment, 148

scope of, 146-147
Series Authority Record Task
    Group, 145-146
series-like phrases, 147, 150
specific fields, 151-152
unique serial identifier, 149
SGML (*Standard Generalized
    Markup Language,* ISO
    8879), 11-13,14,110,115,
    119-121,181
Shared characteristic bibliographic
    relationships, 206-207
Shelflists, 180,181
Singapore, 42-43
Smiraglia, Richard P., 207-208,209,
    210,214
Smith, K. Wayne, 98
Snyder, Samuel, 78
SOAPS (Seals of APproval), 116
Sociology, 219
SoftQuad Corporation, 119
Spicher, Karen, 2,75
Standard availability, publication
    process, 10
Standard, defined, 18
*Standard Generalized Markup
    Language* (SGML, ISO
    8879), 11-13,14,110,115,
    119-121,181
Standards, 2
    characteristics, 5-15
        formal, 6-7
        format standardization, 13-15
        function, 5-6
        informal, 8-9
        key standards for libraries,
            11-13
        recent developments, 9-11
    international
        AACR2, 37-57
        International Federation of
            Library Associations and
            Institutions and, 17-34
        *Library of Congress Rule
            Interpretations,* 61-73

for MARC, 75-86
meta-information structures,
    109-129
national authority file, 131-153
Program for Cooperative
    Cataloging, 91-108
sequential bibliographic
    relationships, 205-219
subject access, 155-173
USMARC classification data,
    177-203
"The Standards Jungle" (Gilchrist),
    168
Stern, Barbara, 2,37
String systems for subject access
    international guidelines, 164-165
    Library of Congress Subject
        Headings, 159-163
    PRECIS, 163-164
    vs. thesauri, 158-159
Subject access
    Finland and AACR2, 49
    language in, 24-25
    for online classification, 180
    standards and guidelines, 155-173
        alphabetical descriptor
            methods, 156,158-169
        classification systems, 169-172
        defined, 156-158
        international, 164-165
        Library of Congress subject
            headings, 159-163
        MARC, 172
        PRECIS, 163-164
        systemic methods, 156
        thesaurus, 165-169
        two-step process, 155-156
    USMARC, 190
Subject Analysis Committee of
    American Library
    Association, 160
*Subject Cataloging Manual: Subject
    Headings* (Library of
    Congress), 160-161
Subject headings

Library of Congress Subject
Headings, 158-163
Library of Congress Subject
Headings (LCSH), 8
for subject access, 156,158-163
USMARC, 181-182,190
Subject-to-name references, 140
Svenonius, Elaine, 166
Sweden, 47, 52-53
Swedish language, 49-50

Taube, Mortimer, 78
TCP/IP, 9
Technical Committee on LC
Classification, 193
Text Encoding Initiative (TEI),
3,12,110
independent header and, 121-124
MARC and, 124-127
Standard Generalized Markup
Language and, 119-121
Thesauri, 156,158-159,165-169
Thesaurofacet, 167
Third World Countries, International
Federation of Library
Associations and Institution
standards, 32
Thomas, Patricia, 95
Thomas, Sarah, 2,91,95
Tillett, Barbara, 2,61,206,207,210,
214,217
Titles
AACR2 and Finland, 50
national authority file, 135,147,
149-150
Toronto, University of, 77,82
Tracings. *See* Cross-references
Training, in Program for Centralized
Cataloging, 104-106
Tucker, Ben, 63

UCLA, 102103
UDC. *See* Universal Decimal

Classification
UKMARC, 57
UK/MARC Pilot Project, 85
"Underground Railway" (term), 162
*Unesco Guidelines for the
Establishment and
Development of
Monolingual Scientific and
Technical Thesauri*, 167
UNICODE character set, 8
Uniform Resource Characteristics
(URCs), 115-117
UNIMARC, 36,57. *See also* MARC;
USMARC
function, 25-26
international use, 14
oversight, 26
United States of America Standards
Institute. *See* American
National Standards
Institute (ANSI)
United States, standards
implementation, 31
Universal Bibliographic Control and
International MARC
(UBCIM), 19
Universal bibliographic control
(UBC), International
Federation of Library
Associations and Institutions
(IFLA), 17-34
bibliographic record sharing,
22-23
international standards, 25-28
language and culture in, 23-25
limitations, 28-33, 36
principles in, 20-21
responsibilities, 18-19,28-29
Universal Character Set (UCS),
development, 8
Universal Decimal Classification
(UDC), 24-25,169-172,
184,195
Universal Resource Identifier
(URI), 111

l'Université Laval, 162
University of Chicago, 67
University of Illinois, 67
University of Illinois Chicago
    Library, 76
University of Newcastle, 133
University of Toronto Library, 77,82
URI (Universal Resource Identifier),
    111
U.S. Government Printing Office, 67,
    79,133,145
USMARC, 3. *See also* MARC;
    UNIMARC; USMARC
    for classification data, 177-203
        advantages, 181-183
        development, 183-184
        distribution issues, 202
        enhancements, 200-202
        modifications, 195-198
        pilot study and LCC
            implementation, 178,
            192-202
        potential uses, 178-181
        problems to be resolved,
            198-200
        structure and content, 184-192
    development, 7
    harmonizing with UKMARC, 57
    international use, 14
    linking structures, 215-219
USMARC Format for Authority Data
    (Library of Congress), 131
USMARC Format for Bibliographic
    Data (Library of Congress),
    209
USMARC Format for Classification
    Data (Library of Congress),
    178,182,184,186

Vietnamese names, 52
Voluntary international associations,
    29-30

West, Linda, 95

Whole-part bibliographic
    relationships, 206
Williamson, Nancy, 3,155,199
World Wide Web (WWW), 12,115,
    116, 119

Yale University, 133
Yoshimura, Karen Smith, 94

Z39, ANSI/NISO,
    6,7,11-12,15,167-168

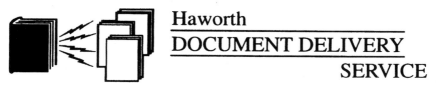

Haworth
DOCUMENT DELIVERY
SERVICE

This valuable service provides a single-article order form for any article from a Haworth journal.

- *Time Saving:* No running around from library to library to find a specific article.
- *Cost Effective:* All costs are kept down to a minimum.
- *Fast Delivery:* Choose from several options, including same-day FAX.
- *No Copyright Hassles:* You will be supplied by the original publisher.
- *Easy Payment:* Choose from several easy payment methods.

Open Accounts Welcome for . . .
- Library Interlibrary Loan Departments
- Library Network/Consortia Wishing to Provide Single-Article Services
- Indexing/Abstracting Services with Single Article Provision Services
- Document Provision Brokers and Freelance Information Service Providers

---

MAIL or *FAX* THIS ENTIRE ORDER FORM TO:

Haworth Document Delivery Service
The Haworth Press, Inc.
10 Alice Street
Binghamton, NY 13904-1580

or FAX: 1-800-895-0582
or CALL: 1-800-342-9678
9am-5pm EST

PLEASE SEND ME PHOTOCOPIES OF THE FOLLOWING SINGLE ARTICLES:
1) Journal Title: _____
    Vol/Issue/Year:_____Starting & Ending Pages:_____
Article Title:_____
_____

2) Journal Title: _____
    Vol/Issue/Year:_____Starting & Ending Pages:_____
Article Title:_____
_____

3) Journal Title: _____
    Vol/Issue/Year:_____Starting & Ending Pages:_____
Article Title:_____
_____

4) Journal Title: _____
    Vol/Issue/Year:_____Starting & Ending Pages:_____
Article Title:_____
_____

(See other side for Costs and Payment Information)

COSTS: Please figure your cost to order quality copies of an article.

1. Set-up charge per article: $8.00
   ($8.00 × number of separate articles)   _____

2. Photocopying charge for each article:
   - 1-10 pages: $1.00   _____
   - 11-19 pages: $3.00   _____
   - 20-29 pages: $5.00   _____
   - 30+ pages: $2.00/10 pages   _____

3. Flexicover (optional): $2.00/article   _____

4. Postage & Handling: US: $1.00 for the first article/
   $.50 each additional article   _____

   Federal Express: $25.00   _____

   Outside US: $2.00 for first article/
   $.50 each additional article   _____

5. Same-day FAX service: $.35 per page   _____

   GRAND TOTAL: _____

METHOD OF PAYMENT: (please check one)

❑ Check enclosed   ❑ Please ship and bill. PO # _____
(sorry we can ship and bill to bookstores only! All others must pre-pay)

❑ Charge to my credit card: ❑ Visa; ❑ MasterCard; ❑ Discover;
                            ❑ American Express;

Account Number:_____ Expiration date:_____

Signature: ✗_____

Name: _____ Institution: _____

Address: _____

_____

City: _____ State:_____ Zip:_____

Phone Number: _____ FAX Number: _____

MAIL or *FAX* THIS ENTIRE ORDER FORM TO:

Haworth Document Delivery Service	**or FAX:** 1-800-895-0582
The Haworth Press, Inc.	**or CALL:** 1-800-342-9678
10 Alice Street	9am-5pm EST)
Binghamton, NY 13904-1580	